SPINOZA: A GUIDE FOR THE PERPLEXED

Continuum Guides for the Perplexed

Adorno: A Guide for the Perplexed – Alex Thomson

Deleuze: A Guide for the Perplexed – Claire Colebrook

Existentialism: A Guide for the Perplexed – Stephen Earnshaw

Gadamer: A Guide for the Perplexed – Chris Lawn

Hobbes: A Guide for the Perplexed – Stephen J. Finn

Husserl: A Guide for the Perplexed – Matheson Russell

Kierkegaard: A Guide for the Perplexed – Clare Carlisle

Levinas: A Guide for the Perplexed – B. C. Hutchens

Merleau-Ponty: A Guide for the Perplexed – Eric Matthews

Quine: A Guide for the Perplexed – Gary Kemp

Rousseau: A Guide for the Perplexed – Matthew Simpson

Sartre: A Guide for the Perplexed – Gary Cox

Wittgenstein: A Guide for the Perplexed – Mark Addis

SPINOZA: A GUIDE FOR THE PERPLEXED

CHARLES E. JARRETT

continuum

Continuum International Publishing Group
The Tower Building   80 Maiden Lane
11 York Road   Suite 704
London SE1 7NX   New York, NY 10038
www.continuumbooks.com
© Charles Jarrett 2007

Thanks are due to the following publishers for permission to reprint
portions of Samuel Shirley's translations of Spinoza's works.

Spinoza. Complete Works; translated by Samuel Shirley and others; edited,
with introduction and notes, by Michael L. Morgan.
Copyright © 2002 by Hackett Publishing Company, Inc.
Reprinted by permission of Hackett Publishing Company, Inc. All rights
reserved.

Baruch Spinoza. Tractatus Theologico-Politicus, translated by Samuel Shirley.
Copyright © 1989 by Koninklijke Brill NV
Reprinted by permission of Koninklijke Brill NV. All rights reserved.

British Library Cataloguing-in-Publication Data
A catalogue record for this book is available from the British Library.

ISBN-10:   HB: 0-8264-8595-2
            PB: 0-8264-8596-0
ISBN-13:   HB: 978-0-8264-8595-3
            PB: 978-0-8264-8596-0

Library of Congress Cataloging-in-Publication Data

Jarrett, Charles E.
Spinoza : a guide for the perplexed / Charles E. Jarrett
p. cm.
Includes bibliographical references and index.
ISBN-13: 978-0-8264-8595-3
ISBN-10: 0-8264-8595-2
1. Spinoza, Benedictus de, 1632–1677. I. Title.

B3998.J37   2007
193–dc22

2006033963

Typeset by Servis Filmsetting Ltd, Manchester
Printed and bound in Great Britain by MPG Books Ltd, Bodmin, Cornwall

For Delrie
and for Alex, Amy, and Julie

CONTENTS

Preface   viii
Abbreviations   x

Part I.   Introduction

1. The Netherlands in the seventeenth century   3
2. Spinoza's life and thought   9
3. The *Treatise on the Emendation of the Intellect*   16

Part II.   The *Ethics*

4. Introduction to the *Ethics*   31
5. The *Ethics*, Part I: God   35
6. The *Ethics*, Part II: Mind and knowledge   61
7. The *Ethics*, Part III: Emotions   95
8. The *Ethics*, Part IV: Ethics   119
9. The *Ethics*, Part V: The mind's power and
   blessedness   155

Part III.   The political works

10. The *Tractatus Theologico-Politicus*   177
11. The *Tractatus Politicus*   190
Postscript: A note on Spinoza's influence   196

Notes   198
Bibliography   210
Index   221

PREFACE

This work is an introduction to Spinoza's philosophy. It is intended primarily for those with little or no prior knowledge of his philosophy or even of philosophy itself.

As a 'Guide for the Perplexed', it is also designed as an aid for those who have begun to read Spinoza, but who have been unable to proceed very far. Some of the reasons for this difficulty will be discussed later in this work, as will the means by which I hope to dispel it.

Readers who turn to Spinoza's *Ethics*, but who have very little background in philosophy, may well be puzzled by unexplained terminology and references to metaphysics, epistemology, the ontological argument, or the problem of universals. This work therefore begins each chapter on the five parts of the *Ethics* (Chapters 5–9) with a very brief overview of the subject or topic under consideration. Each of these chapters also provides an informal statement of some of Spinoza's main theses, a recommended order of readings, and a short discussion intended to clarify Spinoza's major claims and some of his arguments. A brief comparison of Spinoza's views with those of others and a discussion of disputed issues are also provided.

Spinoza's two political works are less highly structured than the *Ethics* and my presentation of them is correspondingly somewhat different. For each of these, I provide an introduction, a presentation of Spinoza's main claims, and a short discussion of some of the issues he raises.

I have tried to bring out the major theses and themes of Spinoza's philosophy without delving unnecessarily into the technical details of his arguments or proofs. It may be helpful to new readers to point out that there is general agreement about many of the main elements of his philosophy. There are also, however, many disagreements about important doctrines. These include questions concerning what, precisely, Spinoza's God or substance is, the relations between the human mind and body, the nature of his ethics, and his doctrine of the eternity of the intellect.

Like others who have written introductions to Spinoza, I hope that this work will be of some interest not only to a general audience, but also to those with a special interest and background in Spinoza, philosophy, or the history of philosophy generally. For the most part, however, scholarly debates are avoided. Interpretations that differ from my own are noted, but only briefly discussed. References to more advanced scholarly discussions are also provided.[1]

ABBREVIATIONS

This book generally follows the style of abbreviation used in Yovel (1999). One exception is that 'cap' is used for the numbered sections of the Appendix to Part IV of the *Ethics*.

C	Spinoza, Benedictus de (1985), *The Collected Works of Spinoza*, vol. 1, ed. and trans. Edwin Curley (Princeton N.J.: Princeton University Press).
CM	*Cogitata Metaphysica* (*Metaphysical Thoughts*). This is the appendix to PPC.
E	*Ethica* (*Ethics*). 'E' is followed by part number (I–V) and one or more of the following:
App	Appendix
ax	axiom
c	corollary
cap	*caput* (heading in E IV App)
d	demonstration
def	definition
def.aff.	definition of affect (in E III)
exp	explanation
gen.def.aff.	general definition of affect (in E III)
lem	lemma
p	proposition
post	postulate
Pref	Preface
s	scholium

Thus, for example, 'E I p 14c2' refers to the second corollary to proposition 14 of the first part of the *Ethics*, and 'E II p 10cs' to the scholium following the corollary of II p 10. A comma indicates 'and'. Thus 'E IV p 1,d' refers to proposition 1 and its demonstration in Part IV.

Ep	*Epistolae* (*Letters*). These are numbered as in Spinoza (2002).
G	Gebhardt, Carl (ed), *Spinoza Opera* (Heidelberg: Carl Winters Universitaetsbuchhandlung, 1925) 'G' is followed by volume (I–IV), page, and line number. Thus 'G II. 10. 8–16' refers to Volume II, page 10, lines 8–16.
KV	*Korte Verhandeling van God, de Mensch en deszelvs Welstand* (*Short Treatise on God, Man, and his Well-Being*). 'KV' is followed by part number (I or II), chapter number, and section number (1, 2, etc.). Thus 'KV I. 6.3' refers to Part I, chapter 6, section 3.
M	Mignini, Filipo (ed. and trans.), *Benedictus de Spinoza: Breve trattato su Dio, l'uomo e il suo bene* (L'Aquila: L. U. Japadre, 1986).
PPC	*Principia Philosophiae Cartesianae* (*Principles of Cartesian Philosophy*), that is, *Renati Des Cartes Principiorum Philosophiae Pars I & II* (*Parts I and II of René Descartes' Principles of Philosophy*). 'PPC' is followed by part number (I, II, or III) and proposition, etc., as in E.
S	Spinoza, Benedictus de (2002), *Spinoza: Complete Works*, ed. Michael L. Morgan, trans. Samuel Shirley (Indianapolis and Cambridge: Hackett Publishing Company).
TdIE	*Tractatus de Intellectus Emendatione* (*Treatise on the Emendation of the Intellect*).
TP	*Tractatus Politicus* (*Political Treatise*).
TTP	*Tractatus Theologico-Politicus* (*Theologico-Political Treatise*).

PART I

INTRODUCTION

CHAPTER 1

THE NETHERLANDS IN THE SEVENTEENTH CENTURY

ORIGIN OF THE NETHERLANDS

The modern state of The Netherlands arose from the union of seven of the 17 provinces that Philip II of Spain inherited in 1555 from his father, Charles V.[1] The Eighty Years War against Spain, which was actually a series of three different revolts,[2] began in 1568 and in 1579 the seven northern provinces formed the Union of Utrecht. This was an agreement to act as one, at least 'in matters of war and peace'.[3] In 1581 they adopted the Act of Abjuration, their declaration of independence from Spain.[4] These provinces achieved official independence in 1648 with the Treaty of Münster, although de facto independence dates from 1609.[5]

The seven northern provinces were Holland, Zeeland, Utrecht, Gelderland, Overijssel, Friesland, and Groningen.[6] They became what is now known as The Netherlands, while the southern provinces are now mainly Belgium and Luxembourg.

GOVERNMENT

Each of the seven provinces had its own governing assembly and each had one vote in the States General, the governing body of the republic.[7] There was also a *stadholder*, or governor, for each province as well as for the provinces as a whole. From 1572 to 1795, the States Stadholder was nearly always the Prince of Orange, including Frederik Hendrik and William I through William V.[8]

The provinces were largely self-governed, however, and The Netherlands itself was a loose confederation, with a relatively weak central government.[9] Holland was the wealthiest and politically most powerful of the provinces and its head of state, the Grand Pensionary Jan de Witt, was the effective ruler of The Netherlands from 1650 to 1672.[10]

RELIGION

Catholicism in Western Europe had a monopoly on religious orthodoxy until the Protestant Reformation. This was initiated by Martin Luther (1483–1546) when he posted his 95 theses on the Wittenberg church door in 1517. Although Luther's primary complaint concerned the sale of indulgences, it eventually led to the establishment of a new orthodoxy, Lutheranism. Another reformer, John Calvin (1509–1564), agreed with Luther that priests may marry, gained political control of Geneva, and established a new Protestant religion, Calvinism. This teaches that the Bible alone has religious authority, that is, it contains everything needed for knowledge of God and of our duties to God and our neighbours. In addition, it holds that good acts can be done only with the grace of God. It also holds that everything which happens is divinely predestined.

The northern provinces became officially Calvinist,[11] despite the large number of Catholics within their borders,[12] while the south remained Catholic.

Religious tolerance was selective and it was extended, sometimes, to Jews, but not to Catholics, Arminians (Remonstrants), or others. An interesting story about this is recounted by Nadler.[13] In the late sixteenth or early seventeenth century, the authorities in Amsterdam investigated a report of a strange language being used in a nearby house. They investigated, took the occupants of the house to be Catholics praying in Latin, and arrested them. When informed that the occupants were Jews who were praying in Hebrew, the authorities released them. Indeed, they gave the Jews permission to set up a congregation. Permission to build a synagogue, however, was evidently refused in 1612.[14]

POLITICS

The major political division was between Orangists, who favoured a strong central government with a powerful sovereign from the House of Orange, and the republicans, who advocated local control and 'true freedom'.[15] Members of the Reformed Church, the Calvinists, were in the former camp, while Spinoza, his friends, and Jan de Witt were in the latter. Tolerance of others, freedom of speech, and freedom to practise one's own religion were major issues in dispute.

1672 was the *annus horribilis*, or 'disaster year', for The Netherlands. The French and the English attacked in concert, the stock market crashed, the art market collapsed, and there was rioting in the streets.[16] On 4 August, Jan de Witt resigned as Grand Pensionary and on 20 August, a mob got hold of him and his brother. They were 'beaten, stabbed, and shot to death'[17] and then hung upside down and mutilated. Parts of their bodies were cooked and eaten.[18]

When Spinoza learned of the killings, he told Leibniz that he planned to go outside and post a notice at the site which read 'ultimi barbarorum' (greatest of barbarians). His landlord, however, locked him in the house to prevent his 'being torn to pieces'.[19] As Nadler relates, Spinoza was linked to de Witt and a 1672 pamphlet 'proclaims that de Witt basically gave Spinoza the protection he needed to publish the *Theologico-Political Treatise*'.[20]

In the end, the French gained little, the English fleet was defeated, and William III's defence of the republic resulted in increased prestige and power for himself and the Orangists.[21] In 1689, following the 'Glorious Revolution', he became King of England and co-ruler with Queen Mary II, thus replacing her father, James II.

THE DUTCH GOLDEN AGE

The seventeenth century, or most of it, is also known as the Dutch Golden Age. It was a period during which Dutch naval power became dominant and, not coincidentally, its economy became the strongest in Europe.[22] The Dutch East Indies Company gained control of trade in Taiwan and Japan, as well as parts of South-east Asia and Eastern Africa, and it established a settlement, initially for 'refuelling', at the Cape of Good Hope.[23] The Dutch West Indies Company established settlements in North and South America, as well as in the Caribbean. These companies had warships and an army, not merely merchant ships, and they committed mass murder[24] in their effort to control trade. They were major participants in the slave trade.[25]

Dutch art and architecture experienced its golden age as well, starting in the 1590s.[26] Rembrandt Harmenszoon van Rijn

(1606–1669) and Johannes Vermeer (1632–1675) are now, surely, the best known among the many Dutch painters of the time.[27] Rembrandt, incidentally, lived for a while 'around the corner from Spinoza',[28] although there is no evidence that they knew each other more than in passing.[29]

SEVENTEENTH-CENTURY PHILOSOPHY AND SCIENCE

Aristotelianism was the dominant philosophy taught in the universities both during and well before the time of Spinoza and Descartes. (Descartes died in 1650, when Spinoza was 17.) Descartes, in fact, went to the Jesuit school at La Flèche in France, where he was no doubt strongly influenced by the work of Francisco Suárez (1548–1617), the principal theorist of the Jesuits. Suárez was the last in a long line of eminent theologians and philosophers that includes Thomas Aquinas (1225–1274), Duns Scotus (1266–1308), and William of Ockham (1285–1347). His *Disputationes Metaphysicae* (1597) is an admirably comprehensive and detailed work on metaphysics and on Aristotle.

Aquinas had combined a primarily Aristotelian philosophical framework with Catholicism in the thirteenth century, comparable to Augustine's synthesis of Plato and Christian doctrine in the fourth and fifth centuries.

The Aristotelian and indeed Christian worldview promulgated a cosmology, or theory of the structure of the universe, that we call 'Ptolemaic'. It was set out in perhaps its most refined form in the *Almagest* by Claudius Ptolemy (*c*. 90–*c*. 168), although Aristotle had advanced it in the fourth century BC. It is said to be a 'geocentric' conception because it holds that the earth is the centre of the universe and the sun, moon, and planets revolve around it. The Aristotelian worldview also regards natural phenomena as having both efficient and final causes. Everything, that is, is 'due to' an antecedent cause as we ordinarily understand it and everything is also 'for something' in the sense that it has a purpose or goal.

The Ptolemaic view was challenged by Nicholaus Copernicus (1473–1543) in his book *On the Revolutions of the Heavenly Spheres*, published in the year of his death. This maintained, or suggested, that the sun is the centre of the universe and that the planets, including the earth, revolve around the sun. This 'heliocentric' or sun-centred conception was later advocated by Galileo in his *Dialogue* and by

Descartes in *Le monde*. Galileo (1564–1642) published his work and got into trouble with the Inquisition because of it. Descartes, on hearing about this, decided against publication of his own treatise.

Descartes' later works were not well received by the Dutch authorities. Indeed, the teaching of Cartesianism was prohibited in the universities.

A short list of some of the other most famous natural philosophers or scientists of the age includes the following:

1. Johannes Kepler (1571–1630), astronomer and astrologer, who formulated three laws of planetary motion.
2. Robert Boyle (1627–1691), perhaps the first modern chemist. Spinoza corresponded indirectly with him, through Henry Oldenburg, secretary of the Royal Society. Oldenburg sent Boyle's book to Spinoza and Spinoza sent back some criticisms. A short exchange followed, always mediated by Oldenburg.
3. Christian Huygens (1629–1695), physicist and mathematician. Spinoza made some lenses for him.
4. Anton van Leeuwenhoek (1632–1723), 'the father of microbiology'. He was born in the same year as Spinoza, in Delft.
5. Isaac Newton (1643–1727), or 'the incomparable Mr. Newton', as John Locke put it in his *Essay*. He produced a unified theory that accounts for both terrestrial and celestial motion and was the co-inventor, with Leibniz, of the calculus. The question of priority has long been controversial.
6. Gottfried Leibniz (1646–1716), physicist, philosopher, and mathematician. He once met and conversed with Spinoza and he corresponded with Spinoza about optics. Spinoza was quite reluctant to allow him to see a manuscript of the *Ethics*.

Extraordinary advances in mathematics were also made in the seventeenth century. Descartes invented analytic geometry, while Leibniz and Newton, as just noted, created the calculus. Other notables in this field include Pierre de Fermat (1601–1665), Blaise Pascal (1623–1662), and Christian Huygens. Lesser known but still notable are John Hudde (1633–1704) and Ehrenfried Walther von Tschirnhaus (1651–1708). Spinoza corresponded with both of them as well as with Huygens.

Several scientific societies were established in the seventeenth century. In England, the Royal Society was founded in 1660 and granted a charter to publish by King Charles II in 1662.[30] Oldenburg was its first secretary and he was an extremely active correspondent with others throughout Europe. Other scientific societies that were formed in the seventeenth century include the French Académie des sciences, the German Leopoldinische Carolinisch Akademie der Naturforscher, and the Italian Accademia dei Lincei (Academy of the Lynxes).

CHAPTER 2

SPINOZA'S LIFE AND THOUGHT

SPINOZA'S LIFE

Family and early life

Spinoza was born in the Jewish quarter of Amsterdam on 24 November 1632. His parents were Sephardic Jews, that is, descendants of Jews who in the Middle Ages lived on the Iberian peninsula (primarily Spain and Portugal). At the time of Spinoza's birth, the Sephardic community in Amsterdam was relatively well established, while the Ashkenazi Jews were more recent, and poorer, immigrants.[1]

Spinoza's mother was Hanna Deborah Senior and it is apparently from her father, Baruch Senior, that Spinoza received his Hebrew name.[2] 'Baruch' means 'blessed' and is 'Benedictus' in Latin. At home and within the Portuguese community he was called 'Bento', which is Portuguese for 'blessed'.

His father was Michael d'Espinoza (also 'Miguel d'Espinosa'), who was born in Vidigere, Portugal in 1587 or 1588.[3] Spinoza's paternal grandfather, Isaac, had left Portugal with Michael to escape the Portuguese Inquisition. In 1497 Jewish children in Portugal were forced to convert to Catholicism and in 1547 the Pope established 'a free and unimpeded Inquisition' in Portugal.[4] Members of the Espinosa family, like many others, had been imprisoned and tortured in Portugal.[5]

Aside from Spinoza's mother and father, his immediate family, at his birth, included an older sister, Miriam (born 1629) and an older brother, Isaac (born between 1630 and 1632).[6] A younger brother, Abraham (also known as Gabriel), was born between 1634 and 1638.[7] Finally, he also had a sister or half-sister, Rebecca. It is unclear, according to Nadler, whether her mother was Hanna (Michael's second wife) or Esther (Michael's third wife).[8] Rebecca moved to Curaçao between 1679 and 1685 and she and one of her sons died there in a yellow fever epidemic in 1695.[9]

Spinoza's father was a fairly successful merchant, who imported a variety of goods such as citrus fruits, raisins, and oil.[10] He was also active in the leadership of the community.

Spinoza went to the local school, run by the Talmud Torah congregation. This had six levels or grades, the two highest of which were mainly for rabbinical training. Spinoza seems to have attended only the first four, after which, at around age 14, he apparently worked in his father's business,[11] which he later ran with his brother, Gabriel.

The years from 1649 through 1654 must have been difficult. Spinoza's older brother died in 1649 and this was followed by the death of his older sister Miriam in 1651, of his stepmother Esther in 1652, and of his father in 1654.

In perhaps 1654 or 1655,[12] and maybe as early as 1652,[13] Spinoza began to attend a private school set up by Franciscus van den Enden. There Spinoza studied Latin, as well as Descartes' philosophy, and he participated with others at the school in the production of various plays. Klever holds, on the basis of new documents that he and Bedjai independently discovered, that van den Enden is 'a proto-Spinoza; the genius behind Spinoza'.[14]

There is also a story about van den Enden's daughter, Clara Maria. Colerus portrays Spinoza as being in love with her and wanting to marry her, but many commentators are sceptical. Nadler is among them and he notes that if this is supposed to relate how Spinoza felt in 1657, Spinoza would have been 25 and Clara Maria 13.[15] Colerus also says that another student, Keckkering, was jealous. Keckkering was 18 at the time and in fact married Clara Maria in 1671.[16]

Van den Enden moved to Paris in 1670. He was charged with plotting to assassinate Louis XIV and was hanged in 1674. One of his alleged co-conspirators was beheaded and the other was shot while resisting arrest.[17]

Spinoza was excommunicated by the Amsterdam synagogue on 27 July 1656. The complete explanation of this is still debated. There is no doubt, however, that at least a central part of the reason for it was Spinoza's heretical views. According to Lucas, Spinoza had revealed some of his views and attitudes to others and they then reported him to the authorities of the congregation.[18] These views included rejection of the orthodox conception of God as a lawgiver and of the Jews as a chosen people.[19] In 1659 a report was made to the Spanish Inquisition concerning Spinoza and Juan de Prado, who had also been excommunicated. They were reported to have said that they had been excommunicated 'because of their views on God, the soul, and the law'.[20]

After his excommunication, Spinoza stayed in Amsterdam, probably at van den Enden's, but he may instead have lived in Leiden. He 'studied at Leiden', according to the Inquisition report.[21] He may have helped in teaching at van den Enden's school and he participated in 1657/58 in various plays.[22] He may also have translated Margaret Fell Fox's *A Loving Salutation to the Seed of Abraham among the Jewes* and one of her letters from Dutch into Hebrew.[23]

Spinoza's closest friends or 'intimate circle', as Wolf puts it, were not numerous.[24] Simon Joosten de Vries (1633?–1667) was a merchant who at his death left Spinoza an annuity, only part of which Spinoza accepted. Lodewijk Meyer (1630–1681) received both a Ph.D. and an M.D. in 1660 from the University of Leiden. He became the director of the Amsterdam Theatre, founded a society of arts, and was an author himself. Another author was Pieter Balling, an agent for merchants. Jarig Jelles (d. 1683) was a merchant, but hired a business manager 'to devote himself to the pursuit of knowledge'.[25] Finally, there were Johan Bouwmeester (1630–1680) and Georg Hermann Schuller (1651–1679). Both were doctors and it was the latter, apparently, who attended Spinoza during his last illness and was present at Spinoza's death.

Rijnsburg

Spinoza moved to Rijnsburg, which is near Leiden, in the summer of 1661. The earliest piece of his correspondence that we have is a letter from Oldenburg, dated 26 August 1661. It is from this letter that we learn that earlier in the summer Oldenburg visited Spinoza and conversed with him about philosophy.

While in Rijnsburg Spinoza dictated to a student the first part of what would become the *Principles of Cartesian Philosophy* (PPC).

The house in which he rented a room still stands and is preserved by Het Spinozhous Vereniging (the Spinoza House Association).[26] They have reconstructed his library and have set up his room, which is rather large, as it was when Spinoza lived there. It is on the ground floor, to the right of the entrance to the house, and it has direct access to the back yard. Among the furnishings is a lens-grinding instrument.

Voorburg

Spinoza moved to Voorburg, which is close to The Hague, probably in April of 1663.[27] There he continued work on what would become the *Ethics*. He also finished composing the *Principles of Cartesian Philosophy* and an appendix to it, the *Metaphysical Thoughts* (CM), which his friends encouraged him to publish. It appeared in 1663, published in Amsterdam by Jan (Johannes) Rieuwertsz.

In 1665 Spinoza began work on the *Theologico-Political Treatise* (TTP).

The Hague

Spinoza's final move was to The Hague, probably in 1669 or 1670, where he again rented a room, first in one house and then, about a year later, in another.[28]

In 1670 he published the *Theologico-Political Treatise*, which was immediately attacked and condemned as godless and blasphemous.[29]

In 1673 Spinoza was offered, but declined, the chair of philosophy at the University of Heidelberg. He accepted, however, an invitation to visit the military headquarters of the Prince of Condé, whose French forces had invaded The Netherlands. The prince was not there, however, and although Spinoza stayed for a while, his mission remains a mystery.[30]

As we learn from Ep 68, Spinoza had the *Ethics* ready for publication in 1675, but because rumours got out that he was going to publish an atheistic work, he decided to wait. He began work on the *Political Treatise* (TP), which he did not finish.

Spinoza became ill about a week before his death and he died on 21 February 1677. The cause of his death was evidently phthisis (tubercular and/or fibrous). He may also have had silicosis as a result of grinding lenses for many years.[31]

His papers were sent to Rieuwertsz in Amsterdam, edited by his friends, and published in 1677 as his *Opera Posthuma*, in Latin, and *Nagelate Schriften*, in Dutch.[32] The *Opera Posthuma* contains his

Ethics, an edited selection of his correspondence, and three incomplete works: the *Treatise on the Emendation of the Intellect*, the *Political Treatise*, and the *Grammar of the Hebrew Language*. The *Nagelate Schriften* contains all of these except the last.

Brief chronology

1632 24 Nov.	Birth of Spinoza in Amsterdam
1638	Death of Spinoza's mother, Hanna Deborah Senior
1652?	Spinoza begins to attend van den Enden's school
1654	Death of Spinoza's father, Michael d'Espinosa
1654–56?	Spinoza runs his father's business with Gabriel
1656 27 July	Excommunication by Amsterdam synagogue
1656–61	Spinoza remains in Amsterdam[33]
1661	Spinoza moves to Rijnsburg, where Oldenburg visits him. He works on the *Principles of Cartesian Philosophy*, the *Metaphysical Thoughts*, and the *Ethics*
1663	Publication of the *Principles of Cartesian Philosophy* and its appendix, the *Metaphysical Thoughts*. Spinoza moves to Voorburg, near The Hague
1665	Spinoza begins work on the *Theologico-Political Treatise*
1669 or 1670	Spinoza moves to The Hague
1670	Publication of the *Theologico-Political Treatise*
1673	Spinoza goes to Utrecht (a diplomatic mission?). He declines the chair of philosophy at Heidelberg
1675	Spinoza considers publication of the *Ethics* and begins the *Political Treatise*
1676	Leibniz visits Spinoza
1677 21 Feb.	Death of Spinoza in The Hague
1677	Publication of the *Opera Posthuma* and the *Nagelate Schriften*

THE CHARACTER OF SPINOZA'S THOUGHT: PHILOSOPHY, SCIENCE, AND THEOLOGY

Spinoza's thought deals with nearly every major issue and field in philosophy. It addresses central issues in metaphysics, philosophy of mind, the theory of knowledge, ethics, and political philosophy. It also provides a cosmology, a psychology, and at least a partial physics. Although we now regard the former subjects as parts of philosophy and the latter as parts of science, he recognizes no sharp division between them.[34]

In this he is like other thinkers of the seventeenth century, who do not think of philosophy, or at least 'natural philosophy', as distinct from the various sciences. Descartes, for example, explicitly maintains that philosophy encompasses everything we can know.[35] Newton's main work is entitled *Mathematical Principles of Natural Philosophy*.[36] We, in contrast, regard it as one of the greatest foundational works in science.

Perhaps this should be expected. For modern science originated partly in the sixteenth and primarily in the seventeenth centuries. It arose with the work of Copernicus, Tycho Brahe (1546–1601), Kepler, Galileo, Descartes, Leibniz, Newton, Huygens, Boyle, Leeuwenhoek, and many others. It was a revolution in thought and the revolutionaries had just begun to create the modern sciences of cosmology and astronomy, physics, chemistry, and biology.

A third field, however, is also prominent in Spinoza's thought. It is theology, taken in its most basic sense as an account, or as knowledge, of God. Spinoza's philosophy thus seems to us a curious mixture not just of two fields, but of three: philosophy, science, and theology.

But in this, too, Spinoza is not unique. Both Plato and Aristotle invoke a concept of the divine to account for features of the physical world. Plato's Demiurge arranges the heavens for the best and Aristotle's unmoved mover, or movers, accounts for motion. In addition, Descartes himself holds that all knowledge depends on knowledge of God. Indeed, he attempts to derive a principle of the conservation of the 'total quantity of motion' from the constancy of God's will. Newton, in turn, takes space and time to be 'God's sensorium' and appeals solely to God to account for the paths of comets, or at least to explain why, as he thinks, the comets do not collide with the planets.

This apparent failure to distinguish philosophy, science, and theology seems quite odd to us, but it is a reflection of the attempt to provide a unitary, reasoned, and comprehensive account of the world, including ourselves.

It seems odd to us partly because we are so accustomed to the specialization and division of labour that has arisen since the seventeenth century. Astrophysics, quantum physics, evolutionary biology, and organic chemistry, to name just a few, are highly specialized fields of scientific enquiry, as are philosophy of mind, ethics, and philosophical logic, in philosophy. Theology, in turn, has its subfields as well and the 'Renaissance person' who combines them all seems an ideal of the past. Graduate training in a moderate number of these fields would normally take a lifetime.

Questions about the nature of philosophy, of science, and of theology, and of their relations to each other, are matters of deep disagreement and I will not try to settle the issues here. My own view, however, is that philosophy, if it does nothing else, raises and attempts to answer the big questions about ourselves and the universe. It is a systematic and reasoned attempt to understand the world, including ourselves. This makes it a theoretical enterprise and continuous, at least in part, with modern science.

Its aim, however, is not just to understand. The quest for knowledge has usually, and quite rightly, been conjoined with the conviction that while knowledge is intrinsically valuable, it is useful as well. 'Reason', as Spinoza and many others have held, has both theoretical and practical aims.

CHAPTER 3

THE *TREATISE ON THE EMENDATION OF THE INTELLECT*

INTRODUCTION

A natural starting point for a consideration of Spinoza's philosophy is his early work, the *Treatise on the Emendation of the Intellect* (TdIE).[1] Its full title is *Treatise on the Emendation of the Intellect and on the Way by which it is Best Directed to the True Knowledge of Things*.[2] As this indicates, one of its primary concerns is with philosophical method. However, its first 30 sections, out of 110,[3] are devoted primarily to a discussion of value and of a change in Spinoza's plan of life. Here Spinoza sets out his conception of the highest good and in the course of this he explains why the subject of the treatise, the emendation or improvement of the intellect, is important.

This part of TdIE may be outlined as follows:

§§1–11   The change in Spinoza's plan of life
§§12–13   The true good and the highest good
§§14–16   The general means by which to attain the highest good
   §17   Provisional rules of life (to be accepted while pursuing the true good)
§§18–24   The four kinds of knowledge or perception
§§25–30   The means to the highest good

THE CHANGE IN SPINOZA'S PLAN OF LIFE (§§1–11)

The *Treatise* begins with an extraordinary sentence:

After experience had taught me that all the things which regularly occur in ordinary life are empty and futile, and I saw that all the things which were the cause or object of my fear had nothing of good or bad in themselves, except insofar as [my] mind was moved by them, I resolved at last to try to find out whether there was anything which would be the true good, capable of communicating itself, and which alone would affect the mind, all others being rejected – whether there was something which, once found and acquired, would continuously give me the greatest joy, to eternity.[4]

Spinoza's philosophy is thus motivated by the search for the true good or, as he later characterizes it, the highest good.

As his first sentence indicates, this is not something that is 'good in itself', or good independently of its effects on us. Indeed, Spinoza holds that nothing is good or bad in itself. Instead, he maintains that things are good only insofar as they affect the soul with joy and they are bad only insofar as they affect the soul with 'negative' (unpleasant) emotions.

Spinoza's subsequent discussion (through §11) contains an account of his struggle to devise and even think about a new goal as well as to free himself from the pursuit of ordinary goods. In the course of this discussion, he criticizes these ordinary pursuits and he also considers the question of the attainability of his new goal.

THE TRUE GOOD AND THE HIGHEST GOOD (§§12–16)

§§12–13. §11 ends Spinoza's 'autobiographical' or 'historical' account of his thoughts. §§12–16 set out his conception of a true good and the highest good, but first he makes some preliminary remarks.

These prefatory remarks and Spinoza's initial identification of the supreme good are as follows:

> good and bad are said of things only in a certain respect, so that one and the same thing can be called both good and bad according to different respects. The same applies to perfect and imperfect. For nothing, considered in its own nature, will be called perfect or imperfect, especially after we have recognized that everything that happens happens according to the eternal order, and according to certain laws of nature.

But since human weakness does not grasp that order by its own thought, and meanwhile man conceives a human nature much stronger and more enduring than his own, and at the same time sees that nothing prevents his acquiring such a nature, he is spurred to seek the means that will lead him to such perfection. Whatever can be a means to his attaining it is called a true good, but the highest good is to arrive – together with other individuals if possible – at the enjoyment of such a nature. What that nature is we shall show in its proper place: that it is the knowledge of the union that the mind has with the whole of nature.[5]

Spinoza here expresses a view that is now sometimes called 'anti-objectivist' or 'anti-realist'. The idea is that things as they are in themselves are neither good nor bad, nor are they perfect or imperfect. To maintain that nothing, 'considered in its own nature', is good or bad can also be expressed by saying that being good and being bad are not 'real properties' of things. Nevertheless, he holds, we can construct an idea of a 'stronger human nature', and can legitimately call a thing 'good' or a 'true good', insofar as it is a means of attaining such a nature. Such a view can also be called 'constructivist', insofar as it requires construction of an ideal with reference to which things are to be evaluated as good or bad.

Spinoza's position is set out quite briefly here, but it is reiterated and characterized more completely in both the *Ethics* and the *Short Treatise on God, Man, and his Well-Being* (KV). We will consider it further when we turn to the *Ethics*.

Another remarkable feature of Spinoza's thought about ethics is also found in this passage. For Spinoza claims or suggests that ethics rests, in part, on ignorance. Our failure to understand the order of nature, that is, our 'human weakness' (*humana imbecillitas*), is apparently cited as a precondition either of our constructing an ideal (or 'exemplar' as he puts it in the *Ethics*[6]), or of seeing no reason why we cannot attain it, or of both. That we are ignorant of the causal order of nature is stressed by Spinoza in several places.[7]

§§14–15. The means by which the highest good is to be attained are enumerated in §§14 and 15. They include: (1) understanding as much of nature as is required; (2) establishing a social order to allow as many as possible to attain the supreme good; (3) the development of moral philosophy and the education of children; and (4) medicine and (5) mechanics (to save time and effort).

This seems to be the outline of a programme. Spinoza's *Ethics* contributes primarily to (1) and to the development of moral philosophy, specified in (3). His political works seem to provide a necessary preliminary to (2).

§16. Most important, however, is the development of a method for emending or healing (*medendi*) the intellect and for purifying it. Thus all sciences are to be directed to one goal, the attainment of the 'highest human perfection', and whatever does not advance this is to be rejected as useless.

PROVISIONAL RULES OF LIFE AND KINDS OF KNOWLEDGE (§17)

§17. Spinoza here sets out provisional rules for living (*vivendi regulae*). These include: (1) speak to the understanding of the multitude (*ad captum vulgi loqui*); (2) indulge in pleasures only to the extent that they promote health; and (3) seek money only insofar as it is necessary for life and health and for following the customs of society (when they do not conflict with his overall aim).

THE FOUR KINDS OF KNOWLEDGE OR PERCEPTION (§§18–24)

§§18–24. These sections provide a survey of kinds of knowledge ('perception') that we have. These are: (1) from hearsay or conventional signs; (2) from casual experience; (3) when we inadequately infer the essence of one thing from another thing; and (4) 'when a thing is perceived through its essence alone, or through knowledge of its proximate cause'.[8]

THE MEANS TO THE HIGHEST GOOD (§§25–30)

§25. Spinoza recounts what is necessary for his goal. This consists generally in the knowledge necessary for determining the extent to which we can change things, and 'This done, the highest perfection man can reach will easily manifest itself'.[9]

§§26–30. What kind of knowledge should we choose? After discussing each kind, he answers in §29 that it is mainly the fourth kind. §30 indicates that the remainder of the work will determine the method for obtaining this kind of knowledge.

SOME ISSUES

The substantive issues raised by Spinoza's discussion in the first 30 sections of TdIE are large and important. A few of these will be considered here, but I should stress at the outset the preliminary nature of my remarks at this point. My aim is to help provide a better understanding of Spinoza's ethics and the issues it raises.

Reasoning about ultimate ends

Spinoza clearly supposes that it is possible to reason about ultimate goals and he seems, furthermore, to be right about this. For this is an essential part of the attempt, which at least some of us sometimes make, to devise a life plan.[10]

Hedonistic criteria

In evaluating ultimate ends, Spinoza makes important use of hedonistic criteria. Indeed, the first sentence of TdIE suggests that a thing is good only insofar as it affects the soul with joy (*laetitia*) and bad insofar as it affects us with sadness (*tristitia*).[11]

Traditional hedonistic criteria include, for example, the quality, duration, and 'purity' of the pleasures compared.[12] Other things being equal, if one activity produces a higher degree of pleasure than another (that is, if it feels better), then that is to be preferred. Similarly, longer-lasting pleasures are to be preferred to shorter ones and a pleasure that is 'unmixed with pain' is to be preferred to one that gives rise to pain.

In the first sentence of TdIE, Spinoza characterizes a true good as one that produces 'the greatest joy, to eternity'. So no other joy will last longer or be of greater quality. His criticism of the pursuit of sensual pleasures is that it necessarily produces the greatest sadness, and the pursuit of wealth and honour can do the same. (It will do so if we are unsuccessful.) Finally, our happiness depends on the quality of what we love. The love of changeable things gives rise to strife, sadness, envy, fear, hatred, or other 'disturbances of the mind' (*commotiones animi*). 'But love toward the eternal and infinite thing feeds the mind with a joy entirely exempt from sadness.'[13]

But while Spinoza's criticisms of the pursuit of wealth, honour, and sensual pleasure are largely hedonistic, it is not obvious that they are exclusively so. For all three engross or 'distract the mind' and 'prevent it from thinking' of a new good (§§3–5). Even this, however, can be regarded as employing a hedonistic criterion, insofar as it assumes that some new and better good could or would be found if the mind were not so distracted.

Alternative descriptions

We see from the descriptions given above that Spinoza characterizes his primary goal (or the highest good) in a variety of ways. A summary of these characterizations is as follows:

§1   supreme and continuous joy to eternity
§2   the greatest happiness
§§9–10   love toward the eternal and infinite thing (or the happiness or joy that arises from this)
§13   a human nature much stronger (and more enduring) than his own
§13   knowledge of the union of the mind with the whole of nature
§14   happiness
§16   the highest human perfection
§25   the highest perfection that man can attain

In TdIE Spinoza says very little about what each of these is. In a note to his identification of the ultimate goal as knowledge of the union of the mind with the whole of nature, he remarks, 'These are explained more fully in their proper place.'[14] The proper place, for this at least, turns out to be KV, not the *Ethics*. Nor does he say very much about happiness, except quite generally. It depends on the quality of what we love. For if the object can change and be destroyed, great sadness, quarrels, etc. can arise from this love; if, instead, the object is something unchangeable, then unmixed joy will arise. But Spinoza does not specify what happiness or even a 'stronger human nature' is in any detail. More complete discussions of these, however, will be found in KV and in the *Ethics*.

Relations among descriptions

Spinoza does not provide an extensive discussion in TdIE of the relations among 'supreme and continuous joy to eternity', 'happiness', 'human perfection', 'a stronger (and more enduring) human nature', and 'knowledge of the union of the mind with the whole of nature'. In §13, however, he does identify 'a stronger (and more enduring) human nature' with 'knowledge of the union of the mind with the whole of nature', and he characterizes this as our perfection. As we have also seen, he seems to suppose, in §§2, 9–10, and 14, that what he seeks is happiness (or the highest happiness, according to §2) and he indicates that this depends on love of the eternal, which 'feeds the mind with a joy entirely exempt from sadness'. In §14 Spinoza also apparently equates his own happiness with his attainment of a stronger and more lasting human nature. Thus Spinoza apparently takes all of these descriptions to be equivalent.

Attainability

The question of the attainability of our goal is a large one, which we have considered very briefly in our remarks on §§12–13 above. For Spinoza seems to suppose there, quite naturally, that we construct or pursue a goal when, and perhaps only when, we do not see anything that prevents our attaining it. Ignorance of the causal order of nature thus appears to be a necessary presupposition of ethics. That our goal should be possible for us – that is, not ruled out by what we know – is also indicated when Spinoza maintains in §13 that it is a stronger *human* nature that we seek. For he holds that individuals cannot persist through changes in their species.[15]

We have also seen that Spinoza provides several different descriptions of his ultimate goal and, indeed, he sometimes leaves open what precisely the highest goal is. In §25, for example, he indicates that what the goal is will become apparent after we come to know the extent of our power over natural things.[16] The question thus arises whether we can, or should, specify our highest goal independently of its attainability.

In the *Ethics*, we might add, Spinoza's ideal is one of complete self-determination.[17] This, however, would require that we not be parts of nature, or that we be unaffected by anything outside of ourselves, and Spinoza himself recognizes that this is impossible.[18] But he also holds that blessedness can be achieved.

Of course, if we think on our own about the construction of an ideal, we might well say about some alleged ideal that it is to be rejected, as an ideal to be seriously pursued, precisely because it is not 'realistic' or attainable. This is a familiar objection to 'utopian' schemes, for example.

An equally standard reply is to say that it may not be attainable, but it can still define what is better and worse. So even if it is not fully attainable, it is valuable even to move toward it.

It is perhaps tempting to suppose this to be a successful defence only for certain types of goals (or goal-specifications). These are goals whose attainment admits of degree, such as being happier, wiser, or richer. If, in contrast, the goal is to be happy, wise, or rich, then however difficult it may be to define these precisely, one either succeeds or doesn't.

Even with a goal that is all-or-nothing, however, it can be replied that if one can approach them more or less closely, then even these notions can be used to specify a viable non-utopian aim. Thus if one can be said to be closer to or further from attainment of the goal, then the goal might still be a useful (or rather 'viable' or 'reasonable') one to propose, even if attainment of it is impossible.

Some of Spinoza's goal-characterizations in TdIE seem to be all-or-nothing, while others seem to admit of degree. 'Knowledge of the union of the mind with the whole of nature' sounds like one item of knowledge that one either does or doesn't have.[19] So, too, the attainment of supreme and continual joy to eternity seems to be an all-or-nothing affair, as does 'love of the eternal and infinite thing'. But love admits of degree or quantity; the question can always be raised about how much of it you have. 'A stronger human nature' is like this as well; for after you have achieved it, we can ask how much stronger you have become and we can always seek to become even stronger. Compare this with the endeavour to preserve yourself for an indefinite period of time.

Another question concerns a subclass of goals that are fully attainable. Consider a goal that is all-or-nothing, does not admit of degree, and does not consist in continuous activity. If this is the supreme good, the ideal perfection for which we strive, or our highest goal, the question is simply this. Suppose this goal to have been attained. Then what?

Consider a goal such a winning a gold medal at the Olympic games, marrying a certain person, or attaining a net worth of a billion dollars. What is one to do if – or after – such a goal is attained?

The same question arises when, like the Buddha or the Platonist within sight of the Good, your highest goal has been achieved, but you are still alive. Are you simply to remain in an enlightened state as long as you can or are you to teach and help others, rule the state, or, for that matter, engage in farming or fishing? Although these alternatives may not be exclusive, it has often enough been thought that they are – that continued contemplation or the vision itself is the ideal state. If so, then the goal is not only to attain perfection. It is not just to become perfect or enlightened, but to become and remain so indefinitely.

Spinoza insists in KV that we must always achieve more and in the *Ethics* that while the goal of complete self-determination is strictly speaking impossible to attain, it is a model by reference to which we make assessments. So it seems that there is, or can be, an advantage to setting out an ideal that cannot be fully attained.

Existence and uniqueness

Spinoza seems simply to assume that there is a highest good and that there is only one. Furthermore, he speaks as if this must be the same for each person. All of these claims can be challenged.

Hobbes, for example, denies that there is an ultimate end or highest good and he denies that happiness consists in the attainment of it. Human life itself consists in a succession of one desire after another, which comes to an end only in death, and happiness he regards as a 'progress' from the satisfaction of one desire to the next.[20]

In TdIE Spinoza, as we have seen, describes the highest good in a variety of ways. On one of these, it is that when possessed which will provide 'supreme and continuous joy to eternity'. On another it is the attainment of a greater (or the greatest) human perfection. The former suggests a state that excludes unsatisfied desires; the latter, in contrast, does not.

One conception of a highest good is of that for the sake of which all else is done and which itself is not done for the sake of anything else. Not being done for the sake of something else is also said to be something that the agent, at least, regards as 'intrinsically good'. In contrast, being done for the sake of something else is said to be 'extrinsically good'. The question whether there might be more than one highest good is then settled by definition. For if achieving A and achieving B were highest goods in this sense, they would have to be the same.[21]

The question whether there is a highest good in this sense, for one person or for all, appears to be a psychological one. Is there some one goal that a given person aims at in everything that person does? This seems exceedingly unlikely, but if there is, then that person regards achievement of it as the sole intrinsic good.

If we ask you for your motivation for doing something, an answer is typically forthcoming. If we keep asking it, it frequently becomes unclear, quite quickly, what is to be said. For example, if I am asked why I am writing this now, I might say that it is in order to complete this work. But why do I want to do that? To publish it, perhaps. Why? To heighten my reputation or to inform others and to help them see the truth. But again, why? At this point or some other I might well say 'Just because' or 'Just because I want to' or even 'Because I enjoy it'. The former two answers seem to indicate that I have no further reason and even that it is a most basic desire. The latter answer suggests that doing something because you like or enjoy doing it is itself an ultimate explanation. If you persist in asking yet again why that is so, you seem to be asking for a cause, not a reason.

In §3 of TdIE Spinoza remarks that the things ordinarily pursued by people, and regarded by them as the highest good, if we judge by their actions, are wealth, honour, and sensual pleasure. He did not, or would not, I expect, think that *every* act of a person might be motivated solely by one of these. Surely a more plausible view is that the desire for wealth, for example, is very strong, or even dominant in the sense that this desire is stronger than others in most cases of conflict. For surely you may take shelter from the rain, for example, because you think you will be uncomfortable if wet, not because, and certainly not solely because, of your desire for money.

Life goals: A preliminary discussion

If *we* ask the question seriously it is hard to know where to begin. People have different attitudes toward the construction of a life plan and they have different degrees of interest in it. Some plan in detail their careers, their love lives, and even the timing and number of the children they will have. Others are content to see how things turn out. Systematic and detailed planning is perhaps exceptional.

The question seems most pressing, perhaps, for those in transition to adulthood, where greater economic and emotional independence from parents is expected. It is also characteristically addressed by those who must deal with a variety of other important life changes, such as the loss of an important job or a loved one. But Tolstoy reminds us that it can also arise for those who have, by any ordinary measure, achieved great success in life.[22]

As the question is typically presented you must decide 'what to do with your life', or with the rest of it, but this form of expression seems odd. It seems to reveal a conception of your life as an object to be used, as if you are one thing and your life is another. However that may be, the choice at first is between school and work. One can of course do both, but it is not easy, and the question, 'In what field?' remains. If one is in college or university, for example, one must decide on a subject. Do you want to be a lawyer, a physicist, a teacher, a businessperson, or what? But this is to classify people, and indeed oneself, primarily in terms of an occupation.

The life plan of many, to judge by their reports, includes getting a good job, getting married, and perhaps having children.[23] This, apparently, is how we conceive of our lives. An ideal life is a successful one and this most importantly includes success in an occupation and success in love. It is thus a conception that seems to reflect or embody a division within us between our public and private lives.

If we enquire into the meaning of 'a good job', we find that it is one that provides a great deal of money, or at least 'enough'. Even more ideally, the job is both lucrative and enjoyable. But it is also important to succeed in your personal life, that is, in love, so that you have someone with whom to share life and perhaps with whom to have and raise children. Thus marriage, as a public mark of success or acceptability, can also be an important element of a life plan.

Variations on this 'decision problem' of course exist and other circumstances or attitudes are possible. Your life may have already been planned out for you by your parents or, in varying degrees, by a tradition in your society. So you may be expected to follow the occupation of your parents or to have no occupation, but instead marry someone who does. This of course does not obviate the decision problem, because it remains true that whether you do what is expected is up to you.

Questions about our career and family life are enormously important to us, of course, but Spinoza says little about them.[24] He himself is said to have had one possible love interest during his life, but he never married.[25] Although he evidently earned some money by grinding lenses, his own primary activity was the development of his philosophy.

That he says so little about careers is due, at least in part, perhaps, to his view that we need very little on which to live and that the more important question is how we live, not what our job or marital status is. The classification he proposes in TdIE, as we noted, contrasts those who value money, honour, or physical pleasures above all with those who know and love God. But the more general contrast, indicated in §§9–10 of TdIE, is between those who love what is destructible and those who love God.

Thus Spinoza can and probably does recognize that people have different abilities and interests and that a life devoted to art, political affairs, particular sciences, engineering, medicine, raising children, or teaching is a worthy one. Spinoza's question concerns the kind of person you are and has little to do with your occupation or with whether you are to marry or have children.

The construction of an ideal

An ideal can be constructed in varying degrees of abstraction from the real and it appears to be endemic to that construction that it involves such abstraction. Some types of things from which we can abstract, in the construction of a concept of an ideal life, are:

1. natural laws – physical, biological, and psychological. Violations of logical laws doom the construction to incoherence. Violations of exceptionless laws of nature make the ideal purely imaginary.

2. general external circumstances, including political, economic, social, religious, historical, and technological circumstances.

3. particular or personal characteristics and circumstances – including gender, height, weight, wealth, intelligence, personality, talents, interests, beliefs, the character and circumstances of one's parents, and so on.

Generally we keep constant our species,[26] the general character of ourselves as having needs and a desire to live well or prosper, and of the world as containing scarcity and threats.

Since an ideal life is and must be a life within a world or environment, we can distinguish changes in us and changes in the world. Indeed, we must consider how changes of one sort mesh with changes of the other.

If we focus on the question of how it is best to be or what kind of person to be, we must face the problem of determining what the alternatives or the relevant kinds are. In TdIE, as we have seen, Spinoza answers this by classifying people in terms of their dominant desire (the avaricious, the sensualists, etc.). We will see that in later works this idea seems to be retained, although it is expressed differently. In the *Ethics*, for example, Spinoza's primary classification is between those who are active and live under the guidance of reason as opposed to those who are passive and live as prompted by the imagination or by passive emotions. He also suggests a division into (1) almost another species, analogous to a Nietzschean 'overman', (2) ordinary people, and (3) beasts.

It is noteworthy that none of these kinds is tied to people in virtue of their types of jobs or careers, such as 'businesspeople' (which cannot be identified with the greedy or 'money-makers'), artists, athletes, teachers, plumbers, and so on. Here there may be mixed motives: those of any of these types may be driven by, or may primarily seek, honour or wealth, but they may also, for diverse reasons and from diverse causes, just be absorbed in the activity.

If the question is, 'What is it best to devote our time and lives to and to try to achieve in our lives?', there does not seem to be just one answer. There are many. This raises a further question, of the unity of our lives, or the lack of it.

It is difficult to conceive that the best kind of life can be divorced or separated from a kind of life that others do, or perhaps rather should, respect.[27] But the nature of this respect depends on who the others are and thus it has the same drawback that Spinoza, with Aristotle, finds in the quest for honour: that you must live in accordance with how others judge, that is, in accordance with what they approve or disapprove. But this type of drawback is one we should expect. For the best kind of life for an individual is surely dependent, in part, on the human environment in which we live and this is not completely within our own control.

More could be said here about public conceptions of who we are to respect. We categorize people on the basis of their jobs and this seems very deeply ingrained within our own society. But we should treat ordinary or commonsense notions with caution. We can of course consider various types or categories of jobs as well, for example, 'skilled or unskilled', 'trades or professions', etc., but more important is what kind of person someone is. The justifiable bases of respect are tied to this, that is, they are tied to character.

PART II

THE *ETHICS*

CHAPTER 4

INTRODUCTION TO THE *ETHICS*

A PREVIEW OF TOPICS

The *Ethics* is one of the world's great books and an acknowledged masterpiece of philosophy. It contains five parts, whose titles are as follows:

   I. Of God
  II. Of the Nature and Origin of the Mind
 III. Of the Origin and Nature of the Emotions
 IV. Of Human Bondage, or the Power of the Emotions
  V. Of the Power of the Intellect, or of Human Freedom

Part I provides a metaphysics, conceived as an account of what sorts of things are real and how they are related to each other. It also provides at least a partial cosmology, since it characterizes the structure of the universe, as well as a theology or theory about God.

Part II sets out an account of what the human mind is and what kinds of knowledge we have. It thus consists of a philosophy of mind and a theory of knowledge, but it also contains, curiously, a physics.

Part III is concerned with the 'affects', that is, our emotions and desires, and provides a psychology of motivation or of 'conation'.

Part IV deals primarily with ethics, understood as an enquiry into the very practical question of how it is best to live and what is of most value in life. In doing so, it explicitly eschews a distinctively or specifically 'moral' concept of obligation, or of 'moral' right and wrong, in opposition to most moral philosophy after Greek and Roman times.

Part V describes, in the first section, the practical means by which negative emotions such as fear and anger can be weakened or eliminated. These are, if you will, psychotherapeutic techniques. It then turns, in the second section, to what Spinoza calls 'another part of ethics'. It deals with freedom of mind and the power of our intuitive knowledge of God. In this section, Spinoza speaks of the eternity of the intellect, that is, as some interpreters hold, of the mind without relation to temporal existence.

Thus, as we noted earlier, Spinoza's philosophy crosses over whatever lines now exist between philosophy, theology, and the sciences, including, perhaps most prominently, physics, cosmology, and psychology.

COMPOSITION

The *Ethics* was published posthumously in 1677, but we know that it was complete, in a form acceptable to Spinoza, in the late summer or early autumn of 1675. For in Ep 68, which is dated September 1675, he relates that when he received Oldenburg's letter of 22 July, he was about to publish it. He delayed doing this, however, for a rumour was spreading that he was planning to publish a book that tries to show there is no God. In addition, complaints to the Prince of Orange and to the magistrates had already been made. Theologians and Cartesians, he says, were plotting against him, so he waited and was uncertain what to do.

We also know, from another letter to Oldenburg,[1] that Spinoza had at least begun to cast his views on God and substance into geometrical form in 1661. If we regard this as the start of the *Ethics* proper,[2] we can conjecture that he worked on the *Ethics* itself, off and on, for at least 14 years.

Spinoza worked on the ideas that it expresses, however, for virtually all of his adult life. For the *Ethics* is a revised and reworked expression of an earlier work, the *Short Treatise on God, Man, and his Well-Being*. This title, in fact, provides a summary of the main topics of the *Ethics*.

READING THE *ETHICS*: TWO OBSTACLES

Two features of the work make it especially difficult for modern readers:

1. it is written in the vocabulary of late medieval scholasticism, and
2. it is set out 'in the geometric order'.

The first is a problem for us because this vocabulary is foreign to nearly everyone now alive.

The geometric order is the order found in Euclid's *Elements*. It begins with definitions and axioms and then proceeds to establish theorems on their basis. This is a problem, in part, because it has no teleological order, that is, it seems to have no direction. It simply proceeds, in theory at least, to churn out theorems without indicating the goal of the author and without indicating which theorems are themselves important, as opposed to those that are important only as a means to others.

The first obstacle

The first of these obstacles is a type of problem that the *Ethics* shares with most works in philosophy. Problems arising from vocabulary are found in nearly all philosophical writings, from the first written philosophical fragments of the ancient Greeks, through Plato, Aristotle, and their successors to modern times. They are more severe, however, in some cases than in others. Kant and Heidegger, for example, depart from plain language much more than do Locke or Searle. But learning the meaning of technical terms is an essential part of the process of coming to understand a philosophy. The same is true in nearly every field, from the arts and law to the sciences.

In the case of Spinoza, we are actually at some advantage here, because he does provide explicit definitions and he makes a great effort, at least, to explain his terms and to use them consistently. This is required, after all, by the geometric method.

On the other hand, it is endemic to this method that the primitive terms remain undefined. In addition, Spinoza sometimes adopts traditional terminology, but uses it in ways that differ radically from its typical seventeenth-century use. This is true, for example, of many of the most important terms, such as 'substance', 'mode', and even 'mind'.

It is like reading Kant for the first time. Once is not enough. And as with Kant, so with Spinoza: it is enormously helpful to have an idea beforehand of what some of the main theses and lines of thought are. It is a main task of this work to provide that.

Spinoza's vocabulary is best discussed and clarified in context, where it is needed. The meaning of his terms, even when familiar to us, like 'idea', is also tied to disputes with his contemporaries. So they are not fully understood except in relation to divergent uses of the terms.

The second obstacle

The virtues of the geometrical order are many. It emphasizes the importance of argument, that is, of reasons for accepting a claim, and thus it seems especially well suited for the presentation of philosophical and scientific results. For the provision and examination of reasons is what marks out philosophy and science from mere dogma.

By its nature, however, the geometrical order cannot provide reasons for its most basic claims, which in theory are found only in the axioms. In addition, it does not exhibit the thought that has led to the selection of some claims rather than others as axiomatic, nor does it speak informally about the problems and perplexities that surround every important philosophical issue. It does not, in short, exhibit the process of discovery, in which so much of philosophical thinking consists.

So in this respect it is often thought to be most inappropriate for philosophy. But if philosophy is conceived not just as a process, but as a process that can and does result in solutions to problems, or answers to questions, then the geometrical method represents the pinnacle of the endeavour. This, ideally, is a comprehensive and unified theory that exhibits the most basic concepts at issue and sets out fundamental claims from which all others are derived.

The problem for readers consists primarily in its apparent lack of direction, although in mathematics there is also often a nagging question about its utility. Spinoza's theory speaks of how it is best to live, however, and of what is of most value in life, so the second of these problems does not seem to arise. The first, however, is solved by providing readers with a clear statement of what Spinoza's most important claims are. This I will try to do in the introductory sections on each part of the *Ethics*.

CHAPTER 5

THE *ETHICS*, PART I: GOD

BACKGROUND

Introduction to metaphysics

Metaphysics is concerned with fundamental questions about what is real. Are there different kinds or types of reality? If so, what are they and how are they related to each other? Are some things more real than others? Is there anything that is most real?

The original source of our word 'metaphysics' is Andronicus of Rhodes, who edited Aristotle's works in the first century BC. Andronicus uses the expression *ta meta ta phusika* to refer to works that were located after (*meta*) Aristotle's *Physics* (*phusika*) in the collection of Aristotle's writings. The expression, which is a transliteration of the Greek, means literally 'the (things) after the physics'.

The word is also sometimes taken to indicate that the subject deals with what is 'beyond' or 'above' physical objects. In Book III of the *Metaphysics*, Aristotle characterizes the subject as the science of 'being qua being'. In contrast to this is physics or philosophy of nature, which studies physical things as physical, not merely as beings or as things that have being. Aristotle also describes his subject as 'theology' (in Book XI) and as the study of the first causes and principles of things (in Book I).

Most of the classical issues in metaphysics are still of contemporary concern and they are typically called 'problems'. Thus we have the problem of universals, the problem of the external world and of other minds, and the mind–body problem.

The problem of universals deals with questions about the existence or ontological status of Platonic forms, that is, the alleged correlates of general terms. If we grant there are or even may be many triangles, for example, does it follow that there must be something else, triangularity, that is mind-independent and common to all triangles? Although debated extensively in the Middle Ages, and almost uniformly resolved in the negative in the seventeenth and eighteenth-centuries, this is still an issue.

The problem of the external world was set out in its most acute form, and most famously, by Descartes. Is there an 'external world', that is, a world of bodies that exist independently of our experiences, and if so, how can we have knowledge of it? The general question of the existence of an objective world is often designated now simply as the issue of 'realism'. But this word is also used for the same set of issues regarding other alleged objects, such as universals and moral properties.

The problem of other minds and the mind–body problem are two other metaphysical problems. How can you really know that there are other beings who have subjective experiences like your own? How are you, or your mind, related to your body?

Other classical issues concern the existence and nature of time, space, events, and God, but this short inventory is by no means exhaustive.

The *Ethics*, Part I in a nutshell

Spinoza maintains that God is absolutely infinite being or substance, that he necessarily exists, and that all other things are modes of God. These modes or modifications of God, such as people, trees, and rocks, are ontologically and conceptually dependent on God. In addition, God or substance is the efficient cause of all modes. God necessarily produces them, but he has no desires or goals, and so does not produce them in order to achieve anything. Unlike people, he does not act purposefully. Thus the world has no purpose or direction. Although God has no free or uncaused will, God is free in the sense that he is completely self-determining.

Substance has infinitely many attributes, of which we know only two: Thought and Extension. Conceived under the attribute of Thought, substance produces an infinite mode (God's intellect or mind); conceived under Extension, it produces Motion and Rest and an infinite body. Each finite body is surrounded by others (since there is no vacuum) and the 'universe', regarded as the totality of all physical things, is an infinite body.

An introduction to Spinoza's views about God: A contrast with traditional views

Part I of Spinoza's *Ethics* is concerned with the nature and properties of God. Although he holds that God exists, Spinoza's conception of God is highly unorthodox. Indeed, it is one of the most radical conceptions that can be found in the Western tradition. What is most radical about it is that on Spinoza's view God

1. has no emotions, goals, or plans;
2. does not have free will;
3. is physical (as well as mental);
4. is not separate from 'the world';
5. has no inherent moral properties (such as justice or benevolence); and
6. is adequately known by us (in his essence).

Spinoza also holds, contrary to prominent theologians such as Maimonides and Aquinas, that there was no first moment of creation. Instead he accepts an infinite regress of finite causes for each finite thing and holds, analogously, that each real thing is a cause of something.

1. Spinoza rejects an anthropomorphic conception of God, according to which God is like a human being. The word 'anthropomorphic' comes from two Greek words, transliterated as '*anthrōpos*' (man) and '*morphē*' (form, shape, or structure).

Although this could encompass any similarity whatever between God and human beings, an anthropomorphic conception is primarily one that takes God to be like people in having desires and emotions such as love, anger, and jealousy, and in having virtues such as benevolence and justice. Sometimes God is also regarded as having hands, eyes, or a face.

In what important respects is God unlike a human being, according to Spinoza? He certainly denies that God literally has hands, eyes, or a face, although in Ep 64 he metaphorically characterizes the infinite totality of all bodies as the 'face of the whole universe' (*facies totius universi*).

In addition, God has no desires and no emotions. He does not love or hate anyone; he is never happy or sad, nor is he angry, vengeful, or jealous. He is also unlike a king, a legislator, or a judge, for he does not issue commands and then seek to reward or punish people for obedience or disobedience.

Ordinary patterns by which we explain human action are thus inapplicable to God's actions. Commonsense explanations of human action, or 'folk psychology', as it has been called, rely on a variety of general theses.[1] One of these is that people typically act in ways that they believe will achieve their goals (or satisfy their desires). Unlike us, however, God has no goals or desires, according to Spinoza. Thus he does not survey alternative courses of action and decide what to do.

Other 'folk psychological' theses are concerned with emotions. A person who hates you, for example, will want to harm you. He will also be pleased when he learns, or even comes to believe, that something bad has happened to you or to one you love. But God has no emotions, according to Spinoza.

Spinoza's general position is interestingly expressed in Ep 56, where he writes, 'I believe that a triangle, if indeed it had the ability to speak, would say . . . that God is eminently triangular, and a circle would say that the divine nature is eminently circular'.[2] Wolf calls attention to similar remarks by Xenophanes of Colophon (570–480 BC).[3] In other letters, Spinoza denies that, philosophically speaking, anything is pleasing to God or that he issues commands or acts like a judge.[4]

It seems clearly to follow from this that on Spinoza's view the universe has no purpose. It is, as we might say, directionless or pointless.

2. Closely related to 1 is Spinoza's thesis that God does not have free will (and we don't either, on his view). Rather than deny that God has a will, Spinoza identifies God's will with his intellect, or understanding. He maintains that for God to will that something be so is the same as his understanding or knowledge that it is so. We might thus call him a 'reductivist' rather than an 'eliminativist' in this respect. For he 'reduces' God's will to his intellect, rather than 'eliminating' it outright.

In addition, Spinoza holds that God's will, like everything else, arises necessarily from God's nature or essence and so it has a determining cause. God necessarily acts as he does because of his nature or essence, not because of his free (that is, uncaused) will. Spinoza also maintains, however, that God is free in the very different sense that he is completely self-determining.

3. Spinoza thinks that God is physical as well as mental. By this he does not mean that God is a body, even an infinite one. It is rather that God has, or rather is, an 'attribute', the attribute of Extension. The idea, following Descartes, is that to be extended (or have extension) is to have length, width, and depth, that is, to be extended in three dimensions. Extension itself is then three-dimensionality. God, however, is also Thought, the other attribute that is known to us. Just as God is not a body, but has one, so too he is not a mind, but he has one.

4. Another important difference between Spinoza's conception of God and more traditional views is that God and 'the world' (or 'universe') are not two beings that are separate from each other. In his language, they are not two 'substances', one of which ('the world') exists, after creation, apart from or 'outside of' the other (God). Instead, God is nature (*natura naturans* in his language), while 'the world' or 'the universe', understood as a totality of all finite bodies (and minds), is a 'modification' of God that is not separate from him.

5. Spinoza denies that things are inherently good or bad. They are good or bad, not in themselves, but only in relation to us (or to some other being). Although Spinoza sometimes calls God 'good', he regards this as true only because God is of benefit to us. Our existence and preservation depend on God, as does our highest happiness. Other moral properties, such as the virtues of justice and benevolence, are simply inapplicable to God. After all, God has no emotions and no desires.

6. We have adequate knowledge of the essence of God, according to Spinoza. In this he departs from the '*via negativa*' or 'negative way', according to which we can only know what God is not. He also departs from those who hold that what we say of God can only be understood by analogy with our talk about other things.

Is Spinoza, then, an atheist? For if his conception of God is so unorthodox, why regard it as a conception of God at all? Why not maintain that 'God' is a misnomer here, since Spinoza's idea of God diverges so much from the orthodox views of Muslims, Jews, and Christians?

One answer is that despite these differences, there are important similarities as well. Spinoza holds, in agreement with more traditional conceptions, that God is omniscient, omnipotent, the creator of all things, infinite, perfect, and unique (i.e. the sole God). In addition, his essence involves existence. According to Spinoza, all of these are properties of God, but not 'attributes that express God's essence'; that is, they do not tell us what God is. In contrast are Thought and Extension, the only attributes that, on his view, we know.

Another answer is certainly possible, however. It concedes that 'God', as ordinarily used, is taken to refer to, and practically means, a non-physical being with emotions and a goal or purpose in creating the world. It then abandons the use of the term 'God' and speaks instead of infinite being or substance. On this view, Spinoza is an atheist.

If he is an atheist, however, he is surely a very unusual specimen of one. For he thinks that our highest happiness depends on, and indeed our salvation or blessedness consists in, knowledge and love of what he calls 'God'.

Thus the issue seems to be at least largely terminological. As we have seen, it was reported to the Spanish Inquisition that Spinoza said, 'God exists only philosophically speaking'.[5] Although I have spoken above of the 'orthodox views' of some of the world's major religions, it should be noted that leading theologians within those traditions often hold views that diverge from the beliefs of ordinary followers. Maimonides, for example, maintains that we can only describe God negatively. We know, for example, that God is not unjust, rather than that he is (positively) just. Aquinas, in contrast, holds that all of our descriptions of God must be understood by analogy with our use of them in describing created things. The word 'just', when applied to God, does not mean quite what it does when applied to Solomon or any other person.

Ordinary believers, on the other hand, sometimes seem to suppose that positive descriptions of God can be given and that they have the same meaning when applied to God as when applied to anything else. The claim that God is just or that God loves you is taken to imply just what it would if you were speaking of another human being.

The extent to which ordinary believers would recognize the God of the philosophers, or of the theologians of their own faith, is not easy to determine.

A RECOMMENDED ORDER OF READINGS FOR PART I OF THE *ETHICS*

This section provides a recommended order of readings for Part I of the *Ethics*. It is intended as a guide for an initial reading, to help you to see for yourself the structure of the work and to understand some of Spinoza's main theses and arguments. Explanatory comments on these readings and the issues that arise will be found in the next section.

It is sometimes useful, when you read the propositions for the first time, to read the demonstrations and scholia as well. Sometimes it is not. Detailed consideration and assessment of the demonstrations is not needed at first and it is certainly not expected on a first reading.

Note that Part I has two main sections or divisions. The first division, from p 1 to p 14, attempts to establish the necessary existence and uniqueness of God. The second, from p 15 to p 36, attempts to show how everything else is related to God.

Abbreviated references are used below and are explained in the separate list of abbreviations at the beginning of this book.

Reading	Spinoza's claim
App, 1st sentence	Summary of Spinoza's main theses regarding God.
p 4d, 1st sentence	Everything that really exists is a substance or a mode.
p 11	God, or substance with infinite attributes, necessarily exists.
p 14	God is the only substance that exists or is conceivable.
p 15	Everything is in and conceived through God.
p 16	Infinite things in infinite ways – that is, everything conceivable by an infinite intellect – follows from the necessity of God's nature.
p 17c2	Only God is a free cause.
p 21–p 23, p 28	God immediately produces infinite modes, these infinite modes produce others, and each finite mode is produced by another finite mode.
p 29	Nothing is contingent.

p 32	There is no free will.
p 33	Nothing could have been produced by God in a different way.
Rest of App	It is not the case that all things in nature act purposively.

DISCUSSION OF THE RECOMMENDED READINGS FOR PART I OF THE *ETHICS*

God's properties
App, first sentence: Main theses regarding God.

The first sentence of the Appendix mentions some of the important properties of Spinoza's God. A list of these, along with the places in the text where they are stated or discussed, is as follows:

God necessarily exists.	p 11
God is unique.	p 14 and its corollaries
God acts solely from the necessity of his nature.	p 16; see also p 17
God is the free cause of all things.	p 17c2
All things are in God and depend on God.	p 15
All things are predetermined, not by God's free will, but by God's absolute nature.	p 16, p 29, p 32c1, p 33; see also p 34

Spinoza's substance–mode ontology
p 4d, first sentence: Everything that really exists is a substance or a mode.

Spinoza defines God in terms of substance and he defines both substance and mode in terms of two other notions that are undefined: being in a thing and being conceived through a thing. His definitions can be expressed as follows:

> def6: God is substance consisting of infinite attributes.
> def3: Substance is in itself and conceived through itself.
> def5: A mode is in and conceived through something else.

Spinoza makes it clear as early as this in the *Ethics* (in p 4d) that his official ontology admits exactly two kinds of 'real things', that is, things '*in rerum natura*' or '*extra intellectum*' (outside the intellect). Each real thing is either a substance or a mode (an 'affection' of substance).

His argument in p 4d cites def3 and def5 as well as ax1, which reads:

ax1:   Everything is either in itself or in another.

Thus Spinoza seems simply to assume that whatever is in a thing is conceived through it. But what is it to be in and conceived through a thing?

'Being in' a thing seems to express a notion of ontological dependence, that is, a dependence with respect to the being or existence of a thing. One thing is in another when it depends, perhaps in one certain way, on that other for its existence; a thing is in itself when it depends only on itself, and so not on another, for its existence.

'Being conceived through' something expresses a notion of conceptual or epistemological dependence. Spinoza sometimes takes being conceived through something to concern the formation of a concept, as def3 indicates. Sometimes it concerns the acquisition of knowledge and the explanation of one thing by recourse to another, as ax4 and its uses indicate.

So substance is something that exists or would exist independently of anything else and it can be conceived and known independently of any other concept or knowledge. This substance–mode ontology appears to be quite orthodox for that time.

What is unorthodox is Spinoza's insistence that there could not be more than one substance of the same kind (p 5), as well as his related theses that no substance is finite (p 8) and no substance can produce another (p 6).

This is unorthodox because 'substance' was standardly used in the seventeenth century to characterize particular finite bodies, such as horses and chairs, as well as individual human minds. Spinoza departs from this usage in refusing to call such things 'substances', for they are not truly independent of other things. How could a horse, for example, exist even for a moment, if it were not surrounded by other bodies and not generated from other things?

The ontological argument for the existence of God
p 11 and its first demonstration: God, or substance with infinite attributes, necessarily exists.

Spinoza's first proof of God's existence is quite short. The form of the argument he gives is called a *reductio ad absurdum* (reduction to absurdity), or more simply a *'reductio'*.

This form of argument begins by assuming the falsity of the thesis to be proved. It then deduces from this assumption some 'absurdity', that is, a claim that contradicts what is known to be true. Thus the original assumption must be false and so the thesis is true. (If the denial of a thesis deductively leads to something false, then the thesis itself must be true.)

The argument is as follows:

(1) Suppose that God does not necessarily exist or, equivalently, God can be conceived not to exist.
(2) But according to ax7, if a thing can be conceived not to exist, its essence does not involve existence.
(3) So God's essence does not involve existence.
(4) But God is substance (def6) and so, by p 7,
(5) Existence belongs to the nature of God, that is, God's essence involves existence.
(6) however, (5) contradicts (3).
(7) Hence, God necessarily exists (or cannot be conceived not to exist).

Reductio arguments can also be set out positively. A positive formulation of p 11d might go as follows:

(1) God, by def3, is substance consisting of infinite attributes.
(2) Existence belongs to the nature of substance (p 7).
(3) Hence, existence belongs to the nature of God.

To say that existence belongs to the nature of God entails, however, that God necessarily exists.

Is this just a verbal trick? God seems simply to be defined into existence and if the argument works here, why couldn't just anything be similarly defined into existence?

A related objection might also be made. For Spinoza's demonstration of p 7 holds that since substance cannot be produced by another, it is 'cause of itself' (*causa sui*), and thus (by def1) existence belongs to its nature. But doesn't this just assume that it has a cause? Round squares can't be produced by another either.

Spinoza in effect replies to this in a proof he appends to the argument in p 11d. (This is the first proof labelled '*aliter*', or 'another', by Spinoza. It is translated as 'Second Proof' by Shirley.) Spinoza there maintains that if a thing doesn't exist there must be a cause or reason why it doesn't and this reason must be 'contained in' the nature of the thing or must be outside it. He argues that such a cause cannot be outside God's nature (for it would have to be in another substance that has nothing in common with God). It also cannot be in God's nature, for there would then be a contradiction in the concept of absolutely infinite being that is 'in the highest degree perfect'.

The argument in p 11d appears to be a variation on the 'ontological argument' given by St Anselm in *Proslogion* 1–4.[6] In Anselm's formulation, God is 'that than which nothing greater can be conceived'. Since it is greater to exist in actuality than to exist only 'in the mind', such a God must, allegedly, exist. In Descartes' formulation in *Meditations* V, existence pertains to the essence of God and hence God necessarily exists. Alternatively, God by definition has all perfections. Since existence is a perfection, God exists.

Leibniz criticized Descartes for assuming, and not proving, that all perfections are compatible, that is, that God is possible.

Later thinkers have objected that existence 'adds nothing' to the concept of a thing[7] and that 'exists' is not a predicate.[8] Modern variations of the argument appear to obviate these objections with the help of modal logic.[9]

God's uniqueness

p 14, p 14d, and p 14c1: God is the only substance that exists or is conceivable.

Spinoza holds that there could be no substance other than God and his argument for this is as follows. If there were a substance other than God, it would have to have some attribute that God has. Presumably, this is because God has infinite, and hence all, attributes. But there cannot be two substances with the same attribute (by p 5).

In the first corollary Spinoza states that God is single, or unique ('*Deum esse unicam*'). This is interesting because in CM I.6 he says, 'God can only very misleadingly be called one or single (*unam et unicam*).' He explains this in Ep 50, written to Jarig Jelles in 1674, and says that it is not very important, since it affects only names, not things.[10]

How all things depend on God
BEING IN GOD
p 15: Everything is in and conceived through God.

Spinoza maintains in p 15 that everything is in and conceived through God. His argument for this states that God, the only substance, is in and conceived through itself (by def3). Modes, on the other hand, can neither be nor be conceived without substance (by def5), and so are in and conceived through it. But only substance and modes exist (by ax1).

An apparent difficulty with this is that def5 actually has two parts. One part of it merely states that a mode is what is in and conceived through another, rather than that a mode is in and conceived through substance. The other part of def5 states that a mode is an affection of substance.

In addition, it becomes clear from later parts of the *Ethics* that there are modes of modes. These must be things that are in and conceived through another which is itself in and conceived through a third.

Spinoza's concept of being in a thing seems to be derived from Aristotle's talk, in the *Categories*, of being in a subject. Aristotle holds, for example, that when we say 'Socrates is white', we are saying that the colour, whiteness, is in Socrates as its subject. Spinoza's view, unlike Aristotle's, is that the ultimate subject of everything we say is God.

p 15s is primarily a criticism of the view that God is not physical or not a material substance. Spinoza's opponents hold that material substance is composed of parts and is divisible, hence it can be destroyed. Spinoza's reply is that matter, considered as substance, has no parts and is not divisible.

He also says in this scholium, 'we have concluded that extended substance is one of God's infinite attributes'. There is a glitch here, since Spinoza has not yet even asserted this. This may be a reference to p 14c2, but this corollary merely says that Thought and Extension ('the extended thing and the thinking thing') are either attributes or affections of the attributes of God. It is not until II p 2d that Spinoza tries to establish formally that Extension is an attribute of God.

BEING CAUSED BY GOD

p 16: Infinite things in infinite ways – that is, everything conceivable by an infinite intellect – follows from the necessity of God's nature.

Spinoza's demonstration maintains that many properties follow from the essence of a thing and that the intellect can infer these properties from its definition. In addition, it maintains that the more reality the essence involves, the more properties follow from it. Since God's essence involves infinite attributes, and each of these is infinite in its kind, 'an infinity of things in infinite ways' must follow from God's essence.

This demonstration seems obscure and it invokes important principles that are not found in the axioms. The primary model of a property that follows from the essence of a thing seems to be a geometrical one. Spinoza often illustrates this by saying that it follows from the essence of a triangle that its three angles are equal to two right angles. Triangles have this property because of what a triangle is (its essence or definition), not because of some incidental feature of it. In Ep 83, written in 1676 to Tschirnhaus, Spinoza replies to the objection that only one property follows from the essence of a thing.

It is natural enough, I suppose, to think that there cannot be more than an infinity of things in infinite ways and Spinoza seems to accept this. In II p 17s he is explicit about it and uses the example of a triangle:

> However, I think I have shown quite clearly (Pr. 16) that from God's supreme power or infinite nature an infinity of things in infinite ways – that is, everything – has necessarily flowed or is always following from that same necessity, just as from the nature of a triangle it follows from eternity that its three angles are equal to two right angles.[11]

That God is the cause of all things (that are in him) is asserted explicitly in I p 18d, as based on I p 16. I p 16 is the basis for all of Spinoza's claims about God's causality.

The parenthetical remark in the proposition itself simply assumes that God has an infinite intellect, but this is not established until II p 3.

It is natural for us to object that in fact we cannot infer from the mere statement of what a triangle is that its three angles equal two right angles. We must at least also have a definition of a right angle and, presumably, other axioms of geometry.

Freedom
p 17c2, its demonstration, and Spinoza's definition of 'free' (def7):
Only God is a (completely) free cause.

One conception of freedom is that of doing what you want, or having the power to do what you want. Hume, for example, takes this position. Spinoza does not accept this generally, primarily because our wants and desires so often arise from causes that are external to us. They are not fully 'ours'.

Instead, he proposes a conception of freedom as self-determination. His definition of this in def7 reads, 'That thing is said to be free, which exists solely from the necessity of its own nature, and is determined to action by itself alone.'[12] This is contrasted with a thing that is 'constrained', that is (again by def7), a thing that is determined to exist and act by another.

Thus God is completely free, since God exists by the necessity of his nature (p 11) and God acts solely by the necessity of his nature (p 16). Spinoza here takes acting to be the production or causation of something. Furthermore, only God is completely free, for everything else is produced by God.

Spinoza maintains later in the *Ethics* that human freedom is in a similar sense possible to the extent that we are determined to an action because of our nature (IV p 68, V p 36s). This will be considered in more detail later.

In I p 17s Spinoza argues against a conception of divine freedom as the ability to omit doing things that follow from his nature, that is, things that are in his power. He also rejects the view that God understands more than he can create.

The second part of this scholium maintains that if intellect and will did pertain to God's nature, then they would have to differ entirely from our intellect and will (or would have only the name in common). Note that on Spinoza's view they do not pertain to the essence of God, that is, they are not attributes. In saying that neither intellect nor will 'pertain to the essence' of God, Spinoza does not deny here that God has an intellect or will; he means that they are not God's essence.

It should be added that I p 33s 2 does not grant that intellect or will 'pertain to the essence of God', except for the sake of argument.

In this respect, the White–Stirling translation of an important part of this scholium is at best misleading.[13]

A very different conception of freedom is espoused by others, such as Descartes. On this conception, freedom consists in having a 'free will', where this is taken to be a will that has no cause. It is in this sense that Spinoza denies free will, for everything, on his view, is caused.

God's causality of finite and infinite modes

p 21–p 23, p 28: God immediately produces infinite modes, these infinite modes produce others, and each finite mode is produced by another finite mode.

In p 21, Spinoza speaks of what follows 'from the absolute nature of any attribute'. His claim is that what does follow from this must itself be 'eternal and infinite'.

Note that here and in p 22, p 23, and p 28, Spinoza speaks indifferently of things as eternal, as necessarily existent, and as always existent. Elsewhere, as in the explicatio of def8, he distinguishes eternity from temporal existence.

In p 22 he speaks of what follows, not from the absolute nature of an attribute, but from an attribute 'modified by an infinite modification'. These, too, must be infinite and necessarily existent.

In p 23 we find that any infinite and necessarily existent mode follows from the absolute nature of an attribute (as in p 21) or from the absolute nature of an attribute as modified by an infinite mode (as in p 22).

Finally, in p 28, he maintains that a finite thing must be determined to exist and act by another finite thing.

Ep 64 (in response to a request by Tschirnhaus, relayed through Schuller) gives examples of immediate infinite modes of Thought and of Extension as well as an example of a mediate infinite mode of Extension. God's intellect, or infinite understanding, is an immediate infinite mode of Thought. Motion-and-Rest is an immediate infinite mode, while an infinite body is a mediate infinite mode, under the attribute of Extension. II lem7 offers further explanation.

Spinoza's denial of contingency

p 29 and p 29d: Nothing is contingent.

Spinoza's argument in p 29d is complicated, partly because it takes into account the idea that even if determined by God to act in a certain way, a thing might determine itself to act differently. The central idea of the argument is that everything has been determined to exist and act by God's nature; hence it exists and acts as it does necessarily, not contingently, most basically because of p 16.

The idea of contingency used here is that of something that is not necessary and not impossible. A thing, for example, exists contingently at a certain moment just if it is possible for it to exist at that moment and also possible for it not to exist at that moment. In p 33s 1, Spinoza reiterates his view that nothing is contingent and explains that we say that things are contingent only because of our ignorance of the essence of a thing or of the causal order of nature.

The scholium to p 29 introduces the terms *natura naturans* and *natura naturata*. The former is equivalent to 'substance' and the latter to 'mode'. These expressions were also used by Aquinas and by Giordano Bruno.

p 32, its demonstration and corollaries: There is no free will.

Spinoza's argument is straightforward in outline. The will is a mode and so it must be determined to exist and act by another. p 27 establishes this for a finite will and p 23 for an infinite will.

If the will is not a mode, then it 'pertains to God's essence', that is, it is God or God's essence. p 33s 2 argues against the view that God acts by free will, that is, by an uncaused will, even if the will did pertain to God's essence.

p 33 and its demonstration: Nothing could have been produced by God in a different way.

Spinoza's argument for this claim is interesting. He maintains that since things have necessarily been produced by God's nature, if God could have produced things differently then God's nature could have been different. But that nature would then also have to exist (by the ontological argument in p 11d). So there would be two Gods, which by p 14 is impossible.

It is tempting to formulate part of this argument as follows:

(1) Every God that is possible is actual.
(2) A God that creates a different world is possible.
(3) Hence, a God that creates a different world is actual.

There would then have to be two Gods, on the assumption that a God that creates a different world is different from the God that creates this one.

In the very last part of p 33s 2, Spinoza contrasts two views that are opposed to his own. On one, created things have arisen from God's arbitrary or indifferent will; on the other, they have arisen from God's will to do what is good. The latter, he says, subjects God to fate, for it supposes that there is something, namely goodness, that is independent of God, and is like a target at which he aims. The former is thus closer to the truth than the latter, he says. In fact the former is Descartes' position, while the latter is Leibniz's.

The denial of purposiveness, except in people
Rest of App: It is not the case that all things in nature act purposively.

Spinoza states that his main aim in the Appendix is to expose the prejudices that prevent acceptance of his views. He holds that these depend primarily on one prejudice, namely, that all things, even God, act as we do: to achieve a goal. His explicit aims, which provide the structure of the Appendix, are to show (1) why people are so prone to accept this; (2) that it is false; and (3) that it is the source of misconceptions about 'good and bad, right and wrong, praise and blame', and so on.

1. Spinoza maintains, very much in outline, that people recognize that they act to achieve something and they then extend this model of explanation to everything else. So they constantly seek the final causes or goals of natural things. Since many of these are useful to people, but not created by them, they suppose that there must be some being like themselves who created them for a purpose. In short, the model we use to explain human action (in terms of goals) is extended or projected to other natural objects and even to the world itself.

2. Spinoza argues on several grounds that God does not act for the sake of an end, that is, that God has no goal or purpose in acting. One of the most powerful of these is that God's acting for a purpose requires that he lack something that he desires and hence is imperfect.

3. The supposition that things were created for the benefit of people has led to 'abstract notions', by which ordinary people attempt to explain things. These are 'good, bad, order, confusion, hot, cold, beauty, ugliness'. (Because they also mistakenly believe they have free will, other notions have arisen, namely, the notions of praise, blame, right, and wrong. These are discussed in IV p 37s 2.) Spinoza's view is that these terms are applied to things because of they way they affect our imagination, as opposed to the intellect. They do not indicate the nature of a thing as it is in itself; rather, they indicate how it affects us. On his view, things are not inherently good or bad, for example; they are so only in relation to us.

COMPARISON OF SPINOZA WITH OTHERS: SPINOZA'S PHILOSOPHICAL ALLIES AND OPPONENTS

We have already considered the major differences between Spinoza's conception of God and the conception promulgated by Islam, Judaism, and Christianity. Spinoza's conception in fact represents a reversion, in important respects, to 'pagan' conceptions advanced by some of the ancient Greeks.

Aristotle, for example, characterized divinity as an 'unmoved mover', that is, as a being that sets other things in motion because it is an object of desire. Its sole activity is thinking and the sole object of its thought is simply itself. God, so conceived, would evidently not deign to concern itself with human beings or human interests. So too, the ancient Stoics and Epicureans suppose that the gods take no part in human affairs. We are just not important to them. Thus we can put aside our fear of God, or the gods, as well as our hopes for divine intervention on our behalf. This has important political implications, as we will note later, for the power of the religious authorities is in large part dependent on hope and fear, that is, on the idea that God will reward or punish us.

Aristotle's philosophy, however, is especially relevant for understanding Spinoza, and indeed all other philosophers of the seventeenth century, on a variety of important topics. In large part this is because it was the dominant philosophy taught at the universities of the time.

There are at least three major elements of Aristotle's philosophy that are relevant here: (1) Aristotle's views on explanation, (2) his substance–mode ontology, that is, his metaphysics, and (3) his theory of knowledge.

1. Of special importance is Aristotle's doctrine of the four causes. These causes are factors we cite to explain a thing and they correspond to the answers to certain questions, as follows: (1) the formal cause: 'What is it?'; (2) the material cause: 'Of what is it made or composed?'; (3) the efficient cause: 'Who or what produced it?'; and (4) the final cause: 'What is it for?' or 'What is its goal or purpose?' Thus it may be a statue, made of ivory and gold, by Phidias, to honour Zeus.

Abandonment of the search for final causes is the battle cry of seventeenth-century physics and cosmology and it appears to be the hallmark of modern science. Descartes and others call for the abandonment of the search for final causes, but Descartes, at least, does so on the grounds that we cannot presume to discover, or know, God's purposes. Spinoza, in contrast, holds that God has no purposes. Although Spinoza grants that people act purposively, or for the sake of an end, he holds that the final causes of human action are really their efficient causes, that is, human desires.

Whether Spinoza in fact fully succeeds in abandoning all use of the concept of a goal or purpose can be disputed. What we have seen, however, is that physics and cosmology have proceeded with great success without the notion. Although biology has long been thought to require the idea, even as late as Kant and into the nineteenth century, Darwin took at least a major step in undermining it even there. Psychology remains a major holdout.

2. Aristotle also provides an astonishingly influential theory of categories, according to which the most basic beings are substances. 'Primary substances' are individual things such as a horse or a house, but Aristotle also supposes that the species of these are 'secondary substances'. All other things are dependent on primary substances and fall into one or another of the less basic categories, such as quality, quantity, relation, place, and time.

This distinction is an important one in the metaphysics of all philosophers of the seventeenth and eighteenth centuries. Descartes, for example, holds that while only God, strictly speaking, is a substance, other things, such as human minds and bodies, can be called substances as well. He holds, in fact, that the human mind and human body are entirely distinct substances, whereas Spinoza, as we have seen, denies they are substances at all. Hobbes, in contrast, thinks that only bodies are substances, Leibniz and Berkeley that only mental substances exist, and Hume that there are no substances. All major philosophers of the period, except Hume, maintain that the most basic beings in the world are substances and that everything else is an 'accident' or mode of a substance. Only Spinoza is a radical 'monist', however, in holding that there is just one substance, and all other things, including ourselves, are mere modifications of it.

3. The final major element of Aristotle's thought that is important in understanding Spinoza is one that Spinoza endorsed without modification. It is 'foundationalism', the doctrine that real knowledge must, like a building, have secure foundations. It must have a structure consisting of essentially two parts: the most basic truths, which are known with certainty, and less basic truths, the knowledge of which is derived ultimately from the basic truths. For if we know anything by inference from other things, we must know some things without inference (otherwise we would face an infinite regress or a circle).

It seems, then, that all knowledge must be capable of being set out 'geometrically', that is, in the manner of Euclid's *Elements*. Although this has been disputed (for example by Hegel in the nineteenth century and by the pragmatists and Quine in the twentieth), Euclid provided the ideal, for Spinoza and Descartes, of a fully worked-out theory. Indeed, even Locke accepted this ideal, at least for knowledge of the 'relations of ideas', and hence, in his view, for our knowledge of ethics.

Spinoza's relations to other philosophers and traditions are of course complex, even within metaphysics, and this discussion, which has focused primarily on Aristotle, is very far from complete.[14]

DISPUTED ISSUES OF INTERPRETATION

The problem of the attributes

One of the oldest and most celebrated difficulties in understanding Spinoza's metaphysics is 'the problem of the attributes'. The problem is essentially this.

Spinoza maintains in I p 4d that only substances and modes exist and that, as I p 14 states, the only substance is God. He also holds, however, that God has an infinity of attributes, that each attribute 'constitutes the essence' of God, and that among these are Thought and Extension.

If an attribute is something real, then by Spinoza's 'official ontology' it must be a substance or a mode. It cannot be a substance, because there is only one substance, but an infinity of attributes. It also cannot be a mode, for a mode is conceived through another, while an attribute is conceived through itself (alone).

Two attempts to solve this problem are well known. The 'subjective interpretation', in what is perhaps its main version, holds that the attributes are actually subjective ways in which we think of substance, not objective properties of it. It notes that the definition of an attribute (I def4) contains a reference to the mind and takes the proper translation of this definition to be 'what the mind perceives as if (*tanquam*) constituting the essence of substance'. One trouble with this is that Spinoza clearly does take an attribute to constitute the essence of substance, as I p 20d makes clear.

The 'objective interpretation', in contrast, regards the attributes as actually constituting the essence of substance and maintains or suggests that substance simply is its attributes. There is one substance, however, and an infinity of attributes. This seems to undermine the alleged unitary nature of substance, for it is not easy to see how one thing can also be an infinity of things.

An attempt to combine these interpretations may also be made. This holds that the distinction between the attributes is subjective although each attribute is actually the (single) essence of God. In Spinoza's language (following Descartes and Suárez), there is only a distinction of reason between them. This means that our concept of Thought and our concept of Extension are distinct concepts, although their objects, Thought and Extension themselves, are the same.

There remains a problem, however, for there are attributes (indeed, an infinity of them) of which we have no concept. In what mind, then, is there a distinction of concepts between attributes X and Y which are unknown to us? Spinoza seems to hold that it is God's mind. For in Ep 66 to Tschirnhaus, he states, 'although each thing is expressed in infinite modes in the infinite intellect of God, the infinite ideas in which it is expressed cannot constitute one and the same mind of a particular thing, but an infinity of minds'.[15]

In other words, God conceives of each mode in infinitely many ways, and each distinct concept he has of a mode is a mind of that thing. Thus, on the solution here proposed, God's conceiving something under the attribute of Extension and his conceiving it under the attribute of X (unknown to us) are distinct, even though Extension and X are one and the same.

This may seem the only possible view if we suppose that attributes are real, that they are not themselves modes, and that everything is a substance or a mode. There is an alternative, however, if we reject 'absolute identity' in favour of 'relative identity'. We will then represent Spinoza as holding (or as best holding) that Thought is the same substance as Extension, but they are not the same attribute.

It might be noted that if this solution is correct (and I am uncertain about this), then Spinoza's notion of a distinction of reason diverges in at least one important way from that of Suárez. For Suárez maintains that God makes no distinctions of reason, on the grounds that such a distinction requires inadequate concepts of the object.[16]

Spinoza himself was asked about the problem, but his answer, in Ep 9, does not seem to resolve it completely. There he takes 'substance' and 'attribute' as two names for the same thing (except that it is called 'attribute' in relation to an intellect that attributes a specific nature to it) and he gives another example of how one thing can be called by different names.

What is God?[17]

We have seen above that God is substance, that is, something that is in itself and conceived through itself. Commentators have disagreed, however, about what more can be said. Some have held that for Spinoza substance, conceived under Extension, is matter. Others have held that it is space, the laws of nature, or even 'all things'.

My own view is that Spinoza takes substance to be matter, when conceived under or conceived as the attribute of Extension.

Spinoza indicates this in several passages. In I p 15s, for example, he speaks of 'matter, insofar as it is substance' and 'water . . . insofar as it is substance'. He also maintains, where he is talking of quantity,

> if . . . we conceive it, insofar as it is substance . . . it is found to be infinite, single, and indivisible, which will be sufficiently evident to those who know how to distinguish between the imagination

and the intellect, especially if one attends to this as well: that matter is everywhere the same, nor are parts distinguished in it, except insofar as we conceive matter to be diversely affected, whence its parts are only distinguished modally, not, however, really.[18]

Further support is found in this qualification, in a passage from TTP 6: 'Note that by "Nature" here I do not understand matter alone, and its affections, but besides matter, other infinite things.'[19]

"Nature", as Spinoza often uses it, is either *natura naturans* (substance) or *natura naturata* (the modes or affections of substance). This distinction is set out in I p 29s. In TTP 6 he uses 'nature' to refer to matter – that is, to substance as extended, and its affections, as well as to 'other infinite things'.

But what are these other infinite things? Spinoza holds that there is an infinity of attributes, although we know of only two: Thought and Extension. Substance is matter, when conceived under Extension. What is it when conceived under Thought? It must be some analogue, in Thought, of matter. It must be, for lack of a better expression, 'mind-stuff', which, like matter, can 'take on' or give rise to a variety of forms (its modes or affections).

The distinction between mass terms and count nouns is relevant here. A count noun, like 'book' or 'lamp', characteristically can be preceded by the indefinite article ('a', 'an'), can take a plural form, and can be used to ask, 'How many ____ do you have?' None of this is characteristically true of mass terms, like 'milk' or 'gold'. Thus we say 'a book', 'the books', and 'How many books do you have?' We do not say, 'a milk', 'the milks', or 'How many milks do you have?' We use mass terms to ask how much, not how many.

In addition, some nouns can function in both ways. We can ask, for example, how many chickens you have in your yard as well as how much chicken you bought at the store. The latter would typically be answered with the help of a count noun, such as 'pounds' or 'kilograms'.

This is relevant to our understanding of Spinoza because some of the important terms he uses can function in both ways. We can ask, for example, how much thought you put into your remarks, but we can also talk about a thought, the thought that $1 + 1 = 2$, and how many truly original thoughts you have had. 'Thought', 'substance', and 'being' can all function as mass terms. Instead of regarding God as a substance and as an absolutely infinite being, perhaps God should be regarded as substance and absolutely infinite being.

As noted above, others have held that according to Spinoza, God or substance consists of the laws of nature,[20] that it is space,[21] or that it is 'all things'.

The first of these encounters a textual problem. For Spinoza explicitly identifies the laws of nature with God's will and intellect, as TTP 6 indicates.[22] But this is an infinite modification of substance, not substance itself.

The thesis that substance is space takes physical objects to be constructions from 'strings of place-times'[23] and supposes this to be similar to the view that fields are most basic. On this interpretation Spinoza has a 'field metaphysic'. A popular expression of it states, 'Matter (particles) is simply the momentary manifestation of interacting fields'.[24]

This view is not easy to assess, but two comments might be made. First, Spinoza denies that matter has parts or consists of particles, so it is not evident that the field metaphysic conflicts with the view that Spinoza's substance is matter. Secondly, Spinoza maintains in V p 29s that we conceive things as actual in two ways: (1) insofar as we conceive them in relation to a certain place and time and (2) insofar as we conceive them to be contained in God. The field metaphysic, because of the priority it accords place-time, seems to take (1) as most basic and as a way of conceiving of things to be in God. Spinoza, in contrast, seems to regard (2) as most basic and as opposed to (1). Thus Spinoza seems to reject the view that in conceiving of things with the help of place and time, we are thereby conceiving of them as in God, or substance.

Other interpretations hold that God is either each thing or the totality of all things.[25] In KV I.2, for example, Spinoza regards God as 'all that is Anything'[26] although even in that work he more often writes as if there are many things other than God. He speaks in KV I.1, for example, of God as 'the subiectum of all other things'.[27]

Many doctrines and passages in the *Ethics* also contradict this reading. Modes, for example, are in and conceived through another, while God is not; some modes are finite, but God is not; and so on. Indeed, in Ep 73, written in 1675, Spinoza explicitly rejects the view that God could be, or become, a human being. He writes,

For the rest, as to the doctrine which certain Churches add to these, namely, that God assumed human nature, I expressly warned them that I do not understand what they say. Indeed, to confess the truth, they seem to speak no less absurdly than if someone were to tell me that a circle assumed the nature of a square.[28]

So the extreme pantheistic interpretation, according to which each thing is God, seems impossible to sustain.

A view similar to this regards God as a whole, or as the totality of 'all being' (*omne esse*), as stated in TdIE: 'This certainly is a single, infinite being, that is, it is all being, besides which no being is given.'[29] Here, one might suggest, we are to think of all bodies (or minds) as summed up into one infinitely extended (or thinking) being.

This infinite being, however, is not *natura naturans*. It is instead *natura naturata*, according to I p29s. That is, the totality of finite beings is an infinite being that is a mode, not a substance. Our intellects, for example, are parts of God's infinite intellect, according to II p11c and V p40s. But by I p31, God's intellect is a mode, not a substance.

II lem7s should also be considered here. For Spinoza there suggests a way of regarding apparently separate things as one thing and then adds: 'And if we proceed in this way to infinity, we shall easily conceive that the whole of nature (*totam naturam*) is one Individual whose parts, that is, all bodies, vary in infinite ways, without any change in the whole Individual.'[30]

This *totam naturam* is not, however, substance. For no substance has parts and no substance is divisible (by I p12 and p13). It is instead a mediate infinite mode, the face of the whole universe (*facies totius universi*), as Spinoza's reference to II lem7s in Ep 64 shows.

Additional disputes

Three other disputed issues might also be mentioned here, although I will not discuss them at any length.[31] The secondary sources cited here will be difficult for new readers.

Being in a thing
Curley (1969) maintains that being in a thing, or at least being in God, is nothing other than being caused by God and that modes,

according to Spinoza, are not in God in the way that a property is in a subject.

One difficulty with this is that it makes I p 15 practically equivalent to I p 16. Spinoza's demonstrations of these propositions, however, are quite different and so are his uses of them. Indeed, in I p 18d, Spinoza cites I p 15 and I p 16 separately in arguing for the thesis that 'God is the cause of everything that is in him'. This, however, is trivially true if being in something is the same as being caused by it.

In addition, it is clear from Ep 83 that Spinoza is willing to regard the things that follow from God, which includes all modes, as properties of God.[32]

Necessity

The second dispute concerns Spinoza's doctrine of necessity, for some hold that Spinoza rejects the absolute necessity of all things,[33] but others disagree.[34]

Teleology

Interpreters disagree as well about Spinoza's views on teleology, final causes, or purposiveness.

Spinoza explicitly maintains that God has no purposes, but that people, at least, do act purposively or have desires. He also thinks, however, that all such purposiveness is reducible to efficient causation. In Aristotelian language, this is to say that final causes are really efficient causes.

Bennett supposes that Spinoza intends to reject all purposiveness, but does not succeed. On his view, Spinoza uses the concept of a desire in an objectionably teleological way.[35]

CHAPTER 6

THE *ETHICS*, PART II: MIND AND KNOWLEDGE

BACKGROUND

Introduction to philosophy of mind

Philosophy of mind is currently one of the most prominent and active areas of philosophy. The central issue is the mind–body problem, that is, the problem of understanding what the mind is and how it is related to the body. How is consciousness and how are you, or your 'self', related to the physical world?

A popular religious answer is that you are essentially a mind or soul, which is not physical, but which is temporarily connected or 'attached' to a particular body. When the body dies, you continue to exist and will eventually be sent to heaven or hell, depending on how you have lived.

Plato sets out a version of this in his myth of Er in the *Republic*. St Thomas Aquinas, principal philosopher of the Roman Catholic Church, also accepts a modified form of it. On his view, a person is a combination of a soul and a body and when the body dies, the soul continues to live. The body will be resurrected, however, and reunited with the soul at the Last Judgement.

A less popular answer is that the soul consists in the functioning of the body or of some part of it, such as the brain. Aristotle accepts a view like this (except for his doctrine of the 'active intellect'). It is also the dominant conception accepted by materialists, from the ancient atomists and Epicureans, through Hobbes and La Mettrie, to twentieth and twenty-first century philosophers such as Smart and Matson.

The issue has been at the forefront of modern metaphysics since its inception, that is, since the time of Descartes. Although

Descartes' formulation and discussion of the problem have been enormously influential, his solution was widely and almost immediately rejected. He maintains that the human mind is a 'thing' or substance whose whole essence is to think. The body is also a substance, but its essence is to be extended, that is, to be three-dimensional. Bodies take up space, have a shape, and move; minds do not. Minds think, affirm, doubt, and will; bodies do not. They are distinct things whose essences are completely different. Hence, they are capable of existing apart from and without each other, at least by the power of God.

Descartes also holds that changes in the body cause events in the mind, and vice versa. Dryness of the throat, for example, or damage to the foot, produces a sequence of changes in the body, culminating in a certain change in the brain. This change in the brain, which perhaps occurs in the pineal gland, then immediately causes a change in the mind: the sensation of thirst or the experience of a pain in the foot. Similarly, a mental decision to look at something at a great distance causes a change in the brain that leads to change in the eyes, thus allowing us to focus on the object.

Cartesian dualism, that is, Descartes' dualism, thus maintains that minds and bodies are distinct things, and distinct kinds of things, but that they causally interact. Mental changes produce physical ones, and vice versa. 'Interactionist dualism' is another name for this view.

In *Meditations* VI Descartes says in addition that the mind and body are so intimately joined (not like a pilot in a ship) that they constitute a single thing. How this is possible, given his view that they are 'really distinct', remains unclear, however.[1] Spinoza criticizes Descartes' conception of this union in E V Pref, taking it to consist, according to Descartes, in being causally connected.

Many reactions to Descartes are possible and most of them are actual. How, for example, can completely different kinds of things causally interact? This was immediately perceived as a problem and a variety of solutions have been proposed.

Nicholas Malebranche (1638–1715) supposes that finite minds and bodies cannot causally interact and, indeed, that no finite thing can really be a cause of anything. He holds instead that only God is a real cause, apparently taking the omnipotence of God to consist in his having all power. How an infinite mind can cause physical changes seems nonetheless problematic.

Arnold Geulincx (1624–1669) maintains, with Spinoza, that there can be no causal traffic between the mental and the physical. Instead, there are two separate series of events, which are arranged so that, for example, pain (a mental event) immediately follows, but is not caused by, your burning your hand (a physical event).

Leibniz in contrast holds that monads, like mental atoms, are the only simple substances, that they are not physical, and that they do not causally interact. Although all perceptions and changes in a monad arise internally, God has arranged the perceptions of each to correspond with the perceptions of all of the others. It may seem that you and I see the same tree and that our experiences are caused by it. But in fact my experience arises from within me and yours arises from within you. God has simply arranged things so that they correspond. This is the 'pre-established harmony'. Bodies are collections of monads or 'well-founded' *phenomena* (appearances). Thus Leibniz rejects Cartesian dualism and denies causal interaction between minds and bodies.

Hobbes, on the other hand, takes 'immaterial substance' to be a contradiction in terms and regards thought and perception simply as the motion of matter.

Spinoza does not regard any mind or body as a substance. He holds instead that a mind is a mode of Thought, while a body is a mode of Extension. He often speaks of them as if they were distinct. For example, he maintains that a finite mind is one of God's ideas, but he is not prepared to say that a body is an idea in God. So, too, he holds that bodies, not minds, move, while minds, not bodies, think. But in several passages, such as II p 21s and III p 2s, he maintains that the mind and body are 'one and the same thing, conceived now under the attribute of Thought, now under the attribute of Extension'.

The standard classification of types of theory of mind and body is as follows.

1. Dualism. Minds and bodies are both real and they are different, mutually exclusive types of thing. An alternative formulation speaks of mental and physical events, rather than minds and bodies. Types of dualism include the following.

A. Cartesian dualism (or 'interactionist dualism'). Minds and bodies causally interact, that is, mental events cause physical events, and vice versa.

B. Epiphenomenalism. Physical events cause mental events, but not vice versa. (T. H. Huxley).

C. Parallelism. There are no causal relations between mental and physical events. Instead, there is a series of causally related physical events, and a completely distinct series of causally related mental events. When you step on a tack, a moment later you feel pain, but this is not because the former (a physical event) causes the latter (a mental event). It is rather that God has arranged the two series of events to run 'in parallel' (Geulincx).

Spinoza accepts this, but only in a modified form, since he is not a dualist. There is actually just one series of events, on his view, but it is 'conceived in different ways'.

D. Occasionalism. The more radical theory proposed by Malebranche that there are no causal relations between finite things, and that only God is a real cause of anything. Note that some authors, such as Matson,[2] use 'occasionalism' more broadly and regard what I have called 'parallelism' as a form of it.

2. Materialism. All events are physical.

A. Reductive materialism. There are mental events, and so they are all physical (Hobbes, Smart, Armstrong, Matson, Davidson).

B. Eliminative materialism. There are no mental events (Churchland).

3. Idealism. All events are mental.

A. Reductive idealism. There are physical events, such as motion, and so they are all mental (Berkeley, I think, and Leibniz, on most interpretations).

B. Eliminative idealism. There are no physical events.

4. Neutral monism. An event, or the most basic stuff or type of real thing, is inherently neither mental nor physical. Being mental or physical is reducible to, or a construction from, neutral entities (Bertrand Russell, William James; Spinoza is sometimes regarded as a neutral monist, but he maintains instead that each thing is inherently both mental and physical).

5. The dual aspect theory. The mind and the body are 'two aspects' of one thing. This view is quite commonly ascribed to Spinoza (and to Spinoza alone), but as indicated above, this does not seem right to me.

Introduction to epistemology (theory of knowledge)

Epistemology, or the theory of knowledge, is concerned with what knowledge is and how, if at all, we can come to have any.

Other questions quickly follow. Are there fundamentally different kinds of knowledge, for example in history, mathematics, science, and ethics? How is knowledge that something is the case related to knowledge of how to do something? Is there some knowledge that is inexpressible in language? Are there inherent limits to what we can know? To what extent is knowledge essentially a social phenomenon, how can it be transmitted to others, and how is it related to power?

Scepticism is the doctrine that we do not, or at least may not, have any real knowledge and the refutation of this is a major concern of Descartes. His famous 'method of doubt' begins by doubting everything that can (for good reasons) be doubted. Anything that survives the attempt will then be certain and so an item of knowledge. Implicit is the thesis that knowledge involves certainty and, on the face of it, that it consists in justified certainty.

Descartes' search for certain knowledge begins by casting doubt on the existence of a physical world. If we cannot distinguish dreams from waking experiences, how can we be sure right now that the objects we seem to see are real? Indeed, how can we know, on the basis of sense perception, that there are objects that continue to exist when we do not perceive them?

His resolution of this and other doubts begins with his idea that at least he himself must exist, insofar as he is thinking. This is the '*cogito, ergo sum*': 'I think; therefore I am'. In addition, he finds a guarantee of truth in everything that he clearly and distinctly perceives. He can regard this as a mark of truth, at least, after establishing the existence of a God who is not a deceiver.

Descartes thus leaves modern philosophers with 'the problem of the external world' and, by extension, 'the problem of other minds'. For we have no immediate access to the feelings and thoughts of others. On what basis, then, can you suppose that there are other beings whose subjective experiences are like yours?

He also leaves us with the idea that what we are immediately aware of in perception are not qualities of bodies, but rather the contents of our own minds. Thus Locke, who follows Descartes here, writes, 'Whatsoever the mind perceives in itself, or is the immediate object of perception, thought, or understanding, that I call *idea*'.[3] When you look at a dog, what you see is not the dog, but your idea of the dog. When you think of the moon, the 'immediate object' of your thought is not the moon, but your idea of the moon.

Spinoza is almost unique among seventeenth- and eighteenth-century philosophers in rejecting this. He holds instead that the immediate objects of perception and thought are the things of which we have ideas. So it is not by perceiving an idea, but by having one, that we are conscious of bodies. He holds, in addition, that the ideas that represent external bodies to us are ideas of changes in our own bodies and these changes are caused by the external bodies.

A traditional proposal about knowledge is that it consists in justified true belief. But what is it for a belief to be justified? One answer, which is called 'foundationalism', maintains that knowledge is like a building. A building requires a strong foundation, on which the walls and then the roof depend. In the same way, knowledge consists of two types of belief: fundamental beliefs, which are self-evidently true, and less basic beliefs, which are derived from and depend on the fundamental beliefs.

Aristotle and Descartes are foundationalists, and, as noted earlier, so is Spinoza. His ideal of knowledge is Euclidean geometry, which, like the *Ethics*, is an axiomatized theory. Allegedly self-evident axioms are set out, and all of the rest is derived from them with the help of definitions and rules of inference.

A different analogy is used by a 'coherence theory' of justification. This holds that knowledge is more like a raft of logs or a cobweb. No one part, or small number of parts, is most basic in the sense that all others depend on them. It is rather that the parts are all interrelated and mutually dependent on each other. The question whether a belief is justified or is to be added to one's existing beliefs is to be answered by determining how it 'fits in' or 'coheres' with them. But piecemeal adjustments can be made to the existing set, as a log on a raft can be repaired or even replaced without modifying any other and without dismantling the whole thing.

The *Ethics*, Part II in a nutshell

Philosophy of mind
Spinoza holds that the human mind is one of God's ideas, that is, it is an idea that is in God's infinite intellect or mind. Its object is the human body and represents the human body, as actually existing, to

God. It is, in short, God's affirmation of the temporal existence of the body.

God's idea is composite and necessarily contains ideas of each part of the human body as well as of each change within it. Some of the ideas of these changes represent external bodies to us.

Human beings are not in principle different in this way from other things, however. For God has an idea of each body, not merely of each human body. Thus everything, according to Spinoza, has a mind or is 'animated' (*animata*) and Spinoza accepts panpsychism, the doctrine that each body has a *psyche*, or soul. He is quick to point out, however, that there are important differences between our minds and those of other things, since our bodies are of much greater complexity than those of other things.

Theory of knowledge

Spinoza is very much a foundationalist, as the structure of the *Ethics* itself strongly suggests. His ideal of knowledge is geometry, which is set out axiomatically. The most fundamental truths are stated as axioms and all other claims (the theorems or propositions) are deduced from them by means of definitions and self-evident principles of inference. Real knowledge carries certainty with it, and if we know, then we know that we know.

Spinoza maintains that we have three types of 'knowledge' (*cognitio*). The first kind he calls 'opinion' or 'imagination'. The second kind of knowledge is 'reason' (*ratio*) and the third is 'intuitive knowledge' (*scientia intuitiva*).

The first type consists of ideas that arise primarily from sense perception and from what we read or hear from others. This knowledge is concerned with individual things as actually existing in time. Such knowledge is inadequate or partial and reveals individual things only insofar as they affect us, not as they are in themselves. This kind of knowledge, or 'knowledge', is sometimes false or 'the cause of falsity'.

In contrast to this is knowledge of the second and third kinds, which is necessarily adequate and true.

The second type consists of knowledge of what is common to everything and what follows from this. Thus it is inherently general, although it can be applied to individuals. It includes knowledge of the attributes and general claims about all bodies, for example, that each body is in motion or at rest. It also includes the 'common notions' (or 'axioms') of Euclid.

Spinoza characterizes the third type as knowledge that 'proceeds from an adequate idea of the formal essence of certain attributes of God to adequate knowledge of the essence of things' (II p 40 s 2). Thus it is knowledge of the essence of individual things, as contained in the attributes, about which Spinoza speaks primarily in the last half of Part V.

An introduction to Spinoza's views about the mind and about knowledge

The mind

Spinoza's conception of the human mind is at least as unorthodox as his conception of God. For while he grants that the mind is a thinking thing that has a variety of properties, he does not regard it as a substance or as an ultimate subject of predication. It is instead a mode of God, conceived under the attribute of Thought, just as the human body is a mode of God, conceived under the attribute of Extension. Thus your mind, he holds, is one of God's ideas. Indeed, it is God's idea of your body.

Ideas, however, are not like pictures. They are affirmations or denials and God's idea of your body is his affirmation of the actual, temporal existence of your body. Since God's ideas are perfect representations of their objects, this entails that God affirms the existence of your body just while your body exists. So your mind begins to exist when your body does and it ceases to exist when your body is destroyed.

Spinoza takes an additional step, however, which is no easier to understand. He holds that the human mind and body are 'one and the same thing', although conceived in different ways. The mind, for example, is conceived as a thing that thinks and does not move, while the body is conceived as a thing that moves and does not think.

He also holds that the relationship between the human mind and body is not unique to us. For God has an idea of each body, or affirms the existence of each body, when it exists, and thus each body has a mind. As noted earlier, Spinoza says (in II p 13s) that all things are *animata*, using a Latin word related to *anima*, that is, 'soul'. Each thing is 'animated' or, we might say, ensouled or even alive.

This view is an example of Spinoza's naturalism, that is, of his tendency to regard human beings as parts of nature that are not in principle different from other things. But while we are not unique in this respect, he grants that human beings have a greater power to think, or to understand, than do other species. He tries to account for this difference by appealing to the greater complexity of the human body and its power to do and suffer many things without being destroyed. His view is very close to what we might say today: that this difference is due to the greater complexity and plasticity of the human brain.

Spinoza thus rejects the orthodox religious view of his time and ours: that the human mind can or will survive the destruction of the body. Heaven and hell, insofar as they require our continued existence in time after death, do not exist.

Somewhat surprisingly, perhaps, Spinoza nevertheless retains a conception of the eternity of the intellect. Although the nature of this conception and its coherence with the rest of his thought is a matter of considerable debate, Spinoza maintains that 'something' of the human mind, or a part of it, is eternal in the sense that it exists atemporally in God. This will be discussed at more length when we turn to Part V of the *Ethics*.

Knowledge
Spinoza departs yet again from religious orthodoxy in claiming that we have adequate knowledge of the essence of God. Every idea of a body, for example, 'involves' the concept of extension, and thus Extension, the essence of God, can only be adequately known. So we have adequate knowledge of God's essence.

In addition, we have intuitive knowledge (*scientia intuitiva*) of the essence of at least some things, that is, of their atemporal reality in God. This, however, is knowledge of a modification or feature of God and Spinoza regards this as knowledge of God as well. Indeed, he holds that all knowledge is knowledge of God.

A RECOMMENDED ORDER OF READINGS FOR PART II OF THE *ETHICS*

Part II of the *Ethics* has two main parts. In the first, from p 1–p 13s, Spinoza provides a characterization of what the human mind is. In the second, from p 14 to the end at p 49s, he sets out his epistemology, that is, he explains how we get ideas, what kinds there are, and to what extent they constitute 'true knowledge'.

Reading   **Spinoza's claim**

Division 1: The human mind (p1–p13)

p 13   The human mind is God's idea of the human body
                   or, as Spinoza puts it, 'The object of the idea
                   constituting the human mind is the body, or a
                   certain mode of Extension actually existing, and
                   nothing else.' Important propositions leading up to
                   this are as follows.

p 1–p 2   Thought and Extension are attributes of God.

p 3–p 4   God has a single idea of himself and of everything
                   that follows from God. This idea is his intellect or
                   mind.

p 5–p 6   God causes an idea, but only insofar as God is a
                   thinking thing and, more generally, God causes a
                   mode in any attribute only insofar as God has that
                   attribute.

p 7s   The order and connection of ideas is the same as
                   the order and connection of things.

p 8d,c,s   An idea of a non-existing mode is contained in
                   God's intellect just as its formal essence is
                   contained in an attribute of God.

p 10,c   People are essentially modes, not substances.

p 11   The human mind is God's idea of an actually
                   existing thing.

p 12   Everything that happens in the object of the idea
                   constituting the human mind is perceived by that
                   mind.

p 13   The object of a human mind is the human body.

p 13s   Panpsychism: each body has a soul or mind.

Division 2: Knowledge (p14–p49)

p 40s 2   An outline of Spinoza's classification
                   of kinds of human knowledge.
                   The first kind of knowledge is opinion,
                   discussed from p 16 to p 32.
                   The second kind is reason, dealt with from
                   p 38 to p 40. The third kind is intuitive
                   knowledge, which is briefly mentioned in
                   p 40s 2, but discussed more extensively in Part V.

Additional claims regarding these
kinds of knowledge are found in
p 32–p 36 and p 41–p 44.

OPINION

p 16   The idea of a bodily change or affection
                        caused by an external body involves the
                        nature of our body and the nature of the
                        external body.

p 17   An idea of an affection of the body
                        caused by an external body represents the
                        external body to us as actually existing.

p 18,s   If once affected by two bodies at once,
                        the mind, when it recalls one, will
                        remember the other.

p 25   Our perceptual ideas of external bodies
                        are inadequate.

REASON

p 38   We have adequate ideas of things that are
                        common to everything.

p 40   Any idea that follows from an adequate
                        idea is also adequate.

p 41   Opinion is the cause of falsity. Reason
                        and intuitive knowledge are necessarily
                        true.

p 43   If you know something to be true, you
                        know that you know it and cannot doubt it.

p 44   Reason conceives things as necessary,
                        not contingent.

ADEQUATE KNOWLEDGE OF GOD'S ESSENCE AS THE FOUNDATION OF
INTUITIVE KNOWLEDGE

p 47   The human mind has adequate
                        knowledge of the essence of God.

ON THE WILL

p 48   There is no free will by which we make
                        affirmations or denials.

p 49c1   The will to affirm or deny is the intellect.

DISCUSSION OF THE RECOMMENDED READINGS FOR PART II OF THE *ETHICS*

Division 1: The human mind (p1–p13)

The nature of the mind
p 13: The human mind is God's idea of the human body.

The culmination of Spinoza's discussion of the nature of the human mind is found in p 13. The scholium is also remarkable, but we will turn to that and to p 13d later. His basic answer here is that the human mind is an idea in God's intellect, that its object is the human body, and that this idea exists in time just while the body exists.

Thought and Extension
p 1–p 2: Thought and Extension are attributes of God.

Spinoza says here what the essence of God is, since by I def6 an attribute is what constitutes God's essence.

That God is essentially a thinking thing was commonly accepted. That he is extended was almost universally rejected and condemned. Spinoza has already anticipated objections to this claim in I p 15s. Spinoza attempts to defend his conception of God as physical against a variety of objections. A central objection is that God would then be divisible and composed of parts, hence capable of ceasing to exist. In reply, Spinoza denies that matter (or quantity), insofar as it is substance, is divisible or composed of parts.

A terminological difference is worth noting. Descartes and others maintain practically as a matter of definition that a mind is a thinking substance, and so that God is a mind. Spinoza, however, uses 'mind' to refer to a modification of God. He agrees that God is a thinking substance, but rejects the ordinary use of 'mind' to refer to a substance.

God's infinite intellect
p 3–p 4: God has a single idea of himself and of everything that follows from God. This idea is his intellect or mind.

God's idea of himself and of everything that follows from God is an immediate infinite modification of God. It is an example of what Spinoza is talking about in I p 21.

The denial of causal interaction

p 5: God causes an idea, but only insofar as God is a thinking thing.

p 6: God causes a mode in any attribute only insofar as God has that attribute.

II p 6 is a generalized form of p 5. It will follow that there is no causal interaction between the mental and the physical – indeed, p 6 is practically an expression of this view. Spinoza asserts this and discusses it more explicitly in III p 2, p 2d, and especially p 2s, which we will consider in Chapter 7. In V Pref Spinoza returns to this and to the contrary views of Descartes.

Spinoza makes crucial use here of the expression 'insofar as' (*quatenus*) and it is important for understanding his thought to see that this functions like the word 'because'. Consider Smith, who is rich, lives in Cambridge, and can buy a very expensive car. It would be true to say that Smith, insofar as he is rich, can buy the car. It would be false to say that Smith, insofar as he lives in Cambridge, can buy the car. His being rich, not his living in Cambridge, is what explains his being able to buy the car.

So too, Spinoza holds that God is extended, or physical, and also thinks, but the fact that he is physical does not explain, nor does it cause, his having a certain idea. In fact, Spinoza holds, the concept of a physical object cannot help us explain anything that is mental (and vice versa).

This is a controversial claim. For we all seem to suppose that if you decide to walk across the room, your decision (which is mental) is a cause of your walking (which is physical). Similarly, we think that your hearing the tree fall is caused by the tree's falling.

Spinoza, in contrast, thinks that your hearing the tree, which is an experience that the mind undergoes, can also be described in physical or neurophysical language. The neurophysiological events in your brain are caused by the air vibrations, and the events in your brain are your ('mental') experience, but your experience is not caused by the air vibrations. An alternative and perhaps better way to express this is to say that the brain event, insofar as it is physical, is caused by the air vibrations, but the same event, insofar as it is conceived as an experience, is not.

Relations between God's ideas and their objects
p 7s: The order and connection of ideas is the same as the order and connection of things.

Spinoza is speaking here of the temporal order of God's ideas and the causal connections between them. The proposition means or entails that God's ideas and their objects have the same temporal and causal order. So God's idea of X exists in time just when X itself exists in time. In addition, if X causes Y, then God's idea of X causes God's idea of Y, and vice versa.

Spinoza writes elsewhere, as in p 11d, that an idea of an existing individual thing is an affirmation of its existence. According to p 8, p 8c, and p 8s, which are briefly discussed below, the notion of existence intended here is that of duration, that is, of existence in time. This affirmation is not in words, of course, but in thought (or Thought).

One conception of God's omniscience is thus expressed here. Suppose for a moment, as I suspect, that Spinoza's God does not employ a concept of negation and does not think of things as in time. The content of what God thinks will then never include negation or a temporal reference, although our reports of his thought may include them.

God will then affirm the existence of your body just while your body exists. At a time when your body does not exist, however, he will not affirm that your body does not exist then. He will instead simply not then affirm that it does exist. So too, God will not think, 'Adam does not exist now (or in 2006)'. Instead, he will not now, or in 2006, think 'Adam exists'.

p 7s is especially important, for Spinoza here makes it clear that, on his view, a mode of Extension (a body) and God's idea of it are 'one and the same thing, expressed in two ways'. Elsewhere, as in p 21s, he says that they are 'one and the same individual, conceived now under Thought, now under Extension'. In Cartesian language this is like saying that the objective reality of God's idea of a thing (that is, the 'representational content') is the same as its formal reality.

It should be noted that there is a difference, on the face of it, between saying that the mind and the body are one thing that is expressed in two ways and saying that they are two different expressions of one thing. The latter is attributed to Spinoza by those who believe he held a dual aspect theory. On this view, the mind is one expression or aspect of a thing and the mind is another. They are two things. The former, in contrast, expresses an identity theory. It maintains that the mind and body are one thing which, when conceived under Thought, is called a 'mind', but when conceived under Extension, is called a 'body'. 'Mind' and 'body' denote one thing, although conceived differently, rather than two things that are aspects or expressions of something else.[4]

Spinoza's distinction between two kinds of existence
p 8d,c,s: An idea of a non-existing mode is contained in God's intellect just as its formal essence is contained in an attribute of God.

Spinoza speaks here of non-existing things whose formal essences are contained in an attribute. Some explanation of his language will no doubt be helpful.

In TdIE Spinoza often talks of the essence of a thing as if it were the thing itself. In E II def2 he defines what 'pertains to the essence' of a thing as that which, when given, the thing is given, and vice versa. He follows Descartes, however, in opposing the terms 'formal' and 'objective'. For example, the 'formal reality' or 'formal being' of a thing is its 'actual' reality, while its 'objective' being or reality is its being, or the thing, 'as it exists in the mind'. Thus the 'objective being' of a thing is actually an idea of it.

When Spinoza speaks here of the formal essence of a thing as contained in an attribute he is expressing the view that the thing itself exists in the attribute, whether or not it now exists in time. So too, he holds that there is an idea of the thing, even if the thing does not now exist, in God's intellect.

In the corollary, Spinoza distinguishes, or seems to distinguish, existence as it is comprehended in the attributes and existence as in time. Spinoza calls the temporal existence of a thing its duration (*duratio*), as I def5 with its explication indicates, and he supposes that if you were to 'take away' part of a thing's duration, you would be taking away that much of its existence. This is the basic idea of bodies as four-dimensional objects.

Thus Spinoza distinguishes the atemporal existence of a thing as it is in God and the temporal existence of that thing. The distinction between these types of existence is illustrated in p 8s with the help of Book III, proposition 35 of Euclid's Elements. The distinction may seem to be a distinction between potential and actual existence and some, such as Donagan (1973), have taken it this way. But E V p 29s seems to me to show that this is wrong and that it is instead a distinction between two types of existence or two ways of conceiving a thing as actual or real.

This is especially important to note because Spinoza uses the distinction in his attempt in Part V to show that the human mind, or a part of it, is eternal. The basis for this is his claim that the idea of the formal essence of our body (as contained atemporally in God) is eternal.

People as modes of God
p 10,c: People are essentially modes, not substances.

The demonstration of and the scholium to p 10 (p 10d and p 10s) point out that substance has properties that people do not have. Substance necessarily exists, only one substance of the same nature exists, and substance is infinite, indivisible, and so on. Hence people must be modes, not substances.

In p 10d Spinoza cites ax1 to show that it is absurd to say that people necessarily exist. The axiom states that it may as much happen, from the order of nature, that a certain man exists as that he does not. This might be thought to deny or conflict with the thesis that each thing is absolutely necessitated by God.

The apparent conflict is resolvable, I think. For, first, the denial that people necessarily exist is here just the denial that their essence 'involves' existence. Secondly, it does happen from the order of nature that a certain man exists at one time and that he does not exist at another. Hence it may and can happen. This is not incompatible with saying that that order is necessitated by God (as I p 33 holds) and that that order necessitates the existence or non-existence of that man at a given time (as remarks in I p 33s maintain).

The object of the idea that is our mind
p 11: The human mind is God's idea of an actually existing thing.

The mind is not merely an idea of an existing thing or an idea of something that in fact does exist. It is an idea of it *as* actually existing or, in other words, it is an affirmation that it actually exists.

In p 11c, Spinoza provides a translation schema for (1) 'the human mind perceives this' and (2) 'the human mind perceives this inadequately'. It is the basis for nearly all of Spinoza's assessments of ideas as 'inadequate'.

1. Spinoza maintains here that for the human mind to perceive something is for God to have an idea of it, insofar as God 'constitutes the essence of the human mind'. Nothing very fancy is meant here by this phrase. For God to constitute the essence of the human mind, according to Spinoza, is simply for God to have the idea that is the human mind.

This seems to be a fairly natural claim to make, once the human mind has been identified with one of God's ideas. For suppose that the human mind perceives something, that is, it has an idea of the thing. Then that idea is in the human mind, and so God, in virtue of having the idea that is the mind, will have that idea. This assumes that God's idea of a thing is 'complete' in the sense that whatever is 'in' (or represented by) that idea is 'in' God's idea of it.

The reverse of this sequence seems plausible as well, on the assumption that God's idea of a thing is always 'accurate', that is, whatever is 'in' God's idea of it is 'in' or represented by that idea.

This part of p 11c is put to immediate use in Spinoza's argument for the claim that the object of the idea that is the mind is the human body and nothing else. This will be considered in a moment.

2. We perceive something inadequately, Spinoza holds here, when God has the idea of it, not merely insofar as he has the idea that is our mind, but also insofar as he has (simultaneously) the ideas of other things as well.

An example will no doubt help. When we see a tree, light is reflected from the tree to our eyes and this produces a change in our body. The idea of this change is what represents the tree to us. But what this change is depends not merely on our body, but also on the nature of the external body. So God has the idea of this change not merely in virtue of having the idea of our body, but also in virtue of having the idea of the external cause of the change. Hence we perceive it inadequately, according to the definition of this in p 11c.

This argument is very similar to Spinoza's argument in p 25d, although he does not there explicitly cite p 11c.

Our ideas of everything that happens in the body
p 12: Everything that happens in the object of the idea constituting the human mind is perceived by that mind.

p 13: The object of a human mind is the human body.

p 9c maintains that God, insofar as he constitutes the idea of a thing, has knowledge, or an idea, of everything that happens in the thing. (Indeed, he has such an idea only insofar as he has the idea of that thing.) Hence by p 11c, the idea or mind of that thing will perceive it.

In p 13d Spinoza uses p 12 to support his claim that it is only the body that is the object of the idea that constitutes the human mind. He uses ax4, which maintains that we have ideas of the affections of the body, to support the claim that the body is the object of the idea that is our mind.

Panpsychism
p 13s: Each body has a soul or mind.

In p 13s Spinoza notes that what he has thus far said is quite general, since God has an idea of each body, not merely of each human body. So he grants that all things are 'animate (*animata*), but in different degrees'. He also holds that the human mind is superior to and contains more reality than other minds, where this superiority consists in having a greater capacity 'to understand distinctly'. This in turn varies with the capacity of the body to act and be acted on in a variety of ways at the same time and its capacity to act in ways that depend only on itself.

Spinoza thus inserts a very short 'physics', according to which each of the simplest bodies is at rest or moves at one or another speed. When various bodies are pressed together by others, so that the pressed bodies retain their close relations to each other, we regard them as united and as forming one body.

We might note that Spinoza supposes that one body can move another or change its speed or direction only by contact. He uses no notion of gravity, or of a concept of 'action at a distance', later employed by Newton (over the objections of many). So complex bodies are 'held together' by, and dependent for their continued existence on, the bodies that surround them.

Spinoza also distinguishes hard, soft, and liquid bodies and explains how a complex body can be regarded as continuing to exist or as retaining its form (the characteristic relations of its parts to each other), despite a variety of changes. These changes include change of place and constant replacement of its parts.

He also goes on to remark in lem7s that we can conceive of individuals of ever increasing complexity and, indeed, we can conceive of 'the whole of nature as one individual'.

Division 2: Knowledge (p14–p49)

The three kinds of knowledge
p 40s 2: Outline of the three kinds of human knowledge: opinion, reason and intuitive knowledge.

This scholium provides an outline of Spinoza's classification of kinds of human knowledge:

1. Opinion or knowledge of the first kind, discussed primarily in p 16–p 31.
2. Reason or knowledge of the second kind, treated in p 38–p 40.
3. Intuitive knowledge or knowledge of the third kind, mentioned here and again in p 47s, but explicitly discussed primarily in the later portions of Part V (V p 25–p 33).

Additional claims regarding these kinds of knowledge are found in p 32–p 36 and p 41–p 44.

Opinion
p 16: The idea of a bodily change or affection caused by an external body involves the nature of our body and the nature of the external body.

Spinoza's argument maintains that the affection or change is caused partly by the external body and partly by our own body. Hence the idea of the change 'involves' each, according to I ax4, which states that the knowledge of an effect depends on and involves the knowledge of its cause.

He states in corollaries 1 and 2 that we therefore perceive both the external body and our own, but the idea of the change indicates the nature of our own body more than that of the external body.

Here and in p 47d Spinoza supposes that if we have an idea of a thing and that thing 'involves' another as its cause, then we have an idea of the cause. It appears to follow (by I p 28) that we will perceive, or have an idea of, each finite cause in the infinite series leading to each finite thing.

p 17: An idea of an affection of the body caused by an external body represents the external body to us as actually existing.

p 18,s: If once affected by two bodies at once, the mind, when it recalls one, will remember the other.

Spinoza holds in p 17 and p 17d that when we have an idea of an affection of the body that 'involves' the nature of an external body, we will regard that body as present to us or as actually existing. It is unclear, I think, whether Spinoza regards this, and his remarks on memory in p 18s, as an account of our consciousness of external bodies.

Spinoza's assesment of perceptual knowledge
p 25: Our perceptual ideas of external bodies are inadequate.

Spinoza uses similar patterns of argument to show that we have only inadequate perceptual knowledge of external bodies, of our own body and its parts, and of our mind. In p 25d Spinoza implicitly uses, but does not cite, p 11c. In contrast, p 11c is cited in p 24d, for example, and it seems to be needed to draw any conclusion about the inadequacy of our ideas.

Spinoza holds that it is through our awareness or idea of changes in our own body that we perceive or have an idea of external bodies (as well as our own body and the parts of our body).

Since 'idea of' is ambiguous, we might say that the 'direct object' of our idea is the change in our body, while the 'indirect object' is the external body. It is the indirect object that is represented *to us* by these ideas, but it is the direct object that is represented to God by these ideas.

In a similar way it is through a perception of these ideas, that is, it is through an idea of an idea of a change in our body, that we are aware of our own mind.

But this idea does not represent the external object completely; it represents it only to the extent that it causes a change in us. As

Spinoza says in p 11c, in having these ideas the human mind perceives things 'partially or inadequately'.

It is important to note that these ideas portray the external body and other singular things as actually existing, that is, as existing in time. In contrast to these are ideas that represent the formal essences of individual things as contained in the attributes. (The latter are discussed in V p 21–p 40 as intuitive knowledge and will be discussed when we turn to Part V.)

p 29c and p 29s provide a partial summary of Spinoza's theses concerning confused or inadequate perceptual knowledge, but a short summary of his main claims in p 16–p 31 is as follows.

When we perceive things via ideas of the affections of our body, we have inadequate ideas or knowledge of

1. the parts of the human body (p 24);
2. external bodies (p 25);
3. the human body (p 27);
4. the duration of the human body and of external things (p 30–p 31).

Furthermore, it is only through the ideas of affections of the body that we know or perceive the human body (p 19) and external bodies (p 26) as actually existing.

In a similar way, it is only through ideas of ideas of affections of the human body that the mind perceives or has knowledge of itself (p 23). Like our perceptual knowledge of our body, our knowledge of our mind is inadequate (p 29). Unlike Descartes, Spinoza thinks we have unclear or confused knowledge of our own mind as actually existing.

In p 29s, Spinoza ties inadequate ideas to ideas that are externally determined, as opposed to our 'clear and distinct' perceptions, which are internally determined.

Spinoza holds that perceptual ideas 'reflect' or indicate the nature of our own bodies more than that of external ones. They do not reveal the nature of external bodies 'as they are in themselves'; they reveal them only insofar as they affect our specialized sense organs. In I App Spinoza makes it clear that colour, taste, and so on – the so-called 'secondary qualites' discussed by Locke and others – are not 'real properties' of objects. The same is true, he there holds, of our ideas of good, bad, order, and confusion.

There are many reasons for thinking that perception consists of inadequate, or partial, ideas. One of these is that insofar as perception reveals the object at all, it reveals only a 'time-slice' of it. We typically perceive external objects only during a very short period of their existence; we get only a glimpse of them, like seeing one frame of a movie. Secondly, having any perception at all of a thing depends on where our body happens to be. Thirdly, perception only reveals the object insofar as our bodies are affected by it and so, as Spinoza notes, it depends as much on the nature of our body as that of the external body. Without specialized sense organs, for example, we will not see or hear bodies at all. Thus sense perception reveals bodies only insofar as they affect our bodies, rather than as they are in themselves.

Spinoza notes in Vp 21,d that this is our only access to 'the present life', that is, to things as existing in time. For we are able to conceive of things as actually existing in time only while our body endures.

Reason
p 38: We have adequate ideas of things that are common to everything.

Spinoza's argument maintains that what is common to everything is known by God insofar as he has the idea of the human mind and insofar as he has the ideas of the affections of the human mind. It would seem to follow by the second part of p 11c that we inadequately perceive what is common to everything. Spinoza asserts in the proof, however, that the idea of what is common is adequate in God, insofar as he has the idea of the human mind, and hence by p 11c it is perceived adequately by us.

p 38c notes that there are 'ideas or notions common to all men', that is, that all people have adequate ideas of certain common properties of things. Spinoza also indicates what these common properties are. All bodies, for example, 'involve the conception of one and the same attribute' and 'may be absolutely in motion or absolutely at rest' (lem2). Thus, it seems, the attribute of Extension and the property of being in motion or at rest are two of the common properties of all things, or rather all bodies. In p 47s, however, Spinoza seems to distinguish common notions from the idea of God's essence.

p 40: Any idea that follows from an adequate idea is also adequate.

In p 40s 2, Spinoza illustrates the three kinds of knowledge with a problem. You are given the values of a, b, and c. The problem is to find the value of d when $a/b = c/d$. Spinoza writes that we may remember what our teachers told us without proof, namely to multiply b by c and divide by a, or we may find ourselves that this works for simple numbers and figure it will work for others. This illustrates 'knowledge' from what others have said or by an uncertain inference from our own experience of what has thus far worked. The 'common property of proportionals' may also be seen 'from the force of the demonstration of Euclid, Book VII, proposition 19'. This illustrates reason. Finally, we may 'infer in one single intuition' what the fourth number is. This illustrates intuitive knowledge.

In p 40s 1 Spinoza considers 'universal notions' (*notiones . . . universales*), indicated by general terms such as 'man', 'horse', and 'dog'. These, he holds, are confused ideas that arise because the human body can only form a limited number of distinct 'images' (physical changes or states). When that number is exceeded, the mind is only able to have a distinct idea of the 'common characteristics' by which the body was most affected. Thus people have different general ideas of man, horse, and so on.

Like Descartes and the empiricists, Spinoza holds that these ordinary universals, which are instantiated by particulars that we sense, are not real entities existing outside of the mind. They are fictitious (p 48s) or simply confused ideas. He does hold, however, that some things are common to every thing and some of these, such as the attributes, are real beings grasped by reason.

Truth, falsity, certainty, and doubt
p 41: Opinion is the cause of falsity. Reason and intuitive knowledge are necessarily true.

p 43: If you know something to be true, you know that you know it and cannot doubt it.

In p 41 Spinoza makes it clear that the second and third kinds of knowledge are necessarily true, although the first kind (opinion) can be, as he puts it, 'the cause of falsity'.

He explains that the first two kinds of knowledge are adequate (essentially by their definitions in p 40s 2) and hence, by p 34, they must be true. He says that opinion is 'the cause of falsity', rather than that sometimes it is false, because he holds that falsity is a 'privation'. By this he means, roughly, that it is not itself a property that expresses something real; it is instead the lack of a 'real property'. So truth is related to falsity as being to non-being. (He holds a similar doctrine, perhaps objectionably, about blindness.)

Spinoza also thinks that knowledge entails certainty and that if you know something, you know that you know it, as p43, d, s, indicate. Certainty, he adds, is not merely a lack of doubt; it is rather that doubt is a lack of certainty. His position here thus seems to undercut Descartes' 'method of doubt'. This method proposes that we begin by undertaking to doubt everything that can be doubted. We can then conclude that what survives this is real knowledge and must be true (as long as God is not a deceiver). Spinoza's objection, in part, seems to be that if we do not first know something, and know that we know it, we cannot expect to obtain or identify knowledge by applying some general criterion. For this would require that we know the criterion is correct.

On the nature of reason
p44: Reason conceives things as necessary, not contingent.

p44c1: It is only because we imagine things that we regard things as contingent.

Spinoza's argument for p44 is straightforward. Reason conceives things truly, that is, it conceives things 'as they are in themselves'. Since everything is necessary, not contingent (by I p29), reason conceives them this way.

In p44c1s Spinoza provides an illustration of his claim in p44c1. Suppose that a boy sees Peter in the morning, Paul in the afternoon, and Simon in the evening. He will then associate seeing them with those times, especially if the sequence is often repeated. But if one day he sees James in the evening, instead of Simon, then the next morning he will imagine seeing first one in the evening and then the other, that is, 'his imagination will waver'. So he will be uncertain, in turn, which one he will see the following evening, that is, he will regard each as contingent.

Another example is this. We suppose that a tree that is now growing near the house could have been cut down yesterday, and used as firewood, primarily because we know that trees are the sort of thing that can be cut down. For in fact some have been. They can of course also be used as firewood. We suppose, too, that if I had decided to cut it down, or to hire someone to do it, I would have done this. So we know that this type of thing happens and we do not see any reason why it could not have happened on this occasion.

Part of what seems crucial in each illustration is that we think in general terms, for example about one morning or another and about one tree as opposed to another. We think, that is, in general terms (constructed, according to Spinoza, by the imagination), and we do not see the details of the causal sequences in each case. We regard what in fact happened to one thing or at one time as showing that the same type of thing can happen or could have happened to a similar thing.

Adequate knowledge of God's essence as the foundation of intuitive knowledge
p 47: The human mind has an adequate knowledge of the essence of God.

p 47d argues that since we have ideas of actually existing things, we have adequate knowledge of the essence of God (by p 45 and p 46).

In p 47s Spinoza maintains that people do not have so clear an idea of God as they do of 'common notions', because the word 'God' has been joined to images and God cannot be imagined. This is puzzling, partly because our idea or knowledge of God is adequate and Spinoza seems to use 'clear and distinct' as a synonym of 'adequate'. (see, for example, p 36 and p 38c). Thus everyone's idea of God must be clear and distinct. p 47s proceeds, however, to discuss situations where people are mistaken in what they say, but not in what they think.

On the will.
p 48: There is no free will by which we make affirmations or denials.

p 49c1: The will to affirm or deny is the intellect.

Spinoza denies that we have a will that is free, since by I p 28 the will, like everything else, must have a cause. As he indicates in II p 48s,

Spinoza is speaking here of the will by which we affirm or deny something, rather than a desire.

In p48 and p49, Spinoza rejects Descartes' account of error. Descartes' account is found in *Meditations* IV. The scholium to p49 clarifies Spinoza's position by contrasting ideas with images and words and by trying to counter four objections. Finally, he points out the advantages of 'this doctrine'. In doing so, he anticipates many of the important doctrines of Parts IV and V of the *Ethics*.

COMPARISON OF SPINOZA WITH OTHERS: SPINOZA'S PHILOSOPHICAL ALLIES AND OPPONENTS

Major philosophers of the seventeenth and eighteenth centuries have traditionally been divided into two exclusive groups. The Continental Rationalists are Descartes, Spinoza, and Leibniz. The British Empiricists are Locke, Berkeley, and Hume. Kant is then seen as mediating the dispute and providing a synthesis.

This division is perhaps suspiciously neat and simplistic, it is incomplete in important respects, and it has been attacked.[5] It does, however, have some merit. The most important cluster of issues that divide the rationalists and the empiricists is concerned with the origin and nature of our ideas of things and the character of the foundations of our knowledge of the world.

Locke is Spinoza's contemporary and in fact they were born in the same year. Nevertheless, Hume provides a more developed and in many ways a more consistent empiricist account of the origin of our ideas. Locke, for example, holds that our idea of substance is unclear – an idea of 'I know not what' – while Hume more consistently maintains that we have no such idea. We only perceive the alleged qualities of objects, not the objects themselves, so we cannot have an idea of them, according to Hume.

Hume is like Descartes and unlike Spinoza in holding that we are immediately aware only of our own perceptions. There are two types of perception: (1) 'impressions', such as the experience or 'sensation' of colour, and (2) ideas. All of our simple ideas are less vivid or less lively copies of some antecedent impression. All other ideas are constructed from these by combining them or by increasing or decreasing them in some respect. We form the idea of Pegasus, for example, by combining the idea of a horse with the idea of a thing with wings. Like Locke, Hume holds that no ideas are 'innate' or 'inborn' in the mind.

This account of the origin of our ideas is then used as a weapon. For if some alleged idea cannot have originated in experience and cannot be constructed from such ideas, then we really have no such idea. Since words signify ideas, the words used to 'express' such an idea are therefore meaningless. In Hume's hands, this results in the view that we have no idea of substance, that is, of a thing that has qualities as opposed to those qualities themselves. Hence we have no idea of a body and no idea of a mind or self, as things that continue to exist or remain the same thing through change.

This account also leads to Hume's claim that the content of our idea of causation can only consist objectively, or independently of us, in the mere constant conjunction of events. The idea that there is a necessary connection between cause and effect arises not 'from reason', but merely from a feeling that we have. Hume calls this feeling a 'determination of the mind'. This subjective feeling is the expectation that the effect will occur when we perceive the cause and it arises only after repeated observation of one type of event (the effect) following another (the cause).

Hume also divides all knowledge into knowledge of 'matters of fact' and knowledge of 'relations of ideas'. Causal claims and all claims about what exists are matters of fact that can only be known by experience, that is, primarily, by sense perception. Mathematical claims concerning quantity and number can be known independently of particular experiences, by inspection of our ideas, so to speak, but they reveal no substantive knowledge of the world.

Hume's views here foreshadow standard doctrines of twentieth-century empiricism. In updated language, due in large part to Kant, a true analytic proposition is one that is true by definition ('All bachelors are unmarried'), while a synthetic proposition is one that is not ('All bachelors are cads'). Analytic propositions give us no real knowledge of the world; they are true simply in virtue of the meaning of our words. In addition, they, and they alone, can be known to be true 'independently of experience', or *a priori*, that is, without justification that appeals to particular experiences. In contrast are 'synthetic' propositions, which make substantive claims about the world and can be known only by experience, or *a posteriori*. Thus there is no substantive *a priori* knowledge, that is, no *a priori* knowledge about the world.

Spinoza, like Descartes and Leibniz, is opposed to all of this.

Spinoza's conception of an idea diverges quite radically from the conception set out by Locke and Hume. Ideas, he holds, are not 'mute pictures on a tablet' (I p 49s). Instead, they are themselves affirmations or denials and 'conceptions that the mind forms because it is a thinking thing' (II def3; see also II def3exp).

Spinoza contrasts ideas that arise from the mind itself with those that arise because of external forces. He thus draws a sharp distinction between the intellect and the imagination, corresponding to the terminological distinction he draws in II def3exp. The intellect consists of conceptions, where the mind is active, while the imagination consists of perceptions, where it is passive.

The imagination consists of ideas that arise in us when we perceive something. Thus when we see a house, an image, which is physical, is formed in our body and our idea of this image represents the house as existing. But this idea is not a faint copy of the physical image and it is not 'mute'. Instead, it is an affirmation of the actual existence of the house.

Many things, however, cannot be imagined in this way. Spinoza holds, for example, that neither God nor God's attributes can be imagined, as II p 47s indicates.

We might note that it seems clearly to follow that ideas are not components of at least simple affirmations. For example, the affirmation that a triangle has interior angles equal to two right angles is not formed by putting together the idea of a triangle with the idea of having interior angles of this magnitude, simply because the idea of a triangle is this affirmation. A 'compositional semantics' for simple sentences thus seems impossible.

As for the dispute regarding literally innate ideas, Spinoza maintains that the mind is itself God's idea of the body and that it necessarily contains ideas of all parts of the body and of all changes that occur within it. Since the order and connection of God's ideas is the same as that of their objects, the human mind comes into existence exactly when the body does. Thus it begins to exist with the ideas of all of the parts of the body.

The most prominent example of a disputed innate idea, however, is the idea of God as infinite substance. Descartes argues in *Meditations* III that we cannot construct the idea of the infinite from the idea of the finite. 'Infinite' is the more basic term and 'finite' means 'not infinite'. Hence the idea of the infinite cannot be derived from our experience of the finite and God himself must be the cause of it. Hume in contrast argued that we ourselves create the concept of the infinite by augmenting, without limit, the concept of the finite. 'Finite' is the more basic term, and 'infinite' means 'not finite'. Thus the concept of God as infinite is ultimately derived from our experience of the finite.

Unlike Descartes and Hume, Spinoza regards all ideas as affirmations and so it is not clear that he is a party to the dispute as formulated here. He maintains, however, that every idea of an actually existing thing 'involves' the idea of God's essence (II p 45) and that this knowledge of God's essence is adequate (II p 46), and so everyone has adequate knowledge of God's essence (II p 47). To the question, 'From what, or how, do we get the idea of God?', he seems to answer, 'It is implicit or built into every idea we have of an existing thing.'

Spinoza also holds that every idea involves other ideas that can only be adequately known. Among these are the 'common notions' or axioms of Euclid's geometry, such as the claim that if equals are added to equals, the result (the whole) is equal. These are 'the foundations of our reasoning'. Spinoza holds that these common notions, and what follows from them, can only be adequately conceived and that the idea of each thing 'involves' the idea of these common things (see especially II p 38–p 40).

Spinoza thus holds, contrary to Hume and other empiricists, that we have *a priori* knowledge of the world. Such knowledge, on Spinoza's view, is knowledge of the world that does not rest on, or receive its justification from, particular sensory experiences, but is instead implicit in all experiences.

On the other hand, Spinoza accepts Kant's claim that in perception we do not obtain knowledge of particular things as they are in themselves. Our perceptual ideas reveal things, not as they are in themselves, but only insofar as they affect us. But in contrast to Kant, Spinoza thinks we do have 'intellectual intuitions' of the formal essence of things as in God, and thus we do have knowledge of individuals as they are in themselves. He also thinks, contrary to Kant, that reason grasps truths, not merely about things as they appear (*phenomena*), but as they are in themselves (*noumena*). Thus we have real knowledge concerning God, freedom, and the eternity of the intellect.

PROBLEMS AND DISPUTED ISSUES OF INTERPRETATION

Mind and body

It is sometimes said that Spinoza has a dual aspect view of the relation between mind and body. According to this interpretation, the mind and the body are two aspects of one thing. This is not what Spinoza actually says, however. As just noted, what he says is that they are one thing that is conceived in different ways. We talk and think of the mind as thinking, as making affirmations and having experiences, while we regard the body as a thing that occupies space, moves, and has a shape. It is as if we had two different languages, or two vocabularies, for speaking of one thing. In a similar way, he speaks in III p 2s of a decision (*mentis decretum*) and a determination of the body (*corporis determinatio*) as one thing that is conceived in different ways.

Spinoza thus seems to accept an identity theory of mind and body, according to which mental events are identical with physical events in the brain. His account diverges from more recent identity theories, however. For while recent theories typically hold, with Spinoza, that all events are physical, they deny that all events are also mental. Spinoza's view, in contrast, is that everything can be conceived either as mental or as physical. The ultimate source of these different conceptions is disputed, however, and is a part of the 'problem of the attributes', which we considered in Chapter 5.

Another interpretive dispute concerns Spinoza's thesis in II p 8c that the formal essences of things which do not exist are contained in God's attributes and the ideas of these are contained in God's idea.

Spinoza illustrates this in II p 8s, where he holds that in a circle, the rectangles formed from intersecting lines are equal, and so there is an infinity of equal rectangles in a circle. He says, however, that none of them exist except insofar as the circle exists. He then proceeds to suppose that there is a circle with two intersecting lines in it, and he includes a picture of it.

This suggests that the formal essences of things are contained in God or exist in God only potentially, since the lines do not seem actually to exist until after they have been drawn. V p 29s, however, notes that things are conceived by us as actual or real in two ways: (1) insofar as they are contained in the attributes and (2) insofar as they exist or endure in time.

We thus seem to have here another example where Spinoza makes crucial use of a distinction between two ways of conceiving a thing, but says less than we would wish about these ways or their ultimate source. Other examples of this, as we noted, concern his distinction between the attributes, between an attribute and God, and between the mind and the body. For the mind and the body are 'one and the same thing', but conceived in different ways and, indeed, under attributes that are at least conceptually distinct.

A central objection to interpreting Spinoza as saying that the formal essence of an individual as contained in God is a merely possible object is that it makes the 'eternal' part of the mind a merely possible object. V p 29s makes it clear, however, that Spinoza regards eternal existence in the attributes as actual and real.

Mind–body causality

Most commentators take Spinoza to have rejected any causality between the mind and the body. They suppose that on his view, no mental event causes a physical event, and no physical event causes a mental one.

Koistinen and Davidson, however, disagree.[6] They hold that Spinoza sometimes speaks of what causes a thing as what causally explains it. On their view, Spinoza's denial of causal interaction expresses only the thesis that physical events (conceived as physical) cannot be explained by citing mental events (conceived as mental), and vice versa. The concept of causality employed here is said to be the 'opaque' or 'intensional' concept. There is another concept of causality, however, the 'transparent' or 'extensional' concept, on which it is always true that if X causes Y and X is identical with Z, then Z causes Y. Thus if a physical change in your brain causes a muscle in your arm to contract, and that brain change is a (mental) decision, then the decision causes your muscle contraction.

To deny this, when the transparent concept of causality is in question, is a 'logical absurdity',[7] but on this interpretation of Spinoza there is no need to ascribe it to him. We can hold instead that in III p 2 and similar passages, Spinoza merely denies that a mental event causally explains any physical event (and vice versa). He merely denies, in other words, that an event when conceived as mental can be cited to explain an event conceived as physical.

What remains at issue is whether Spinoza has a transparent concept of causality. An alternative to the view of Koistinen and Davidson maintains that he does not. III p 2d cites II p 6 and II p 6d in turn cites I ax4. I ax4 maintains that the knowledge, or concept, of an effect depends on and involves the knowledge of its cause. This seems to make it axiomatic that (minimally) if X causes Y, then the concept of Y involves the concept of X. Spinoza holds, however, that the concept of extension does not involve the concept of thought (and vice versa). It thus seems to follow that nothing conceived as physical can cause anything conceived as mental (and vice versa).

By its nature, however, this argument cannot establish that Spinoza has no transparent concept of causation. It merely shows that the concept of causation set out in I ax4 and used in the demonstrations of II p6 and III p2, among others, is not transparent. For even if this is Spinoza's central concept of causation, it does not follow that it is his only one.

But if he has such a concept, why does he not make important use of it and say, for example, that in one sense the body can determine or cause the mind to think and that the mind can determine the body to motion and rest? Why does he not assert this and then add that the effect cannot be explained by citing its cause? In addition, why does he attack Descartes in V Pref for holding that the mind can cause changes in the pineal gland, if he thinks that in fact there is a sense in which this is true?

It thus seems to me implausible to suppose that Spinoza grants or would grant that there is causal interaction in any sense between the mind and the body.[8]

Epistemology

As we have seen, opinion, or the first kind of knowledge, includes perceptual knowledge, that is, ideas we have because bodies outside of us produce changes in our bodies. In vision, for example, light reflected from a body makes changes in our eyes. These in turn lead to other changes in the body (especially the brain). Spinoza maintains that we have an idea of the change produced in our bodies and this idea represents the external body to us. It is thus one and the same idea that 'represents' the object perceived and that is 'of' a change in the brain.

As we have also seen, we must thus distinguish the 'representative relation' that an idea has to the object that caused the brain event from the relation that the idea has to the brain event. The latter is an instance of the general relation that God's ideas have to their objects. The order and connection of these ideas is the same as the order and connection of their objects, for example. Like the human mind, which is God's idea of the body, such ideas come into existence when their objects do and they cease to exist when their objects do. Indeed, Spinoza maintains that they are 'one and the same thing, although conceived in different ways'.

Ideas that represent objects to us, in contrast, typically come into existence after the object does. The house or building you are now in existed long before you perceived it and you may well continue to believe it exists long after it has been destroyed. Spinoza is a realist in the sense that he believes that physical – and indeed mental – objects exist independently of our ideas of them.

Spinoza, however, says almost nothing about the many questions that can be asked about this account. A body that we see, for example, produces many changes in our bodies. There is an idea of each of these changes, but apparently only one of these represents the object as present to us. If that is so, which one of these is the idea of the external object?

Here I think we must grant that Spinoza provides, and was able to provide, only a sketch of a theory. More detailed answers could only be provided after the development of neurophysiology, which began in earnest only in the twentieth century.

A second question concerns the diversity of the types of our sense perceptions. The idea that arises in us when we hear an object is presumably different from the idea we have when we see it. How do we obtain a unified idea of an object that we both hear and see?

Despite this, it is tempting to think that Spinoza's basic idea may well be right: it is through our awareness of changes in our body that we are aware of external objects. It is by having an idea of a change in our body that we are aware of, or conscious of, external bodies.

A caveat, however, is in order here. For Spinoza does not seem to have a systematic theory of consciousness. He holds that we have ideas of every part of our body and every change that occurs in it, but he is presumably not willing to say that we are conscious of every part and every change in the body. We also have an idea of every idea of an affection of the body, according to II p 27,d, where having such an idea of an idea is surely not the same as being conscious of the idea. In III p 9s and III gen.def.aff. he regards desires as appetites of which we are conscious and suggests, at least, that we are conscious of some and not others.

Spinoza infrequently uses 'conscious' (*conscius*), but when he does, it is at least sometimes a term of praise that cannot simply be equated with 'having an idea'. He writes in V p 39s and V p 42s as if infants, children, and the ignorant are not conscious of themselves, of things, or of God, while the wise are; and he writes of being conscious of something as if it were the same as having an adequate idea of it. But of course his account in Part II maintains that everyone has an idea of everything that happens in the body and such ideas necessarily 'involve' adequate knowledge of God.

Does Spinoza, then, hold that in addition to the conscious mind and conscious mental events, there is an unconscious? Although he does not put it this way, I think we must regard him as committed to that. Indeed, this seems to be the case in two ways. For there are mental acts, namely ideas, which are affirmations or denials that do not consist in consciousness of something. In addition, many of these acts are ones of which we are not conscious.

That Spinoza's theory of ideas does not focus or rely much on a distinction between conscious and unconscious mental events should not be very surprising, in one respect. For with the exception, perhaps, of II ax4, he does not determine what ideas are in the mind by introspection or by 'looking into' the mind. He instead deduces what ideas must be there from a consideration of the nature of God's idea of the body.

CHAPTER 7

THE *ETHICS*, PART III: EMOTIONS

BACKGROUND

Introduction to the emotions

Some questions

The study of the emotions is an important part of many different fields, including philosophy, biology, psychology, sociology, and medicine. Major subfields of philosophy that consider the emotions are philosophy of mind, ethics, social and political philosophy, and aesthetics. Major subfields of biology that investigate them are neuroscience and evolutionary biology.[1] In addition, of course, the emotions are a central concern in the arts, including literature, as well as in everyday life.

Initially, we have three most basic questions about the emotions. What are they? What causes them? What effects do they have? Since we regard them as varying in strength, we also want to know how we can best estimate, or even measure, their strength.

Another class of questions arises from the fact that we assess emotions. On what grounds are we to evaluate them as good, bad, excessive, appropriate, or desirable? Secondly, what can we do to increase or decrease their strength and, more generally, how can we control them?

The expression of emotion is also a fertile field. How do we ordinarily recognize emotions in others and, indeed, in ourselves? Are there facial expressions or other indications of emotions, for example, that are uniformly recognized in all human cultures? How is art related to emotion?

Emotions have historically been assimilated to sensations or experiences that are distinguished on the basis of how they feel; to thoughts or beliefs, distinguished by the content of the belief; or to motivational states like desires, distinguished by their object or the type of act they motivate.[2]

Sometimes they are regarded as purely subjective experiences or feelings that differ from each other in the way that the taste of chocolate differs from the taste of cheese. Feeling angry, for example, is quite different from feeling afraid or elated. Other emotions, however, do not seem to consist in having some characteristic feeling, at least if we generally take motivational states as emotions. You may want to play tennis tomorrow, or reply to a friend's e-mail, but there seems to be no special feeling that you have when you want these things.

In a similar way, some emotions are closely associated with bodily changes, for example sweating palms and a racing heart when you are afraid or very nervous. These are studied by neuroscientists, who have identified the central role that is played here by the sympathetic and parasympathetic nervous system.

The 'expression of emotion' is also an important topic and psychologists have, for example, made cross-cultural investigations of the recognition of facial expressions of emotion. Evolutionary biologists are concerned with this as well, following Darwin himself, who wrote *The Expression of the Emotions in Man and Animals*.[3]

Finally, emotions constitute part of the subject of 'folk psychology', our relatively commonsense psychological knowledge, which includes knowledge of important connections between emotions and beliefs. Anger or hatred, for example, can arise not from the fact, but from the belief, that a person you love has been harmed by another.

Why are emotions important?

Emotions one of great importance for a number of reasons:

1. Imagine for a moment that you are, by almost any measure, a great success. You have made fundamental contributions to some chosen field, you are well respected and indeed famous, you have amassed a small fortune, and you have a loving family as well as good health. But suppose, in addition, that you are constantly depressed or afraid.

Now imagine the contrary. Suppose, for example, that you lose your family, your home, your job, your wealth, your health, and everyone's respect. Although innocent, you are to spend the rest of your life in prison. But add to this that you are and will remain constantly cheerful and can see only the brighter side.

Which life would you choose? Which would be 'the best life'?

The answer may seem clear: a joyous life is better than a miserable one, even if the external circumstances are as described. But this means that what is most important in life depends, not – or not so much – on external success, but rather on our own attitudes and emotions. The quality of our lives is their quality 'from the inside', that is, it is the quality of our own consciousness – of how it feels. So it is hard to see how anything could be more important than our own emotions.

At least two objections can be made to this. One arises from consideration of the 'experience machine' imagined by Nozick.[4] When you 'plug in' to this machine, it produces any experience or sequence of experiences you have selected. So it will seem to you that you are playing tennis, or even winning the singles championship at Wimbledon, although in fact you are in a room plugged into the machine, or even a 'brain in a vat'. Would you plug in for the rest of your life? Nozick thinks not, because we do not want merely to have various experiences. We want actually to do things and to be a certain sort of person. We want, not just experiences, but experiences of 'the real world'.

I suppose that is true. But by hypothesis there is no difference you could detect between your simulated experiences (and false memories) in the machine and your experiences of the real world. You might wonder, when in the machine or out of it, whether your whole life is a dream or illusion of the sort portrayed in the movie *The Matrix*. Unless you wake up, however, and could determine that, there seems to be no way for you to tell, solely on the basis of your own experience.

Some, certainly, would reject doubts of this sort as meaningless, on the grounds that any meaningful hypothesis must in principle be capable of verification or falsification on the basis of experience. Others would respond that if you cannot tell whether your life is a dream or not, then it just doesn't matter. What is of value would remain the same, because that exists only within consciousness.

Another objection arises from consideration of the movie *It's a Beautiful Life*. The main character there proceeds joyously even in the face of the worst circumstances, including internment with his young son in a Nazi concentration camp. One reaction is to think that you ought to feel awful in the face of calamitous events and if you don't there is something wrong with you. We suspect that cheerfulness in the face of calamity is a mark, not of wisdom, but of madness.

Epictetus reminds us in *Enchiridion* that a ceramic cup is the sort of thing that can break.[5] So to avoid distress, it is best not to become too attached to any particular cup. His point, however, is that people, including your spouse and child, are like this as well. It is their nature to die and it is best not to love any individual too much. The Stoics think, and Spinoza is inclined to agree, that it is better not to have loved and lost than to have loved at all. The Stoic ideal of detachment from perishable things is shared by Spinoza. He notes, however, that no distress can arise from the love of an unchanging thing.

2. Emotions are important as well because so much interpersonal, social, and political conflict arises from them.

Murder, by popular accounts, is usually committed because of anger, hatred, greed, jealousy, or ambition. Racial violence, assassination, and war have some of the same causes, although ignorance and fear are important as well.

In the US, the attacks of 11 September 2001 produced fear and terror, followed by anger and a desire for revenge. The use of terror, no matter where it occurs, all too predictably has the same result. Anger and hatred arise, along with a desire for revenge. The suggestion that we should understand the reasons for the attack and respond 'coolly', without anger, is regarded as unpatriotic.

Emotions move us to act and hence they are tools of social control. Fear, perhaps, is the most powerful of them and thus it has often been exploited by religious and political leaders. Gruesome public executions, for example, were long thought to be an important deterrent to crime, including heresy, and the fear of eternal hellfire, along with the hope of eternal bliss, still motivates conformity to religious authorities. But secular governments find it just as useful. Demonization of the enemy is an important step in the preparation for war.

Spinoza lived in a culture that sometimes preached that joy is bad and sadness good. People should be glum and always reminded of their sinful nature, so joyous dancing, and indeed any enjoyment, is suspect at best. But what could be more depressing than that? Indeed, in IV App cap 30 Spinoza himself refers to such a doctrine as what 'superstition reaches'.[6]

3. The importance of the emotions in Spinoza's theory emerges primarily in Part IV of the *Ethics*, which contains an assessment of them and a statement or recommendation of the best way to live.

Part III, in contrast, provides the necessary preliminaries. What are the emotions and how are they related to each other, to our thoughts, and to changes in our bodies? Here Spinoza presents parts of folk psychology. As noted earlier, this consists of the general principles by which we ordinarily describe and explain human action and motivation. We ordinarily suppose, for example, that if you love someone, you will be glad when something good happens to him or to her, or more accurately, you will be glad when you come to believe that something good has happened to him or her.

Spinoza does much more, however, than merely present some of these commonsense psychological principles. He attempts to ground them, or exhibit their foundations, in his more basic principles regarding the mind.

The *Ethics*, Part III in a nutshell

Spinoza maintains that we have three primary, or most basic, emotions.

One of these is desire. Our most fundamental desire, and indeed our essence, is the endeavour (*conatus*) or power to persist in existence. Other desires are 'affections' or modifications of this desire. They are, as it were, offshoots of it, in the same way that a desire to help may give rise to a desire to wash the dishes.

Our two other fundamental emotions are joy and sadness. Joy is an increase in our power and sadness is a decrease in it. Love, hatred, and all other emotions are compounds of these with each other and with our ideas. Thus love is joy along with an idea of the cause of our joy, while hatred is sadness along with the idea of its cause.

Spinoza also derives a variety of general principles concerning the relations between our emotions and our beliefs. He maintains, for example, that you will be glad or be pleased if you believe that a person you love is pleased, that you will hate anyone whom you believe to have harmed a person you love, and that hatred is increased if it is reciprocated, but destroyed by love.

It is important to note that Spinoza does not regard all emotions as 'enemies of reason'. He thinks, for example, that reason itself gives rise to certain emotions, which he calls 'active emotions', in contrast to passive ones. In addition, many passive emotions are good, since they increase our power.

A RECOMMENDED ORDER OF READINGS FOR PART III OF THE *ETHICS*

Part III is concerned with the nature and origin of the emotions (*affectus*). It can be regarded as having four main sections, as follows:

Division 1: Preliminaries.
Division 2: The *conatus* doctrine and the three primary emotions.
Division 3: Passive emotions: general principles regarding the origin of important passive emotions and their relations to thoughts and other emotions. This takes up the majority of Part III. Note that I list quite a few of these general principles, as samples, but I will not comment on each one separately.
Division 4: Active emotions.

Reading	**Spinoza's claim**

Division 1: Preliminaries (Pref, p1–p3)
Spinoza begins with important preliminaries. These concern his manner of treatment of the emotions, the distinction between actions and passions (*passiones*), and a reiteration of his denial of causal interaction between the mental and the physical.

Pref	The emotions are natural phenomena, not defects in nature or 'faults and follies of mankind'.
p1	Sometimes the mind is active; sometimes it is passive. We act insofar as we have adequate ideas; we are passive insofar as we have inadequate ideas.
p3	Actions arise only from adequate ideas; passions (passive states) arise only from inadequate ideas.
p2	The body cannot cause the mind to think, nor can the mind cause the body to move or be at rest.

Division 2: The conatus *doctrine and the three primary emotions (p4–p11)*

p4	Nothing can be destroyed except by an external cause.
p6	Each thing, insofar as it can, endeavours to persevere in its being.

p 7   The endeavour to persevere is the actual
             essence of a thing.
p 9s   The definitions of 'will', 'appetite', and
             'desire', and a comment on the relation of
             desire to judgements of what is good.
p 11   If a thing increases the body's power of
             action, the idea of that thing increases the
             mind's power of action.
p 11s   The definitions of the three primary
             emotions: desire, joy, and sadness.

Division 3: Passive emotions (p12–p57)

LOVE AND HATRED
p 12   The mind endeavours (*conatur*) to think
             of what increases the body's power of acting.
p 13c   The mind is averse to thinking of what decreases the
             body's power.
p 13s   The definitions of love and hate.

THE ASSOCIATION OF EMOTIONS AND THEIR CAUSES
p 14   We associate emotions experienced at the
             same time.
p 15,s   Anything can be the accidental cause (*per
             accidens causa*) of joy, desire, and sadness.
             Love and hatred can arise from unknown causes.
p 16   We sometimes associate emotions whose
             objects are similar.
p 17   We sometimes love and hate a single object.

THOUGHTS, LOVE, HATRED, JOY, AND SADNESS
p 19   If you think (*imaginari*) that what you love is
             destroyed, you will be saddened; if you
             think it is conserved, you will be joyous.
p 20   If you think that what you hate is destroyed,
             you will be joyous.
p 21   If you think that what you love is joyous or
             sad, you will feel joyous or sad.
p 22   If you think that someone affects one you love
             with joy, you will love him. If you think he affects
             one you love with sadness, you will hate him.

Desire, love, and hatred

p 37	The strength of desire arising from joy or sadness varies with their strength.
p 39	We desire to harm those we hate and to benefit those we love.
p 40	Hatred, when no cause has been given for it, will be returned with hatred.
p 41	Love, when no cause has been given for it, will be returned with love.
p 43	Hatred is increased by hatred and it is destroyed by love.
p 46	If someone of another class or nation causes pleasure or pain, and we regard that person, qua member of the group, as its cause, then we will love or hate everyone of that class or nation.
p 53	Joy arises from the thought of our own power.
p 55	Sadness arises from the thought of our own impotence.
p 57,s	The emotions of one individual differ from those of another to the extent that the essence of one individual differs from that of another. Animals have emotions.

Division 4: Active emotions (p58–p59)

p 58	We have active emotions of joy and desire.
p 59,s	Our only active emotions are those of joy and desire.

The last portion of Part III provides definitions of the various emotions and a general definition of the passive emotions. Emotions are defined as confused ideas that determine the mind to think of one thing rather than another.

DISCUSSION OF THE RECOMMENDED READINGS FOR PART III OF THE *ETHICS*

Division 1: Preliminaries (Pref, p1–p3)

Emotions as natural phenomena
Pref: The emotions are natural phenomena, not defects in nature or 'faults and follies of mankind'.

Spinoza begins by emphasizing that his aim is to understand the emotions and behaviour of people as natural phenomena, in contrast to those who regard us as 'outside nature'. He indicates that his opponents are those who think that we 'disturb' rather than follow the order of nature, that we have absolute power or control over our actions, and that 'human weakness' is due to a defect in our nature, rather than the power of nature.

Spinoza alludes here to those who, like Descartes, think that our actions proceed from a completely free will and so we always have the power to act in one way rather than another. His opponents also surely include those who think that human nature is inherently evil or sinful, at least since the fall of Adam.

His own position, in contrast, is that our decisions have determining causes and, indeed, that everything in nature is subject to causal laws. So there is no 'free will' in the sense of an uncaused will. He also holds, as we will see when we turn to Part IV, that human nature is inherently good (for us), not inherently evil, and that nothing bad for human nature arises solely from that nature. Plenty of bad things happen to people, and people of course do bad things, but the source of this is always external to human nature itself.

The idea that human emotions and behaviour are to be regarded as natural phenomena, and explained in terms of natural laws, is the hallmark of a modern science of psychology.

Active and passive emotions
p 1: Sometimes the mind is active; sometimes it is passive. We act insofar as we have adequate ideas; we are passive insofar as we have inadequate ideas.

p 3: Actions arise only from adequate ideas, passions (passive states) only from inadequate ideas.

III def3 defines an emotion (*affectus*) as an affection (*affectio*) of the body by which its power is increased or decreased, along with the idea of the affection. An affection of something is a mode or modification of it, including changes that occur in it and, I think, states of it. We find out later (in p 9s) that for Spinoza, any increase in the power of the body (or mind) is a form of joy or pleasure and any decrease is a form of sadness or pain. We also find out (in p 11s) that in addition, Spinoza regards desire as an emotion as well.

In p 1d and p 3d Spinoza proceeds to argue for two main claims (primarily on the basis of def1 and def2). (1) We are active, or act, when we are the adequate (or complete) cause of something and this occurs only when we have adequate ideas. (2) We are passive when we are the inadequate or partial cause of something and this occurs insofar as we have inadequate ideas. That we in fact are sometimes active and sometimes passive follows from claims in Part II that some of our ideas are adequate and some are inadequate (as noted in II p 40s 2).

The denial of causal interaction between mind and body
p 2: The body cannot cause the mind to think, nor can the mind cause the body to move or be at rest.

Spinoza's argument in p 2d relies primarily on II p 6. In the scholium to p 2d he argues that the mind does not control the body and that decisions, or 'decrees of the mind', cannot cause physical changes. He explicitly maintains that buildings and pictures, for example, regarded as physical, cannot be caused by mental events, but must instead arise from events considered as physical. Although a decision in the mind is itself the same as a 'determination of the body', they are conceived differently, on his view, and it is only an event regarded as physical that can cause something physical.

If we ask how a building can be regarded as mental, that is, conceived under the attribute of Thought, the answer seems clear. It must be regarded as an idea or affirmation, namely, God's affirmation of the existence of the building. This idea comes into existence when the building does and just as the building contains a variety of parts, so the idea of it contains ideas of all of its parts.

Division 2: The *conatus* doctrine and the three primary emotions (p4–p11)

The conatus doctrine
p 4: Nothing can be destroyed except by an external cause.

p 6: Each thing, insofar as it can, endeavours to persevere in its being.

p 7: The endeavour to persevere is the actual essence of a thing.

Spinoza states in p 4d that the proposition is self-evident, but he explains that the definition of a thing affirms or posits the essence of the thing. When we attend to the thing itself, he says, 'we can find nothing in it which can destroy it'.

In p 6d Spinoza infers from p 4 and p 5 that each thing 'opposes' (*opponitur*) everything that can destroy it, and thus it 'endeavours to persevere in its own being'.[7]

Finally, in p 7d Spinoza argues that from the 'given' or 'actual' essence of a thing – that is, from the existing or instantiated essence – certain things follow, and so its power of action, that is, its *conatus* to persevere in existence, is its given essence.

The details of this whole sequence are difficult to understand. Spinoza takes a similar position, and says similar things, about motion and rest, however. In II lem3c he holds that it is self-evident that a body in motion will remain in motion, and a body at rest will remain at rest, unless affected by another body.

In CM I.6 Spinoza holds that there is only a distinction of reason between a thing and its *conatus* to persevere in its own being. A distinction of reason is a distinction only in our concepts, or way of conceiving a thing, not in the thing itself. He there uses motion as an example and says, 'Motion has a force for persevering in its own state; this force is certainly nothing other than the motion itself'.[8] Those who say otherwise, and suppose that a force distinct from the motion is required to preserve it, are committed, he thinks, to an infinite regress of forces.

Spinoza thus treats the existence of a thing as he does the motion of a body. Each is a state which has, or rather is, a force for continuing. Like other states, and unlike events, existence and motion tend to last. It is a change of state, not the continuation of one, that is in need of explanation.

p 9s: The definitions of 'will', 'appetite', and 'desire', and a comment on the relation of desire to judgements of what is good.

In p 9s Spinoza defines 'will' (*voluntas*) as the *conatus* itself, when 'related to the mind alone'. When related to both the mind and the body, it is called 'appetite' (*appetitus*). Desire (*cupiditas*) and appetite are the same, he remarks, except that we usually ascribe a desire to someone just when the person is aware of his appetite.

Spinoza's distinctions between being 'related to' (*refertur*) the mind alone, to the body alone, and to both is not completely transparent. Sometimes he means by 'related to' that it is attributed to the thing or predicated of it. It also seems that when he speaks of something as related to the mind, he sometimes means 'insofar as it is conceived under the attribute of Thought', that is, as mental. Similarly, a thing is 'related to the body' when it is 'conceived under the attribute of Extension', or as physical. The term 'will' is thus used to denote something conceived as mental. How something can be conceived as both mental and physical at the same time may thus seem problematic, since these are distinct ways of conceiving it. To do that seems like describing it at one and the same time in two distinct languages.

Spinoza indicates that we may be unaware of an appetite, although he regards an appetite, by definition, as both mental and physical. Thus he evidently does not suppose that anything which is regarded as mental must itself be an object of awareness or consciousness.

In the last part of this scholium Spinoza maintains that we do not desire something because we judge it to be good; rather, we judge it to be good because we desire it. In Part IV, however, he takes knowledge of good and evil to be an emotion of joy or sadness (IV p 8) and in the first sentence of IV p 15d he supposes that these emotions are causes of desires. Thus he there takes the judgement that something is good as the cause of our desire for it.

The resolution of this apparent conflict is not at all obvious. It is clear, however, as we will see when we turn to Part IV, that Spinoza rejects the view that objects are inherently good or bad. He holds instead that they are good or bad only insofar as they affect us and, in particular, insofar as they promote or decrease our power and desire to persevere in being. So this general desire must first exist in order for there to be anything that is good or bad, and thus in order to judge correctly that anything is good or bad.

The three primary emotions

p 11: If a thing increases the body's power of action, the idea of that thing increases the mind's power of action.

p 11s: The definitions of the three primary emotions: desire, joy, and sadness.

Table 1. Translations of emotion terms in Part III of the *Ethics*

	Shirley (Spinoza 2002)	Curley (Spinoza 1985)
laetitia	pleasure	joy
titillatio	titillation	pleasure
hilaritas	cheerfulness	cheerfulness
tristitia	pain	sadness
dolor	anguish	pain
melancholio	melancholy	melancholy
gaudium	joy	gladness

The scholium to p 11 provides definitions of *laetitia* (joy or pleasure) and *tristitia* (sadness or pain). Both are said to be passive transitions of the mind. Joy is a transition to a 'greater perfection', that is, to a greater power of acting; sadness is a transition to a lesser perfection or power. We discover later, in III p 58, that in addition to passive joy, there is an active emotion of joy as well.

Spinoza also subdivides each of these (when related simultaneously to both mind and body). *Laetitia* is either *titillatio* (pleasure or titillation) or *hilaritas* (cheerfulness). *Tristitia* is either *dolor* (anguish or pain) or *melancholio* (melancholy). The difference is that *titillatio* and *dolor* affect only some parts of the body, or some more than others, while *hilaritas* and *melancholio* affect all parts equally.

The two standard English translations render some important terms differently, as indicated in Table 1.

I follow Curley's translations of these terms.

It seems clear that there is at least a potentially important distinction between pleasant and unpleasant experiences that affect only a part of us, or of our bodies, and those that affect us as a whole. As just noted, this is the distinction Spinoza draws between *titillatio* (pleasure) and *hilaritas* (cheerfulness) on the one hand, and *dolor* (pain) and *melancholio* (melancholy) on the other. It is the difference between pleasures and pains that are localized or locatable as opposed to those that are not. Stubbing your toe or cutting your finger, for example, is quite unlike hearing that your cat has died. So too, the pleasant taste of an orange differs importantly from good news or the satisfaction of a job well done.

Sometimes we want to jump and shout when something good happens (or rather is believed to have happened) and we want to withdraw and become motionless when something bad happens. Joy is often accompanied by an increase in activity and sadness by a decrease. (Anger, on the other hand, is often expressed by an increase in activity as well.) Whether joy or sadness can be identified with an increase or decrease in power is another question. Although Spinoza makes this identification, he does not suggest a way of quantifying the amount of power we have at a given time, nor does he consider how to measure increases or decreases in it.

Another reservation should be expressed as well. Spinoza does not seem to think of our force or power as being used up when we engage in some activity such as playing tennis. In fact if we enjoy playing tennis, this enjoyment, according to Spinoza, is an increase in our power of self-preservation. How he would explain fatigue, despite this enjoyment, is not entirely clear. He does, however, try to explain a somewhat similar phenomenon. For he explains that we stop eating, even if we enjoy the food, because eating causes a change in the constitution of the body and we then feel disgust or weariness (*fastidium & taedium*).

Spinoza here classifies desire (*cupiditas*) as one of the three most basic emotions, but he has also identified desire with the *conatus* and the essence of each individual. How can desire be both an 'affection' of the essence and also the essence itself of an individual?

The answer to this, I think, is that while the *conatus* (and desire) to persevere in our being is our essence, other endeavours (desires) arise partly or wholly from this as modifications or affections of it. The desire to live, for example, gives rise to a desire for shelter from the snow. It may be wondered how the *conatus* to persevere, that is, our essence and power, can itself be an emotion, but it is clear that a modification or even a specification of it is. Spinoza, however, characterizes it as a desire, and the upshot of this is that we have one most basic desire, the desire to persevere in existence, and all other desires arise from it.

Division 3: Passive emotions (p12–p57)

Love and hatred

p 12: The mind endeavours (*conatur*) to think of what increases the body's power of acting.

p 13c: The mind is averse to thinking of what decreases the body's power.

p 13s: The definitions of love and hate.

Love is joy (*laetitia*) along with the idea of an external cause, while hate is sadness along with the idea of an external cause. Spinoza adds here that if you love a thing, you will want it to be present and will want to preserve it. He makes analogous remarks about hatred.

It may be that Spinoza has in mind primarily love of another person and other 'things', like pets or a favourite cup. We also at least say of people, however, that they love such things as chocolate, money, playing tennis, or winning and it is not entirely clear that, or how, Spinoza's additional remarks apply to such cases. The love of chocolate, for example, may be the love of eating chocolate, in which case we do want chocolate to be present. We want that, however, primarily because we want to eat it or taste it. Unfortunately eating it also destroys it. Perhaps this is like money, in one respect. For the love of money is on the face of it the love of one's own possession of money; the use of it will then be a cause of sadness, insofar as it decreases the amount you have.

Another feature of Spinoza's discussion is worth noting. Since Spinoza defines joy as a transition to greater power, he must evidently regard love as an event. But it seems rather to be a relatively long-lasting state. Falling in love may of course take a long time, or a short time, but being in love is something that lasts, or doesn't. Events occur or happen. States, in contrast, last for a time. So love seems more like a disposition or state, and more like a relatively long-lasting desire than a pleasant event.

The association of emotions and their causes
p 14: We associate emotions experienced at the same time.

p 15,s: Anything can be the accidental cause (*per accidens causa*) of joy, desire, and sadness. Love and hatred can arise from unknown causes.

p 16: We sometimes associate emotions whose objects are similar.

p 17: We sometimes love and hate a single object.

In these propositions Spinoza holds that we form an association of emotions, either because we were once affected by both at the same time (p 14) or because the object of an emotion is similar to some other object (p 16). In the first case, we have in effect a kind of 'emotional memory'. Spinoza's proof relies on the claim that if we have been affected by two bodies at the same time, then when we later think of one we will remember the other. He is asserting, it seems, that the feelings we had when they affected us become associated with each other in the same way. Alternatively, it may be that feelings become tied to our thought of the objects. So if we afterwards think of one of them, then not merely do we think of the other, but we have the same feelings we had before.

Spinoza also holds that if we notice a similarity between a thing that is pleasant and another thing, then we will love the second thing. In short, we will regard the second as a source of pleasure, or with joy, although it is not in fact the cause of our joy.

We can thus love or hate a thing indirectly and without realizing why and, as III p 17 asserts, we can also experience love and hate of a single object at the same time.

This love and hatred, however, cannot occur literally at the same time if they consist of cheerfulness and melancholy (*hilaritas* and *melancholio*) along with the idea of a single cause. For by definition these are an increase and a decrease, respectively, in the power of the whole mind or body.

Thoughts, love, hatred, joy, and sadness

p 19: If you think (*imaginari*) that what you love is destroyed, you will be saddened. If you think it is conserved, you will be joyous.

p 20: If you think that what you hate is destroyed, you will be joyous.

p 21: If you think that what you love is joyous or sad, you will feel joyous or sad.

p 22: If you think that what affects one you love with joy, you will love him. If you think he affects one you love with sadness, you will hate him.

Here and in many other places it is tempting to express Spinoza's claims by talking of what you think or believe. Spinoza himself, however, uses the verb *imaginari*, which both Shirley and Curley rightly translate as 'imagine'. What Spinoza seems to mean, however, is not merely what 'imagine' may easily suggest, namely that something simply occurs to you, as in a daydream, but without your supposing that it is really the case. He uses this term elsewhere, for example, to speak of sense perception and of the beliefs that we acquire by perception.

It is not entirely clear how inclusive Spinoza here intends *imaginari* to be. It may include mere imagining (as we often use the term), thinking that something is so, or coming to have a belief or even having a belief that something is so. It may be that he means all of these. If so, 'thinks' may give the best English rendition. For 'thinks' may characterize an event or process, but it may also be used to describe a belief, that is, a relatively long-lasting state.

Desires, love, and hatred

p 37: The strength of desire arising from joy or sadness varies with their strength.

p 39: We desire to harm those we hate and to benefit those we love.

p 40: Hatred, when no cause has been given for it, will be returned with hatred.

p 41: Love, when no cause has been given for it, will be returned with love.

p 43: Hatred is increased by hatred and it is destroyed by love.

p 46: If someone of another class or nation causes pleasure or pain, and we regard that person, qua member of the group, as its cause, then we will love or hate everyone of that class or nation.

p 53: Joy arises from the thought of our own power.

p 55: Sadness arises from the thought of our own impotence.

p 57,s: The emotions of one individual differ from those of another to the extent that the essence of one differs from another. Animals have emotions.

Some of these propositions seem unproblematic and may constitute a part of our ordinary or 'commonsense' beliefs about emotions. Such beliefs, however, are not ordinarily tied to specific definitions and derived from more basic principles. The details of these I leave aside here.

In p 57s Spinoza notes that other animals have desires and he emphasizes the difference between individuals of the same and of other species. He holds, for example, that human lust is quite different from equine lust and the joy of a drunkard quite different from the joy of a philosopher.

Division 4: Active emotions (p58–p59)

p 58: We have active emotions of joy and desire.

p 59,s: Our only active emotions are those of joy and desire.

Spinoza argues in p 58d that we have adequate ideas and in having them we are conscious of ourselves and of our power. According to p 53, however, joy arises from the thought of our own power. Hence we experience joy, which arises insofar as we have adequate ideas, that is, insofar as we are active.

We also endeavour to persevere in our being, insofar as we have adequate ideas (by p 9). This endeavour is a desire, however, and so some desire is active as well.

Spinoza notes in p 59d that when we feel sad, the mind's power of activity, that is, its power of understanding, is decreased. He immediately concludes from this that we cannot feel sad insofar as we act. Unlike joy and desire, sadness is thus inevitably a 'passion', that is, something of which we are not the adequate cause.

In p 59s Spinoza provides a classification of the virtues, although he speaks of them as actions, desires, or endeavours. His initial concern is with actions that follow from emotions that we have insofar as we understand. All of these he 'refers' to 'strength of mind' (*fortitudinis*) and he divides them into two types: (1) courage (*animositas*, translated by Curley (Spinoza 1985: 529) as 'tenacity'), where we aim only at our own advantage, and (2) nobility (*generositas*), by which we help others. Under courage he explicitly includes moderation, sobriety, and presence of mind in the face of danger; under nobility, he includes courtesy and mercy.

The last portion of Part III sets out definitions of the various emotions and a general definition of the passive emotions. Here he takes an emotion to be (1) a 'confused idea by which the mind affirms a greater or lesser power' of the body or a part of it, which (2) determines the mind to think of one thing rather than another.

Part (1) of this definition, Spinoza notes, expresses the nature of joy and sadness, while part (2) expresses the nature of desire.

COMPARISON OF SPINOZA WITH OTHERS: SPINOZA'S PHILOSOPHICAL ALLIES AND OPPONENTS

Hobbes

In Part I, chapter 6 of the *Leviathan*,[9] Hobbes sets out an account of the emotions, or passions, beginning with endeavour (which in Latin, as we have seen, is *conatus*). He maintains that endeavour consists of motions in the body that lead to visible, voluntary action. When the endeavour is toward something that causes it, it is appetite or desire, and when it is away from something it is aversion. In I.6.2 he holds that love is the same as desire, except that we call it 'desire' when the object is absent, 'love' when it is present. So, too, aversion and hate are the same, except that in aversion, the object is absent and in hate, it is present.

Hobbes also holds, in I.6.11, that pleasure and displeasure are the 'appearance or sense' of good or evil, and that they accompany all desire and aversion. Pleasure or displeasure in expectation of what will happen is joy or grief.

Hobbes lists the 'simple passions' in I.6.13. They include appetite, desire, love, aversion, hate, joy, and grief. In the immediately succeeding sections he proceeds to define a variety of other emotions in terms of the simple ones. These include hope, despair, and fear, as well as what we regard as dispositions or character traits, such as liberality and kindness.

Thus Hobbes seems to hold that there are three most fundamental types of emotion: endeavour, pleasure, and displeasure. As indicated above, he explicitly holds that endeavour consists in physical motions in the body that cause actions and that pleasure and displeasure are the 'appearances' of good and evil. These appearances presumably also consist in motions in the body, however, for Hobbes is a materialist. His general metaphysics maintains that the only real things that exist are bodies that move or are at rest.

Spinoza's theory of emotion is thus remarkably similar to Hobbes's in several ways. Like Hobbes, Spinoza maintains that one of three most basic emotions is endeavour or desire (whether it be toward or away from something), and that when conceived as physical, endeavours are changes in the body. Spinoza also of course holds that endeavour can be conceived as mental, or under the attribute of Thought, as well.

Spinoza is also in agreement with Hobbes, at least verbally, that the two other most basic emotions are pleasure and displeasure or, in Curley's translation, joy (*laetitia*) and sadness (*tristitia*). According to Spinoza, these can also be conceived as physical changes in the body. Spinoza departs from Hobbes, however, in maintaining the additional thesis that joy and sadness consist of transitions to a greater or smaller degree of power (in our endeavour to persevere) and in holding that joy and sadness are causes of our desires, rather than accompaniments of them.

Another important similarity is that Spinoza, like Hobbes, regards our endeavour or desire to preserve our lives as our most fundamental or powerful desire and sometimes speaks as if all of our actions are motivated by self-interest.

It is thus highly likely that Hobbes's theory of emotion was an important influence on Spinoza.

Descartes

Descartes' theory of the passions is set out in the *Principles of Philosophy* and in a separate treatise devoted to the topic, *The Passions of the Soul*.[10] He maintains that there are six most basic passions, namely, wonder, desire, love, hate, joy, and sadness. We have seen above that of this group, Spinoza, in the *Ethics*, accepts as basic only desire, joy, and sadness.

In KV II.3, however, Spinoza's list of passions begins with wonder, or surprise, and he regards it, and indeed all emotions, as arising from judgements or 'knowledge'. In KV II.1 and II.2, he classifies knowledge into three types: opinion, true belief, and clear knowledge. As in the *Ethics*, the first kind of knowledge is further subdivided into hearsay and fallible experience. Wonder, or surprise, arises from what we now call 'inductive generalization'. His example is of someone who has only seen short-tailed sheep and concludes that all sheep have short tails. He is then surprised when he sees Moroccan sheep, which have long tails.

Spinoza continues, in KV II.3, to treat of love, hatred, and desire, which arise from the first kind of knowledge, and then, in subsequent chapters from II.4 through II.14, of other emotions. Later chapters, including II.22, 23, and 26, speak of love of God, which arises from the third kind of knowledge and (sometimes) from the second.

This account is a forerunner of his views in the *Ethics*, although some differences are quite evident. For example, in the *Ethics* Spinoza explicitly denies that wonder is an emotion.[11]

Descartes' general conception of the emotions is that they are perceptions and, indeed, confused ideas, that are typically caused by bodily changes.[12] These perceptions cause the soul to want things or to want to do things.[13] He maintains that although the mind and body are distinct types of thing, physical changes nevertheless directly cause changes in the mind or soul and the soul in turn directly causes physical changes. Thus when you see a vicious dog approach, changes in the body produce awareness or the perception of the dog as vicious, from which your fear of it arises. The fear then causes a desire to run and your desire, which is mental, causes changes in the body such as contraction of the muscles in your legs – that is, it causes you to run.

Accompanying this general account are detailed speculations on the relevant bodily processes that cause and are caused by the emotions. Descartes speaks of nerve pathways, for example, connecting the brain and the heart, and of the animal spirits (subtle matter conveyed by the nerves), as well as the locus of interaction, which he thinks might be the pineal gland.

Descartes also attempts to explain why a certain physical event should cause one mental change rather than another and, more generally, why the causal relations between mind and body are set up as they are. His answer is that while God could have set up the causal relations in any way whatsoever, he chose this one because it results, in normal circumstances, in the health and preservation of the body.[14] He thus provides, so to speak, a 'quasi-Darwinian' account.

Spinoza's main complaint about this is that the claim of causal interaction between the mind and the body is unintelligible. He rejects it in E II p 6 and III p 2 and he discusses it at greater length in III p 2s, and in V Pref where he cites Descartes by name. In the general definition of the emotions, he agrees with Descartes, however, that *passive* emotions, not active ones, are confused ideas that give rise to desires, conceived as modes of Thought.

Spinoza, however, also holds that there are active emotions, of joy and desire only, that arise from adequate ideas. His notion of active as opposed to passive emotions recalls, but is not the same as, Descartes' distinction between 'intellectual joy' and 'animal joy' in *The Principles of Philosophy*.[15]

Descartes there maintains that intellectual joy (*gaudium intellectuale*) arises when we hear good news, and no 'commotion of the body' is involved. Intellectual joy produces a change in the imagination, and 'spirits' (subtle bodies) then account for a sequence of changes, proceeding from the brain to the heart, back to the brain, and finally back to the soul, where 'animal joy' (*laetitia animalis*) arises.

Spinoza holds in IV p 52,d,s that joy arises from reason, the second kind of knowledge, and he states in V p 32c that it also arises (or 'arises') from intuitive knowledge, the third kind of knowledge. The latter kind of joy, when accompanied by the idea of God as its cause, he calls 'intellectual love' (*amor intellectualis*; see again V p 32c). But neither can arise from an external source such as good news and of course neither, conceived under the attribute of Thought, is causally related to physical changes in the body.[16]

PROBLEMS AND DISPUTED ISSUES OF INTERPRETATION

One of the most disputed issues in the interpretation and assessment of Spinoza's philosophy concerns his views on teleology or purposiveness. Recent interest in this is in large measure due to Bennett (1984).

An initial problem arises because Spinoza seems to reject the concept of final causation in Part I of the *Ethics*, but to accept and use it in Part III. In I App he goes so far as to say that 'all final causes are only human fictions'.[17] But in Part III, as we have seen, he employs the concept of an end, that is, of a goal, when he characterizes all particular things as having a *conatus* or desire to persevere in existence.

The resolution of this initial problem does not seem difficult. Spinoza's attack on final causes in Part I of the *Ethics* is an attack on the idea that some abstract or future state of things can by itself be cited as a cause to explain some earlier act, either of God or of anything else. Such an explanation, for example, would cite 'habitation' or 'having a house' as a final cause of human acts of building a house. One of Spinoza's objections, whether a fair one or not, is that this reverses the order of nature. It confuses the effect with the cause.

Spinoza does suppose, however, that a desire to build a house can be cited to explain human actions that bring a house into existence. Such a desire, he holds, is the efficient cause of human action and, ultimately, of the house.

There is thus no conflict between Spinoza's rejection of all final causes, understood as abstract or future states that cause earlier events, and his acceptance of 'ends', that is (by IV def7) desires or appetites as the efficient causes of action. Nor is there any conflict between his rejection of ends or goals of God's action and his acceptance of human goals. For while we have desires, and thus need or lack something, God does not.

A second problem arises, however, because Spinoza seems to use the concept of desire in an objectionably teleological way. Perhaps the primary passages at issue are III p 12, p 13, and their demonstrations. In p 12d, for example, Spinoza seems to argue, very much in outline, as follows:

(1) We endeavour to persevere.
(2) Thinking of things that increase our body's power promotes or leads to our perseverance.
(3) Hence, we endeavour to think of things that increase our body's power.

This is like arguing:

(4) We want to live.
(5) Eating low-fat dinners promotes our lives.
(6) Hence, we want to eat low-fat dinners.

The difficulty is that it is not a desire and a *fact* that something is a means to its satisfaction that generates a desire for the means; it is rather a desire and a *belief* that something is a means to its satisfaction that does this. It is not, for example, (4) and (5) that licenses (6), but rather (4) and the following:

(7) We believe that eating low-fat dinners promotes our lives.

On many other occasions, however, Spinoza recognizes this. In III p 28, for example, he holds that we desire whatever we *believe* (*imaginamur*) leads to pleasure. He does not hold there that we desire whatever in fact does lead to pleasure, despite his use of III p 12 in III p 28d.

Similar theses are set out, with reference to beliefs, not facts, from III p 19 through p 32. For example, in p 22, he holds that we will hate someone, not when he has in fact produced sadness in a person we love, but when we believe this. Thus Spinoza seems generally to maintain that an emotion, along with a belief, not a fact, generates other emotions.

A third and final objection might also be raised. It is that in providing explanations that appeal to the content of our desires (and other psychological phenomena), Spinoza has used the concept of desire in another objectionably teleological way. For a desire to jump, as opposed to a desire to run, is a state that is 'directed toward' the future and is regarded as causing one thing rather than another solely because of its content. A non-teleological use of the concept would instead cite those intrinsic features of the desire in virtue of which it causes us, when it does, to jump.

It might be said in reply that the 'directedness' of desires is no more objectionably teleological than the concept of a vector. The speed of a train, for example, is said to be a scalar quantity (say 60 mph), while its velocity, or speed plus direction, is a vector (e.g. 60 mph to the north). Just as a body moves with a speed in a direction, so too, a desire is a 'force', for lack of a better word, that has a direction. Indeed, in Spinoza's view the *conatus* or endeavour of a particular thing to continue to exist is the same type of thing as the *conatus* of a body in motion to remain in motion.

In addition, it might be replied, the content of a desire or other psychological state, conceived under the attribute of Thought, is an intrinsic feature of it.

It is by no means evident, however, that these replies are adequate.

CHAPTER 8

THE *ETHICS*, PART IV: ETHICS

BACKGROUND

Introduction to ethics

It is customary to distinguish descriptive ethics, normative ethics, and meta-ethics as follows.

Descriptive ethics is an attempt to characterize and explain the actual moral beliefs, attitudes, and practices of an individual or group. Such attempts fall within a variety of social sciences such as psychology, sociology, and anthropology. These sciences at least typically endeavour to be purely descriptive and explanatory, leaving aside all assessment or evaluation of the truth or acceptability of the morality or moralities under study.

Normative ethics, in contrast, is an attempt to characterize a 'true morality', or at least an acceptable one. As a part of philosophy, it is in large measure an enquiry into the truth or acceptability of principles of conduct. These are the principles we accept or might accept for deciding what to do and for assessing our own and others' actions.[1] Normative ethical theories are not just concerned with the assessment of action, however. Equally important is the assessment of intentions, dispositions, emotions, people, and ways of life as 'right', 'wrong', 'good', or 'bad', and as 'honourable', 'dishonourable', 'mean', 'dishonest', 'kind', 'unconscionable', 'nice', and so on.

Meta-ethics, finally, is concerned with questions about the meaning and justification of normative claims. What does 'Lying is always wrong' mean and how, if at all, can we know that it is true?

Thus the claim that the seventeenth-century Batak of Sumatra practised cannibalism, and accepted the practice, while modern Batak reject it, is a statement within descriptive ethics. The claim that cannibalism is wrong (or morally wrong) is a claim within normative ethics. The claim that 'Cannibalism is wrong' means that it is contrary to God's commands, or contrary to reason or nature, is a claim within meta-ethics.

Normative theories can be classified in a variety of ways, but the most generally accepted current scheme makes crucial use of the distinction between an act and its consequences. Indeed, the main classificatory scheme embodies a dispute about the conceptual relations between the rightness of an act and the (non-moral) goodness of the act's consequences. Thus a theory is said to be consequentialist (or teleological) just when it holds that the moral rightness of an act is dependent exclusively on the non-moral goodness (or badness) of its consequences. A theory is said, in contrast, to be deontological just when the rightness of an act is not held to be strictly determined by the goodness or badness of its consequences.

The paradigm consequentialist theory is John Stuart Mill's.[2] He holds that an act is right just when, or just to the extent that, it produces 'the greatest happiness for the greatest number'. In slightly different terms, an act is right when it produces the greatest net balance of good over evil for all concerned. The paradigm of a deontological theory is Kant's.[3] He maintains that the good or bad consequences of an act are irrelevant to the assessment of it as right; instead, an act is right just when it conforms to the supreme principle of morality. This principle, the 'Categorical Imperative,' states in one form that you are to act only on that maxim, or rule, that you can consistently will to be a universal law. An alternative and allegedly equivalent formulation maintains that you are to treat humanity (whether in yourself or in others) never merely as a means, but also as an end.

The above characterization is drawn largely from an account by Frankena, which makes a sharp division – indeed, an exclusive and exhaustive one – between these two theories.[4] Teleological and deontological theories are sometimes less rigidly defined, however. It is sometimes said, for example, that a teleological theory is one that 'focuses' on the consequences of an act, while a deontological theory is 'concerned with' rules in its characterization of acts as right, wrong, obligatory, and so on. This leaves the borders fuzzy, if not fluid, and opens the way for other types of theories, the most prominent of which is now 'virtue ethics'.

Such an ethics takes the primary question to be what kind of person we are to be, and what dispositions we are to cultivate, rather than what kinds of acts are morally right or wrong. Whether this is a genuine alternative to teleological or deontological theories is questionable, however. Frankena maintains that it is not, at least if notions of moral rightness and their kin are retained. For a virtue will be a character trait or a disposition to act in some way and a specification of it will be equivalent, or nearly equivalent, to the specification of a duty. Honesty, for example, will be a disposition to tell the truth, except in some circumstances, perhaps, and to say this is to say, practically, that we ought generally to tell the truth.[5]

The question of what kind of person to be cannot mean 'what kind of person we have a moral obligation to become', if a virtue ethics is to be distinct from deontological or consequentialist theories. Indeed, Frankena's claim that all moral theories are either teleological or deontological may seem impossible to avoid. One alternative, set out by Gary Watson, is to take the concept of virtue as primary and to define concepts of moral rightness and so on in terms of it.[6] Another alternative, which Frankena himself suggests, is to try to proceed without any concept of distinctively moral rights, obligations, and so on.[7] This we may call a 'radical virtue ethics', although Frankena is inclined to deny that it is an ethics, or moral theory, at all.

Preliminary remarks on Spinoza's normative ethics and meta-ethics

Spinoza's normative ethics and meta-ethics are especially interesting, and potentially instructive, for a variety of reasons.

1. Spinoza's ethics is set out within a highly unorthodox metaphysical context. It is unorthodox in the West, at least, since the spread of Christianity. For, as noted earlier, it maintains that there is one substance, of which we are modifications, and while it accepts the existence of God, it rejects a conception of God as transcendent and as like a person who issues orders and then rewards and punishes us accordingly. Even more radically, Spinoza takes everything to be an expression of God's power and every act to be an act of God.

2. It has more in common with the philosophical ethics of ancient Greece than with the Judaeo-Christian ethics of his own culture or even of ours. For it revives and indeed is devoted to the ancient question of how it is best to live, and it answers this question without appeal to divine revelation or a supernatural world.

Like the ancient Stoics, Spinoza takes the distinction between what is and what is not in our power as fundamental in answering this, as attested by a major structural division in the *Ethics*. For the title of Part IV is 'Of Human Bondage, or the Strength of the Emotions', where bondage is our lack of power over the emotions. The title of Part V is 'Of the Power of the Intellect, or of Human Freedom'. Like Plato, Spinoza endeavours to show that virtue is happiness (or blessedness) and is its own reward. Although he advocates action in accordance with rules and principles, he does not regard acts contrary to these as 'morally wrong'. Contrary actions rather reveal lack of power, or even an illness.

3. It appears to contain no concept of moral obligation, or of what is morally right or wrong. It is instead set out more as a description of how a rational, free, or virtuous person will act, and what such a person will value, than as a statement of what people should or ought or must do.

Indeed, an important distinction between moral and non-moral value does not seem to be present in Spinoza, unless you simply and implausibly dub the use of 'good' in 'good person' or 'good character trait' as a 'moral' notion, in opposition to the non-moral use of 'good' in 'good dog' or 'good food'. In contrast to this is Kant's conception of what is 'good without qualification' (the good will), and the placement of this outside the natural world.

4. It is preceded (in TdIE, KV, and earlier passages of the *Ethics*) by meta-ethical remarks that deny, or seem to deny, the objective reality of its favoured terms of assessment. These terms are 'good' and 'bad', along with the associated notions of what is perfect and imperfect, where these express the degree of approximation to an ideal for human beings.

5. Indeed, his exposition sometimes begins, as in TdIE, with an emphasis on the extent to which ethical thought rests on ignorance. It sometimes ends, as in E IV p 68, with the claim that no real knowledge of such matters is possible – that, in fact, the whole enterprise is (ideally?) to be transcended.

The *Ethics*, Part IV in a nutshell

Spinoza holds that human power consists primarily in intelligence or the power of the mind to understand. Our most fundamental desire and power is the endeavour to persevere in existence, not as mere bodies, but as embodied rational beings.

His primary terms of evaluation are 'good' and 'bad' and he rejects the view that things are in any absolute sense good or bad. He instead holds that things are good or bad only in relation to us and, indeed, to a model or ideal of human nature. A thing is good when it brings us closer to this model and it is bad when it takes us farther away from the model. The ideal or model that he himself advocates is that of a person who is completely or maximally rational. Thus a thing is good when it increases our understanding and it is bad when it decreases it.

Spinoza also puts this point by saying that the 'highest' (*summum*) thing we can understand is God and so our highest good or highest desire is to understand God. Whatever promotes this is useful or good and whatever hinders it is bad.

We act freely, from virtue, and under the guidance of reason, when we do things and have active emotions that follow from our essence alone. Such actions and active emotions can only be good. We are passive and have passive emotions when things follow from our essence only when taken in conjunction with other things. These can be good, bad, or neither.

Things are also good for us insofar as they agree with or have something in common with our nature and they are bad insofar as they are contrary to our nature. Since nothing agrees with our nature more, or has more in common with us, than another person who lives under the guidance of reason, nothing is more useful to us than such a person.

In addition, the preservation of our body is essential for the continued existence of the mind and the body needs many things, such as food, that we cannot practically obtain without the help of others. Thus it is crucial that we live in harmony or on friendly terms with others. What promotes this harmony is good and what undermines it is bad. The application of these principles generates Spinoza's assessment of acts, desires, and emotions as good or bad. A sample of these is as follows:

1. Joy or cheerfulness (*hilaritas*), which consists in an increase in the power of the whole body or mind, can only be good.
2. Love and desire can be excessive, hatred is never good, and if we live under the guidance of reason, we endeavour to repay hatred with love.

3. Humility and repentance are not virtues.
4. Pity (in one who lives under the guidance of reason) is bad, as are regret, hope and fear.
5. A free man always acts honestly.
6. Those guided by reason are more free in a state than alone.

A RECOMMENDED ORDER OF READINGS FOR PART IV OF THE *ETHICS*

A short list

Readers who are new to Spinoza's ethical theory might best begin by reading three relatively short sections of Part IV:

1. the Preface
2. p 18s
3. the Appendix

Spinoza explains in the Preface that he will use 'good' and 'bad' only in relation to the concept of an ideal person that we want to become. A thing is good when it promotes our attainment of the ideal and it is bad when it hinders our attainment of it.

p 18s gives a preview of some of his central ideas regarding ethics, including the claim that the foundation of virtue is doing what is truly best for yourself.

The Appendix provides a summary of many of the doctrines that he sets out 'geometrically' from p 19 to p 73. It also contains comments on additional topics, such as sexuality and marriage, that Spinoza does not explicitly discuss earlier in Part IV. Some comments on these short list passages are found below.

A longer list

Reading	Spinoza's claim
Preface	The main aims of Part IV and the meaning of valuational terms.

Division 1: Why we see the better, but follow the worse (p1–p18)

p 7	An emotion can be destroyed only by a stronger, contrary emotion.

p 8   Knowledge of good and evil is an emotion.

p 14   Emotions can be restrained by true knowledge of
        good and evil only insofar as this knowledge is an
        emotion, not insofar as it is true.

p 15   Desire that arises from true knowledge of good and
        evil can be destroyed or restrained by many other
        desires.

Division 2: The right way of living (p18–p73)

SECTION 1: VIRTUE AND THE HIGHEST GOOD (P18–P28)

p 18s   A summary of some important precepts of reason.

p 19   Each person, from the laws of his own nature,
        necessarily desires or is averse to what he judges to be
        good or bad.

p 20,s   A person's *conatus* or power to persevere
        in existence is proportionate to that
        person's virtue.

p 23   A person acts from virtue just insofar as he
        understands, or has adequate ideas.

p 26   Insofar as we reason, or have adequate
        ideas of reason, we endeavour only to
        understand and we regard as good only
        what advances understanding.

p 27   The only thing we know with certainty to
        be good or bad is what advances or hinders
        understanding.

p 28   Our highest good (*summum bonum*) is knowledge
        of God and our highest virtue is to know God.

SECTION 2: SOCIAL HARMONY: RELATIONS TO OTHER PEOPLE (P31–P37)

p 31   Whatever agrees with our nature is
        necessarily good.

p 34,c   Insofar as we have passive emotions, we
        can be contrary to each other.

p 35   Insofar as people live under the guidance of
        reason, they agree in nature.

p 36   The highest good is common to all.

p 37   The good that we want for ourselves,
        insofar as we pursue virtue or live under the guidance
        of reason, we want for all other people.

p 37s 1   We may treat other animals as we will.

p 37s 2   On praise and blame, merit and sin, and justice and injustice.

SECTION 3: THE ASSESSMENT OF ACTS AND EMOTIONS AS GOOD OR BAD (P38–P61)

p 38   Whatever increases the body's power to affect and be affected by external bodies is good; whatever decreases this is bad.

p 39   Whatever preserves the proportion of motion and rest of the parts of the body to each other is good; whatever changes this is bad.

p 40   Whatever promotes social organization and harmony among people is good; whatever produces discord in the state is bad.

THE ASSESSMENT OF JOY AND SADNESS (P41–P43)

p 41   Joy is good in itself, while sadness is bad in itself.

p 42   Cheerfulness is always good and melancholy is always bad.

p 43   Pleasure can be excessive and bad; pain can be good to the extent that pleasure can be bad.

THE ASSESSMENT OF LOVE, DESIRE, AND HATRED (P44–P46)

p 44   Love and desire can be excessive.

p 44s   Some emotions, when excessive, are diseases.

p 45   Hatred toward people can never be good.

p 46   Insofar as we live under the guidance of reason, we endeavour to repay hatred, anger, etc. with love.

THE ASSESSMENT OF HOPE, FEAR, PITY, ETC. (P47–P61)

p 47   Hope and fear are not good in themselves.

p 50   Pity, in a rational person, is bad.

p 53   Humility is not a virtue.

p 54   Repentance is not a virtue and he who repents is doubly wretched (*bis miser*).

SECTION 4: KNOWLEDGE OF EVIL; THE FREE MAN (P62–P73)

p 64   Knowledge of evil is inadequate.

p 68   If we were born and remained free, we
                           would have no concept of good or evil.

p 72   Free men never act deceitfully.

p 73   Insofar as we live under the guidance of
                           reason, we are more free in a state than in
                           solitude.

Appendix

App   Summary of much of Part IV.

DISCUSSION OF THE RECOMMENDED READINGS FOR PART IV

Preface

The main aims of Part IV

As noted above, the title of Part IV is 'Of Human Bondage, or the Strength of the Emotions', and Spinoza indicates in the first paragraph of the Preface that human bondage (*servitudinis*) is bondage to the emotions. It is, he says, a lack of power to control them.

The conflict between reason and emotion is an ancient and still current theme. We noted in Chapter 7, however, that Spinoza does not regard all emotions as the enemies of reason. We are enslaved only to emotions that arise from sources 'outside of' ourselves. These are 'passive emotions'; other emotions, however, arise from our nature alone and are 'active'.

The first paragraph of the Preface indicates Spinoza's main aims in Part IV. His first goal is to explain how it is possible for us 'to see the better, but follow the worse'. This is found in p 1–p 18. His second task is to set out 'what is good and what is bad' in the emotions or, as we learn in p 18s, what the precepts of reason are. This is the concern of p 18s through p 73.

The meaning of valuational terms

Spinoza here explains what he will mean by 'perfect', 'imperfect', 'good', and 'bad'. His 'official' definitions of 'good' and 'bad' are given in IV def1 and def2.

This part of the Preface maintains that 'perfect' and 'imperfect' originally applied only to things that were intentionally built or created by people. A thing is perfect when it is completed or finished and it is imperfect when it is not. But whether it is completed or not depends on the intention of the 'author' or originator (*auctor*).

Later, he says, people created universal ideas and models of things, such as houses and buildings, and began to prefer some to others. To say that a thing is perfect came to mean that it matched or conformed to the model they preferred; to say that it is imperfect meant that it did not match or agree with the model.

But people also developed universal ideas of natural things, not made by people, and supposed that God or nature uses these ideas as models in creating them. When they find an imperfect thing, that is, a thing that fails to match their preferred model, they think that nature has made a mistake.

Spinoza of course rejects the idea that God or nature acts purposefully and so he rejects the idea that nature makes mistakes. He thus holds that perfection and imperfection are just ways of thinking that arise from comparing individuals to each other. But he retains the words: 'By reality and perfection I understand the same thing' (II def2).

Spinoza proceeds to say that 'good' and 'bad' do not express properties of things as they are in themselves. For one and the same thing can, at the same time, be good, bad, and indifferent – that is, it can be good for one, bad for another, and indifferent for a third. Like 'perfect' and 'imperfect', these words indicate ways of thinking that are due to comparisons that we make. He also retains these terms, however, since, he says, 'we desire to form an idea of man as a model of human nature'. A thing will be said to be good, then, when that thing is useful in attaining this model, that is, in becoming like it; a thing is bad when it prevents us from attaining it.

Division 1: Why we see the better, but follow the worse (p1–p18)

How emotions can be destroyed

p 7: An emotion can be destroyed only by a stronger, contrary emotion.

Spinoza's argument for this proposition maintains, in outline, that:

(1) An emotion (conceived under the attribute of Thought) is an idea of an affection of our body (a change in our body's power of action).

(2) This affection can be destroyed only by a physical cause, which produces an affection of the body that is contrary to and stronger than the earlier affection.

(3) But whenever that happens, there will be an idea of the new affection of the body, which will be contrary to and stronger than the earlier idea.

(4) This idea of the new affection is itself an emotion.

(5) Hence an emotion can only be destroyed by another stronger and contrary emotion.

It might also be noted that if an affection of the body can be destroyed only by some other affection of the body, then the idea of the affection of the body can be destroyed only by the idea of that other affection of the body. This is so by II p 7, which states that the causal order of ideas is the same as that of their objects.

Knowledge of good and evil
p 8: Knowledge of good and evil is an emotion of joy or sadness. Spinoza's argument in p 8d goes as follows:

(1) According to IV def1 and 2, when we say that a thing is good, we mean that it helps to preserve our being, and when we call it bad we mean that it is detrimental to the preservation of our being. But by III p 7 this is the same as saying that it increases or decreases our power of acting.

(2) An increase in our power of acting is joy, however, and a decrease in our power of acting is sadness, by II p 11s. So the knowledge or awareness of our own joy and sadness – or our awareness that a thing is producing joy or sadness – is the same as our knowledge that it is good or bad.

(3) An idea of an affect is united to the affect just as the mind is united to the body; that is, they are not really different, but only 'conceptually' (*nisi solo conceptu*) different, by II p 21.

(4) Hence our knowledge of good and evil is the emotion of joy or sadness 'insofar as we are conscious of it'.

Note that this argument shows only that knowledge of our own (present) good or evil is the emotion of joy or sadness, that is, when we know something of the form 'This is good' or 'This is bad'. It does not seem to be applicable to knowledge of the form 'This is good for you' or 'This is always bad'.

Spinoza's views here are strikingly close to emotivism. This holds, in a typical formulation, that what appear to be moral statements, or statements of value, are actually just expressions of emotion. 'This is bad' is like saying 'Ouch' and 'This is wrong' is like saying 'Boo'.

It is natural to object that knowledge of what is good is an affirmation that is true, while an emotion is not, and hence Spinoza's identification of them is false. Although Spinoza's thesis is actually that they are the same, but differ 'conceptually', it remains unclear whether, or just how, this provides an adequate defence.

Reason vs emotion

p 14: Emotions can be restrained by true knowledge of good and evil only insofar as this knowledge is an emotion, not insofar as it is true.

Spinoza's proof of this proposition relies primarily on p 1, p 7, and p 8. Indeed, he anticipates this claim in p 1s, where he provides an example. Fear may disappear when we hear something true, but it does not disappear because it is true. For fear may also be destroyed when we hear false news.

Another example might be useful. You might want to eat some chips, but restrain yourself and decide not to, because someone points out that the fat and salt content is unhealthy (or that they have been poisoned). It is not because your belief is true (which I here assume) that you become averse to eating the chips. For if, unbeknown to you, that belief had been false, your desire for them would still have been destroyed.

It is a belief itself, not its truth, that is relevant to the explanation of our emotions.

Weakness of will

p 15: Desire that arises from true knowledge of good and evil can be destroyed or restrained by many other desires.

This proposition and its demonstration provide Spinoza's basic answer to the question posed in this division, namely, 'How is it possible to know what is best for you and yet not do it?' p 16 and p 17 describe two special cases. Knowledge of a future good (p 16) and of a contingent good (p 17) can be destroyed by desire for present things. See p 17s as well.

Spinoza's demonstration of p 15 cites III def.aff.1 to support the thesis that pleasure and pain give rise to desire. The definition states, 'Desire is the very essence of man insofar as he is conceived as determined to any action from any given affection of itself'.[8] He has already argued for this in greater detail in III p 37d and he cites p 37 itself to support the claim that the strength of a desire is proportional to the strength of the pleasure or pain that generates it.

In the next part of his argument, Spinoza notes that true knowledge of good and evil arises in us insofar as we are active and so the force of it and of the desire it generates must be 'defined' by human power. The force of other desires, however, is 'defined' by the power of external things, which can surpass our power (by IV p 3). Thus a desire that arises from true knowledge of good and evil can be destroyed by other desires.

Spinoza thus explains 'weakness of will' or '*akrasia*' in an apparently straightforward manner. One can 'see the better, but follow the worse' simply because the desire that arises from knowledge of what is better is weaker than other desires. You may know 'intellectually' that smoking is bad for you and yet still smoke, because your desire to smoke, or your addiction, is much stronger than the desire to quit that arises from recognition of its dangers.

There is a problem with Spinoza's premise that true knowledge of good and evil arises in us insofar as we are active. This requires that we be the adequate cause of such knowledge and hence that this knowledge be adequate. But p 64 denies that we can have adequate knowledge of evil and p 68 maintains that if we were born and remained free we would have no concept of good or evil.

Division 2, section 1: Virtue and the highest good (p18–p28)

Precepts of reason
p 18s. A summary of some important precepts of reason

In p 18s Spinoza notes that he has now finished his explanation of human weakness and our failure to act in accordance with the precepts of reason. He then proceeds to state what these precepts are. He states, for example, that each person should love himself and do what is best for himself, and that what is best for himself is to join forces with others and advance the common good. He maintains, in short, that if we do what is best for ourselves, we will be virtuous.

His aim here, as he himself indicates, is to undermine the view that doing what is best for yourself conflicts with what is best for others and is the basis, not of virtue, but of vice or immorality.

Desire and judgement

p 19: Each person, from the laws of his own nature, necessarily desires or is averse to what he judges to be good or bad.

This is a slightly modified restatement of III p 28. Spinoza, however, speaks here of what we judge to be good or bad, rather than what we imagine (or believe) to be good or bad. He also believes that desire (*appetitus*) is the essence or nature of each person and so he adds 'from the laws of his own nature' in the statement of the proposition.

The rationality of suicide

p 20,s: A person's *conatus* or power to persevere in existence is proportionate to that person's virtue.

Spinoza identifies virtue with the power (or the effective power) to persevere in existence and so the more power a person has, the more virtue he has.

In the scholium he maintains that no one kills himself by the necessity of his own nature. The example of Seneca, who was ordered by Nero to kill himself, is an especially interesting one, because Spinoza maintains that in killing himself Seneca desired, or chose, the lesser of two evils. Although Spinoza does not assert here that this was the rational thing to do, he does hold in p 65 that a rational person will choose the lesser of two evils (and the greater of two goods).

Spinoza emphasizes again his thesis that what destroys a thing is never contained within its essence (III p 4) and states that for one to destroy himself solely from the necessity of his nature is as impossible as that something come from nothing. It is also as impossible, on his view, as that the motion of a body give rise to rest, that is, that it destroy itself.

It is sometimes thought that Spinoza's doctrine of the *conatus* to persevere in existence makes suicide impossible or at best irrational.

This does not seem to me to be true. For his *conatus* doctrine holds that the essence of a thing cannot be the sufficient cause of its own destruction. It does not deny that it is a partial cause, which must be cited along with external things, or its environment, to explain the thing's destruction.

Spinoza apparently thinks that Seneca must either obey Nero's command, and kill himself, or else face even worse consequences, such as torture and then death. It would then be rational for him to kill himself. But he does this only in the face of external forces that affect him.

It is also clear from p 72s that Spinoza does not think everyone will avoid doing whatever can be foreseen to lead to his own death. For Spinoza holds that a rational person will tell the truth even if it leads to death.[9]

Acting from virtue

p 23: A person acts from virtue just insofar as he understands, or has adequate ideas.

The basic idea behind the proof, not its details, is as follows.

As IV def8 indicates, Spinoza takes acting from virtue as essentially acting or doing something that follows from our essence or power alone. But a thing follows from our essence alone, that is, we are the adequate cause of it, just in case it follows from adequate ideas, by III p 3. So we act from virtue only insofar as we understand or have adequate ideas.

Spinoza seems very close to saying that our essence, or the essence of our mind, consists in adequate ideas. For he holds that we are the sufficient cause of something just in case it follows from (or is caused by) our adequate ideas alone. But of course he does not maintain that our essence consists only of adequate ideas; he holds instead that our essence is an idea that contains both adequate and inadequate ideas.[10] Indeed, if we had only adequate ideas, it would be hard to see how we could be distinguished from each other. More will be said about this later, when we come to the last section of Part V.

Our highest desire

p 26: Insofar as we reason, or have adequate ideas of reason, we endeavour only to understand and we regard as good only what advances understanding.

The crucial portion of the first part of Spinoza's argument seems to rely on II p 40, which states that any idea which follows from an adequate idea is also adequate. If we grant that only an idea follows from another idea, then only adequate ideas follow from an adequate idea.

This first part of the argument seems to me obscure, but it may, at bottom, go roughly as follows.

(1) Our essence is (only) the endeavour to persevere in existence and to do what follows from our nature.
(2) Only adequate ideas follow from our nature, insofar as we have adequate ideas.
(3) So, the only thing we endeavour to do, insofar as we have adequate ideas, is to persevere in existence and have adequate ideas (or to persevere as a being with adequate ideas).

The second part of the argument merely needs to note that 'good' means whatever is useful, as stated in IV def1, and that to be useful is to be useful for something, that is, for achieving some goal. If our only goal, insofar as we are rational, is to understand or have adequate ideas, then the only thing that will be good, insofar as we are rational, is what promotes understanding.

Instead of maintaining that what is good is what promotes understanding, however, Spinoza here states that the mind, insofar as it uses reason, judges nothing to be good except what promotes understanding.

The highest good
p 27: The only thing we know with certainty to be good or bad is what advances or hinders understanding.

p 28: Our highest good (*summum bonum*) is knowledge of God and our highest virtue is to know God.

Spinoza argues in p 28d that God is the highest or greatest thing that we can understand, since God is absolutely infinite being (or an absolutely infinite being) and nothing can be or be understood without God. Thus, by p 26 and p 27, he says, the knowledge of God is our greatest advantage or good.

Spinoza seems to express here the idea that our ultimate goal is to attain knowledge of God and he nearly says this in his summary in IV App. In IV App cap 4, he says that our final goal (*finis ultimus*) or highest desire (*summa cupiditas*) is 'that by which we are brought' to understand 'all things'. He also says that our highest happiness and blessedness consists in perfecting the intellect, or reason.

What may at first seem problematic about p 28, then, is that Spinoza uses 'good' here to denote our ultimate goal, not what is useful for something or what is a means to an end. He does not, that is, use 'good' here as it is defined in his 'official' definitions. For he defines 'good' in IV def1 as what we certainly know to be useful and in IV Pref he regards as good anything that brings us closer to the model of human nature that we set before ourselves.

His official definitions, then, take 'good' to mean what is often now called 'extrinsically good'. Something is 'intrinsically' good when it is good 'in itself' and it is extrinsically good when it is a means to something that is intrinsically good.

Division 2, section 2: Social harmony: relations to other people (p31–p37)

Things in agreement with our nature
p 31: Whatever agrees with our nature is necessarily good.

Spinoza argued in p 30d that if a thing agrees with our nature or has something in common with it, it cannot be bad. (For it would otherwise be able to decrease our power and hence a thing could destroy itself, contrary to III p 4.) That thing also cannot be indifferent, for then nothing would follow from our nature that preserves our nature (by IV p 6). Hence it must be good.

Passive emotions and being contrary to each other
p 34,c: Insofar as we have passive emotions, we can be contrary to each other.

Spinoza gives an example to establish this. Paul may hate Peter for a variety of reasons, and so it may happen that Peter hates Paul (by III p 40,s). So they may try to hurt each other and thus they are contrary to each other.

Human nature

p 35: Insofar as people live under the guidance of reason, they agree in nature.

Spinoza argues that what we judge, under the guidance of reason, to be good or bad necessarily is good or bad (by II p 41). Hence what we do, insofar as we live under the guidance of reason, really is good for human nature and hence is good for each person. So we agree in nature.

Spinoza explicitly uses a concept of human nature here, but says nothing about its ontological status. Elsewhere, in II p 40s 2, he maintains that we form universal ideas of species, including man, from experience of individuals. We ignore the many differences between individuals, or cannot retain distinct images of all of them, but notice their similarities, and different people form different ideas of them. The species, man, is itself not something distinct from the individuals who are similar to each other.

As noted earlier, he also holds, in IV Pref itself and elsewhere, that to speak of what is good or bad for people, we must set up, or construct, an idea of man as a model of human nature.

In the first corollary, Spinoza holds that nothing is more useful to us than a person who lives under the guidance of reason.

The highest good

p 36: The highest good is common to all.

p 37: The good that we want for ourselves, insofar as we pursue virtue or live under the guidance of reason, we want for all other people.

In p 36 Spinoza proceeds to maintain that 'The highest good of those who pursue virtue is common to all, and all can equally enjoy it.'[11] He has already argued in II p 47 that everyone in fact has adequate knowledge of God and it seems evident that knowledge, unlike food and shelter, is not a 'competitive good'. Possession of it by one does not, that is, conflict with its possession by another.

Spinoza adds in p 37 that what we want for ourselves we also want for all others. This, too, is restricted to desires that we have insofar as we 'pursue virtue', and the basis for this claim is that others who have what we want are most useful to us.

Other animals
p 37s 1: We may treat other animals as we will.

Objections to 'slaughtering beasts' or using them as we will are based on 'groundless superstition or womanish compassion', according to p 37s 1. Right is defined by power, and we have greater power over other species than they do over us. In addition, other species do not 'agree with' our nature and it is most useful for us to be 'in close relationship' only with other people. So even though other animals feel, and have pain, we may treat them in any way we like.

Spinoza's philosophy, in this respect, thus seems a most unlikely basis for an environmental ethics, let alone a 'deep ecology' movement. Nevertheless, his philosophy has been taken by some as the foundation for such a movement.[12]

Sin and injustice
p 37s 2: On praise and blame, merit and sin, and justice and injustice.

Spinoza remarks here that in I App he said he would explain the following pairs: praise–blame, merit–sin, and justice–injustice. He explained praise–blame in III p 29s. (Praise is the pleasure we have when we think that another has acted to please us; blame is the pain we feel when we dislike another's action). Here he explains the others, but he must first, he says, 'speak of man in a state of nature and of man in society' (*de statu hominis naturali, & civili*).

Spinoza follows Hobbes in making use of the notion of a state of nature. Everyone has a natural right, Spinoza says, to do what he thinks will be advantageous for himself. If we all lived in accordance with reason, we would have this right without harming each other. Because we have passive emotions, however, we do harm each other.

Since we cannot very well live without the help of others, we must give up this natural right and form a society, which itself has the right, or power, to preserve itself, to judge what is good and bad, and to establish laws. Even those who do not live under the guidance of reason will then be induced not to harm others, for fear of a greater harm to themselves. A society with this right, or power, is a state (*civitas*).

Wrongdoing or sin (*peccatum*) cannot be conceived in a natural state. It can only be conceived to exist in a civil state, where it consists in disobedience to the law. Obedience, on the contrary, is 'merit' in a citizen.

In a similar way, Spinoza holds that ownership is not a 'natural relation' or that the concept of ownership is inapplicable in a state of nature. Ownership only exists in a state, where there are laws that express the common consent about who owns what. Justice, as Plato held, is rendering to each his own and injustice consists in depriving someone of what they own. But what a person owns is defined only by the laws.

Spinoza thus rejects specifically 'moral' concepts of what is right and wrong, as well as of justice and injustice, in favour of legal concepts. In the *Tractatus Politicus*, which we will consider later, he considers and rejects the terminological suggestion, as he sees it, that wrongdoing be identified with what is contrary to reason, or to what one who lives under the guidance of reason would not do.

Division 2, section 3: The assessment of acts and emotions as good or bad (p38–p61)

The body

p 38: Whatever increases the body's power to affect and be affected by external bodies is good; whatever decreases this is bad.

p 39: Whatever preserves the proportion of motion and rest of the parts of the body to each other is good; whatever changes this is bad.

Spinoza holds that our mind's power to understand is proportional to the powers of the body (II p 14). Hence whatever increases these powers is good and whatever decreases them is bad (by IV p 26 and p 27).

The form of the body consists, on his view, in a certain proportion of motion and rest among its parts (def. before II lem). Whatever preserves this preserves the body and hence makes it possible for the body to affect and be affected by external bodies in more ways; hence it is good (by p 38). Whatever changes this proportion destroys the body and thus destroys its powers. Hence it is bad (again by p 38).

In p 39s Spinoza notes an apparent implication of his view about the form of the human body (or of any complex body). What he suggests, or does not deny, is that a living body can lose its form, and so die or cease to exist, 'without turning into a corpse' (*nisi mutetur in cadaver*). Spinoza suggests that this happened in the case of 'a Spanish poet' who lost his memory and it may happen as well in the transition from infancy to adulthood.[13]

On this view, the poet before his loss of memory is not the same 'man' or human being – and presumably not the same individual – as the person with a memory loss. The infant, similarly, is not the same human being as the adult.

Social harmony
p 40: Whatever promotes social organization and harmony among people is good; whatever produces discord in the state is bad.

Spinoza cites p 35 to show that what promotes harmony promotes living 'from the guidance of reason' (*ex ductu rationis*) and thus, by p 26 and p 27, it is good.

There seems to be a difference, however, between living or acting from the guidance of reason and living in accordance with reason. Similarly, there is a difference between doing something that happens to be right and doing something because you know that it is right.

Spinoza seems to ignore this difference here (although not elsewhere[14]) in citing p 35. For p 35 speaks, or seems to speak, of living from the guidance of reason in the sense that you do things because they follow from reason or because reason 'dictates it'. His argument in p 40d, however, speaks of anything that promotes harmony and this may include acts that arise from many different motives. Suppose, for example, that I want to hit you or steal your property, but I refrain from this because I am afraid of the punishment that the law prescribes. My action, or inaction, is then in accordance with reason, but not from reason. I thereby promote harmony, but I am not, it seems, acting from reason.

An example of a 'positive act' could also be given. Assume that the law requires that I give money to charity (as in effect it does, since taxes are used to provide income and health care for the poor), and I do this, but solely because I fear the punishment. Again I act in accordance with reason, but not from reason.

Thus p 35 seems inapplicable, at least without further argument, to the claim that acting in accordance with reason ultimately promotes acting from reason. I am uncertain whether a successful argument for this can be given.

Joy and sadness

p 41: Joy is good in itself, while sadness is bad in itself.

Spinoza argues that joy (conceived under the attribute of Extension) is an affect by which the body's power of action is increased and sadness is an affect by which it is decreased. Thus by p 38 joy is good and sadness is bad.

Cheerfulness and melancholy

p 42: Cheerfulness is always good and melancholy is always bad.

Cheerfulness consists in joy in which all parts of the body retain their relations to each other, since all parts are equally affected (by III p 11s). Thus, by IV p 39, it is always good and cannot be excessive. Melancholy affects the whole body as well by decreasing its power and so it, too, by IV p 39, is always bad.

Pleasure and pain

p 43: Pleasure can be excessive and bad; pain can be good to the extent that pleasure can be bad.

Pleasure, by III p 11s, affects and increases the power of one part of the body rather than others and thus it can reduce the variety of ways in which the body can be affected by other bodies. So by IV p 38 it can be bad and excessive. Pain, insofar as it can prevent pleasure from being excessive, can be good.

Love and desire

p 44: Love and desire can be excessive.

Spinoza attempts to demonstrate that love can be excessive as follows. Love is joy along with the idea of an external cause (IV def.aff.6). Since pleasure is one type of joy, pleasure along with the idea of an external cause is one form of love. So by IV p 43 love can be excessive.

As for desire, according to Spinoza the strength of a desire is proportional to the strength of the affect (or emotion) from which it arises, by III p 37. Just as an emotion such as love can be excessive, so too the desire that arises from it can be excessive (by reducing the variety of ways that the body can affect or be affected by other bodies).

Emotional diseases

p 44s: Some emotions, when excessive, are diseases.

Spinoza here contrasts cheerfulness (*hilaritas*) with pleasure (*titilla-tio*). Cheerfulness is always good and cannot be excessive, but he indicates here that it is not very common. Pleasure, in contrast, affects only some parts of the body and is much more common.

This scholium is especially interesting because it introduces the idea that excessive love and desire for one object can be a disease. 'Fixations' of this sort prevent people from thinking of anything else. Indeed, sometimes this is so extreme that people mistakenly believe the object of their love to be present, that is, they hallucinate. This scholium is also important because it seems to recommend a shift in our attitude toward such people, from laughing at or hating them to regarding them as sick: 'Greed, ambition, and lust are really species of madness, even though they are not numbered among the diseases.'

Hatred

p 45: Hatred toward people can never be good.

Spinoza's argument notes that by III p 39 we endeavour to destroy a person we hate and he then cites IV p 37 in an apparent attempt to show that destroying another is bad.

The whole demonstration reads, 'We endeavor to destroy a man whom we hate (by prop. 39 of part 3), that is (by proposition 37 of this part), we endeavor to do something which is bad. Therefore etc. Q.E.D.'[15] In the scholium Spinoza explicitly notes that here and in what follows he means by hatred only hatred toward people, which is what I think he means here by 'men' (*hominem*).

If destroying another is always bad, however, it would follow that capital punishment and killing others in self-defence and in war are bad. Spinoza accepts capital punishment, however, when it is done for the good of the state, rather than out of passion.[16] He also seems to accept killing a person who has gone mad from the bite of a rabid dog.[17] Finally, he advocates the fortification of cities[18] and surely accepts the use of force, and the killing of enemies, in their defence.

Thus Spinoza does not hold that killing another person is always bad. In addition, in IV p 59 and its demonstrations he makes it clear that any act that arises from passion can also arise from reason and no act, considered in itself, is good or bad. 'Striking a blow', which may be intended to include hitting another, is his example in p 59s. The second demonstration of p 59 supposes that an act is bad if the emotion from which it arises is bad.

The reference to p 37, in p 45d, is puzzling and seems to be a slip. More useful, perhaps, would be a citation of p 40.

How to respond to hatred and anger
p 46: Insofar as we live under the guidance of reason, we endeavour to repay hatred, anger, etc. with love.

Hatred, anger, etc. (toward people) is bad, by p 45c1, and so under the guidance of reason we endeavour to avoid it (p 19). Thus we desire that other people not experience hatred (p 37). Since hatred is increased by hatred and destroyed by love (III p 43), we endeavour, insofar as we live under the guidance of reason, to repay hatred etc. with love.

Hope and fear
p 47: Hope and fear are not good in themselves.

Spinoza holds that hope and fear are always found together (III def.aff.12,13,exp), for when you hope or fear something, you are in doubt about whether it will occur. So if you hope that something will happen, then you will also fear that it will not, and vice versa.

Since each of these emotions is or entails sadness, neither can be good in itself, by IV p 41.

People as superhuman, human, or inhuman
p 50: Pity, in a rational person, is bad.

Pity is bad simply because it is a kind of sadness (III def.aff.18) and so it is bad (by IV p 41).

Spinoza holds that pity leads people to help those whom they pity, but this is useless or not needed in those who are guided by reason. For they will help others even without pity (by IV p 37).

In the scholium Spinoza mentions those who are moved 'neither by reason nor pity' to help others and he calls them 'inhuman' (*inhumanus*). He thus suggests a threefold classification of people. We might call them 'superhuman', 'human', and 'subhuman'.[19] Those who are 'superhuman' are of course people who act from the guidance of reason, while the merely human are ordinary people or 'the multitude'.

In Spinoza's eyes, the 'inhuman' probably include the people who murdered (and ate) Jan and Cornelis de Witt. As noted in Chapter 1, the sign he wanted to post at the site of the murders would simply have stated *ultimi barbarorum* ('the greatest of barbarians'). In Ep 23, to Blyenbergh, Spinoza spoke of a someone with a 'perverted human nature', who by hypothesis would see clearly that he could lead a better life by engaging in 'villainy'.

Humility
p 53: Humility is not a virtue.

Spinoza defines humility as sadness that arises from considering our own lack of power (III def.aff.26). It is the opposite of 'self-contentment' or 'self-esteem' (*acquiescentia in se ipso*), which Spinoza considers in IV p 52.

Spinoza argues, in a somewhat roundabout way, that humility does not arise from reason and hence 'is a passion, not a virtue'. We might also note that according to Spinoza, because humility is a kind of sadness it is directly bad, by p 41. Hence it cannot arise from our virtue or power (def8).

Repentance
p 54: Repentance is not a virtue and he who repents is doubly wretched (*bis miser*).

The proof of the first claim in p 54 is like that of p 53, Spinoza says. The second claim is true because the person first has a bad desire and then is also sad.

The scholium notes that humility and repentance, like hope and fear, are useful, for people rarely live under the guidance of reason: 'The mob is terrifying, if unafraid'.[20] Spinoza knew this quite well, from the mob's treatment of the de Witt brothers.

Division 2, section 4: Knowledge of evil; remarks on the free man (p62–p73)

Knowledge of good and evil
p 64: Knowledge of evil is inadequate.

p 68: If we were born and remained free, we would have no concept of good or evil.

The proof of p 64 seems straightforward. Knowledge of evil is sadness (IV p 8), that is, a decrease in our perfection (III def.aff.3). Thus it cannot be understood through our essence alone (III p 6 and p 7). Thus it is a passion (III def2), which depends on inadequate ideas (III p 3). Hence by II p 29 knowledge of evil is inadequate.

On the other hand, Spinoza seems unable to establish or even to grant that knowledge of good is inadequate. For knowledge of good is joy, that is, an increase in our perfection, which sometimes can be understood through our essence alone. Self-esteem, for example, is joy that arises when we consider our own power and by IV p 52 it arises from reason. So it depends only on adequate ideas. This knowledge of good must thus be adequate (by II p 40).

In p 68 Spinoza does not explicitly assert that knowledge of good is inadequate, but he comes very close. In p 68d, he argues that if we were born and remained free, we would have only adequate ideas and hence would have no concept of evil, by p 64. From this he infers we would also have no concept of good, 'for good and evil are cor-relative (*correlata*)'.

Lying
p 72: Free men never act deceitfully.

A free man is one who acts from the guidance, or dictates (*dictamina*), of reason, as Spinoza explains in p 66s. If a free person acted decep-tively, being deceptive would be a virtue (by p 24) and everyone would be better off by being deceptive, that is, to agree in words, but to be contrary to each other in fact. But this is absurd, by p 31c.

In the scholium Spinoza maintains that a free person would not lie even to save his or her own life. Spinoza holds that what reason recommends (*suaderet*) to one person it recommends to all, and in that event it would recommend that people not join forces or have common laws.

Spinoza's position here is similar to that of Kant, who holds, to put it roughly, that an act is wrong if and only if it cannot be con-sistently 'universalized'. Like Spinoza, he holds that lying, even to save an innocent person's life, is always wrong. Neither grants that lying might be acceptable in some circumstances, but not others.

We seem to think instead that we do not always owe the truth to others, especially to enemies in time of war and to those who are 'inhuman'.

In addition, this type of position seems already to have been rejected by Spinoza, when he maintains that killing another, when motivated by reason, not passion, is not bad.

The free man and the state

p 73: Insofar as we live under the guidance of reason, we are more free in a state than in solitude.

Spinoza's demonstration cites p 37 to show that insofar as we are guided by reason or are free (p 66s), we desire 'to maintain the principle of common life and common advantage'[21] and thus, by p 37s 2, to obey the laws of the state. He concludes that we endeavour, insofar as we are guided by reason, to obey the law in order to live more freely.

An evident difficulty is that unswerving obedience to the state may require that you act contrary to the guidance of reason. Spinoza replies to this in TP 3.6, where he maintains in response that the advantages of the state will outweigh any disadvantages.

In the scholium to p 73 Spinoza speaks of those who are strong-minded. This is defined in IIIp 59s as doing things that follow from active emotions, that is, emotions that we have insofar as we understand. A strong-minded person 'hates nobody, is angry with nobody, envies nobody, is indignant with nobody, despises nobody, and is in no way prone to pride'.[22] In addition, he regards it as most important

> that everything follows from the necessity of the divine nature, and therefore whatever he thinks of as injurious or bad, and also whatever seems impious, horrible, unjust and base arises from his conceiving things in a disturbed, fragmented, and confused way. . . . And so he endeavors, as far as he can, to do well and to be glad[.][23]

Appendix

The Appendix to Part IV of the *Ethics* provides a useful summary of much of the material set out more formally from IV p 19 through p 73s. It also contains brief comments on topics, such as marriage and childrearing, that are not considered earlier in Part IV.

IV App cap 32 is especially interesting, for after noting that our power is limited, and is not great enough to prevent what is opposed to our interests, it provides a general recommendation. Spinoza here maintains that the intellect is the better part of us, and that if we seek 'only what must be and are content only with truth, then the better part of us will agree with the order of nature.

COMPARISON OF SPINOZA WITH OTHERS: SPINOZA'S PHILOSOPHICAL ALLIES AND OPPONENTS

Spinoza's ethics is most akin to ancient Greek accounts given by Plato, Aristotle, Epicurus, and the Stoics. His primary concern, like theirs, is with how it is best to live and his answer, in outline, is also the same: 'in accordance with reason'.

Generic points of agreement include the following:

1. a conception of happiness and virtue as living in accordance with our nature, which is reason;
2. an ideal of self-determination, with the consequent admonition not to become too attached to perishable things;
3. rationality or wisdom as the antidote to the passions; and
4. an attempt to reconcile true self-interest and morality.

Spinoza is also like them in developing his account from within a fairly intricate metaphysical, epistemological, and psychological framework, in which a distinction between activity and passivity is fundamental.

Like Aristotle, he holds that our capacity to understand is distinctive and definitive of us and, as he put it, 'the better part of us' is the intellect. He does not, however, follow Aristotle's classification of the virtues as 'intellectual' and 'moral'. Ultimately we have only one virtue, which is the power of understanding, or of having adequate ideas. He also characterizes it as the *conatus* or desire to persevere in existence as rational beings. Spinoza divides what we ordinarily call virtues into two types: those that are 'self-regarding' (e.g. courage) and those that are 'other-regarding' (e.g. nobility). In III 59s, where he makes this division, Spinoza speaks of these as desires. If a desire, such as courage, can be general and relatively long-lasting, this may not be a large departure from Aristotle, who takes the virtues to be dispositions or traits of character.

In other ways, however, Spinoza's account of the virtues importantly departs from Aristotle's. Spinoza does not, for example, regard a virtue as a mean between two extremes and he does not think that a virtuous person will ever be angry at anyone. So the Aristotelian virtue consisting of a disposition to be angry in the right circumstances, to the right degree, and so on is not a Spinozistic virtue. Nor is magnanimity, insofar as it requires great wealth.

Spinoza's relations to Kant seem clear. Kant holds that reason itself is the source of the Categorical Imperative, which maintains, in one form, that we must treat others never merely as a means to an end, but always also as an end. Spinoza, in contrast, seems to regard other people as of solely instrumental value.

Kant also thinks that there is something that is good in itself, namely, a good will, and that this will is completely free. It is free, not as a *phenomenon* in nature or in time, but rather as a *noumenon*, or a thing in itself. Spinoza, however, maintains that nothing is good or bad in itself; instead, things are good or bad only insofar as they affect us in time. There is no free will, but there is freedom, conceived as self-determination in time. Both think, however, that we can and do conceive of ourselves, and even experience ourselves, as eternal.

PROBLEMS AND DISPUTED ISSUES OF INTERPRETATION

The character of Spinoza's ethics

I have portrayed Spinoza's ethics as a radical virtue ethics.

It is radical, in our eyes, because it proceeds without using a concept of specifically moral obligation or of what is morally right or wrong and it does not mark out special senses of 'good' as moral as opposed to non-moral.

It is a virtue ethics because the primary question it addresses is how it is best to live and the answer, in one formulation at least, is that it is best to be virtuous. It is true that there is ultimately just one virtue, according to Spinoza, namely, our power to understand or, as I have put it, our power to persevere as rational beings. But many of the ordinary virtues that we recognize are also accepted by him. These include honesty, discussed in IV p 72, as well as chastity, moderation, and sobriety, which are mentioned in III def.aff.48exp and III p 56s. Spinoza's own categorization of the virtues is found in III p 59s.

In the *Ethics*, Spinoza takes on the role of a guide or adviser, not a general. His primary tone of voice, or the illocutionary force of his utterances, is one of advice or counsel, not that of an order or command. At the very beginning of Part II, for example, he says he will proceed now to things that 'can lead us as it were by the hand to the knowledge of the mind and its utmost blessedness'.[24] At the very end of the *Ethics*, in V p 32s, he describes himself as having pointed out the road that leads to wisdom and blessedness.

Spinoza's own attitude to the force of his ethics is nicely expressed by saying that 'in moral service' we want volunteers, not conscripts.[25] It is not so much that you must not be like that, but rather that you are better off this way or, when you realize that, you will prefer this form of life. Confirmation is found in the *Tractatus Theologico-Politicus* and the *Tractatus Politicus*, where Spinoza holds that if we sin, it is against ourselves.

In contrast, some maintain that Spinoza makes substantive use of the concepts of moral obligation and of morally right and wrong action. On this view, which is set out by Curley,[26] Spinoza's ethics provides not just advice or counsel, but orders or commands.

Some support for this comes, perhaps, from Spinoza's talk of the 'right way of living' and the 'dictates' or 'commands' (*dictamina*) of reason. It is also supported, according to Curley, by IV p 18s.[27] For Spinoza there states that 'reason . . . demands that every man should . . . seek his own advantage'. Thus reason does not merely advise us. It makes demands or issues categorical, not merely hypothetical, imperatives.

The idea, in outline, is that reason does not merely state (hypothetically) that you should return love for hatred, if you want to be happy or do what is best for yourself. It states this and then proceeds: since you do necessarily want what is best for yourself, you should, categorically, return love for hatred.

This reading seems quite implausible to me, notwithstanding Spinoza's occasional talk of the dictates or demands of reason. If Spinoza had employed a concept of a morally impermissible or morally wrong act, surely a 'sin' (*peccatus*) would count as one. Spinoza does not, of course, take a sin to be an act contrary to God's commands, for God does not issue commands. He is not a legislator in that sense. Nor is it an act that is contrary to God's laws, taken as the laws of nature by which in fact all things act. For nothing can act contrary to such laws and so there are no such acts. (It would be a miracle, but there aren't any miracles.) It remains open to Spinoza to hold that a sin is an act that is contrary to reason. But this Spinoza explicitly refuses to do.[28] As noted above, he instead defines a sin as a legal wrong and says that it cannot be conceived except with reference to the laws of a state. Thus Spinoza seems to reject a specifically moral concept, as opposed to a legal concept, of an act that is wrong.

We should note as well Spinoza's attitude toward, and his ultimate assessment of, a person who commits an act that we call 'morally wrong'. In Ep 23 Spinoza holds that theft may have as much reality or perfection as almsgiving, but the same is not true of the thief and the charitable person. The thief lacks something, namely knowledge of God, and it is this that makes us human.[29] Similarly he regards those who are avaricious, lustful, and so on not as evil or morally bad people, but as weak, or even sick.

Spinoza has no use and no room, really, for the concept of an evil person, that is, one who is bad in a specifically moral sense – at least if the concept of a morally bad person is tied to the concept of a morally wrong act, that is, if it is necessarily the case that a morally bad person commits morally wrong acts. For on his view there are no morally wrong acts.

To this it might be objected that on Spinoza's view, a person may be good or bad in at least two senses: (1) the person is useful or a hindrance to our becoming more like our ideal; (2) the person matches, or is far from, the concept of the ideal that we have formed of the species.

In the first sense, a person is essentially helpful or harmful to us and is no more morally good or bad than is a cool breeze or a tornado. It is simply good or bad for us.

In the second sense, a bad person may be a defective specimen of the type or imperfect in the sense that he does not match very well our general (imaginative) idea of it. The person may also not measure up to Spinoza's constructed ideal and it is in this sense, it might be thought, that a person can be morally bad.

An important problem with this suggestion, however, is that Spinoza's most basic attitude toward such a person is expressed by this description: he is weak or sick.

The paradigm of evil, or the alleged 'incarnation' of it, is the devil. Spinoza's views and attitudes here are clearly out of tune with his age. He holds, first, that if the devil 'has nothing from God', then he doesn't exist. Secondly, if he 'completely opposes himself to God', then he is very miserable, and 'if prayers could help, we should pray for his conversion'.[30]

Spinoza then proceeds to argue that duration, or existence in time, arises from the perfection of a thing, and from a union with God produced by love. Since devils have none of these, they cannot exist. Others, he says, suppose devils to exist in order to explain emotions such as hatred, anger, and envy, but he can explain them without these 'fictions'.[31]

It may be that one reason that Spinoza has for dispensing with the concepts of a morally wrong act and of a morally bad person is that their application generates or tends to generate outrage and hatred. It is true that this may also be generated by the mere description of their acts. But if we think of murderers as weak or ill, rather than morally bad, our attitude toward them will be different. We will try to help them or if, as a society, we judge that they pose too great a threat to the community, we will destroy them. For as noted earlier, Spinoza accepts capital punishment, when done not out of passion, but for the good of the community.[32]

Spinoza's denunciation of the mob that murdered and then mutilated the bodies of the de Witt brothers, seems to confirm this. The placard he wanted to display was not 'the evil ones', but 'the greatest of barbarians'.

It should also be added that we ordinarily explain murder by supposing that the motive is greed, jealousy, anger, hatred, ambition, or some similar emotion. But these, according to Spinoza, never arise solely from the person. They arise only because the person has been affected by external causes. People are only the partial cause, never the sufficient cause, of these emotions or of the acts to which they give rise.

Morality and self-interest

One of Spinoza's main aims is to resolve the apparent conflict between morality and self-interest.

That they do conflict seems to be entailed by ordinary conceptions of morality as requiring self-sacrifice. Courage and patriotism, for example, are praised as virtues that may lead you, and may require you, to sacrifice your life for your country. Children are taught not to lie and their parents insist that they tell them the truth, even if punishment will follow. When older, however, they are sometimes thought to be idiots if they don't lie, if they can thereby easily escape some legal penalty. Thus successful lying, which is thought to be wrong, is also thought to be in one's own best interests.

One general way in which this conflict can be and often enough is resolved is by holding that after death, the virtuous will be rewarded and the wicked will be punished. Morality thus requires self-sacrifice only in this world. In the longer run, doing what is right is in your own self-interest.

Spinoza, however, rejects the existence of a temporal life after death and he maintains that what is best for each person in this life is to be virtuous. The former is entailed by his doctrine in II p 7 that the order and connection of God's ideas is the same as that of their objects. For the human mind is God's idea of the human body, and so when the body ceases to exist in time, so does the mind. The latter is set out most explicitly in V p 42, where he identifies blessedness, or the highest satisfaction (*aquiescentia*) we can have, with virtue. It is also implicit, perhaps, in IV App cap 4. There are difficulties, however, in the claim that we experience this satisfaction in time.

The major question that remains is how being virtuous can be identified with what is best for you in this life. Doesn't courage, for example, sometimes lead to death and doesn't lying sometimes lead to what is more advantageous for you?

Spinoza tries to identify virtue and self-interest, it is tempting to say, by identifying your 'real self' with your intellect, that is, your adequate ideas, and by regarding your single most fundamental desire as the desire to understand. Our 'highest good' is thus knowledge, which is unlike 'competitive goods' such as money or the material possessions it can buy. These latter are competitive goods in the sense that the possession of them by one conflicts with their possession by another. This allows Spinoza to take our 'true' or 'real' self-interest to be the possession of something that all can possess and so our true self-interest never conflicts with the self-interest of others.

He also, of course, defines 'virtue' as power (IV def 8) and, in particular, our power to understand and do what follows from our nature. 'Virtue' in its current ordinary sense doesn't mean that, but Spinoza does argue that ordinary virtues such as honesty are encompassed by his sense of the term.

A difficulty has been pointed out by Broad, as Steinberg notes.[33] For while the highest good may not be a competitive good, the means to it are. It is still necessary, for continued life, that we have sufficient food, air, and water and in a crisis or an emergency, there may not be enough for all. Indeed, it may be necessary that some devote themselves to agriculture if others are to cultivate the intellect.

Steinberg regards the problem here as arising from an instrumentalist interpretation, which can show only that what is good for one is at best often or typically good for another.[34] It cannot show that this is necessarily the case. Her solution is to suppose that for Spinoza there is a common human nature, humanity itself, which is a complex individual of which we are all parts. She points out that in V p 35d Spinoza seems to argue that what is good for one is good for all, because it is good for human nature, which we all share. Spinoza's conclusion will be correct, she holds, if we regard this common human nature as a complex individual.

What seems puzzling to me is how this helps. For Spinoza himself holds that pleasure (*titillatio*) can be excessive. Pleasure itself consists in an increase in the power of one part of the human body and this can be excessive if it occurs at the expense, so to speak, of the whole. Why, then, can there not be an excess of what is good for an individual person, which increases that individual's power to the detriment of the whole?

There is, secondly, the question of how exactly this resolves the problem of the scarcity of resources. Suppose, for example, that I eat all of the remaining food. This is good for me, because it is a means to the continued, even if short, preservation of my rational life. Why, on this view, is this not bad for you, since it deprives you of what is necessary to preserve your life? Isn't this bad for you, because it hastens your death by starvation? It may be that human nature, conceived as a complex whole, is thereby strengthened, but it seems to be strengthened only at the expense of one of its parts, namely you.

It may be that Spinoza assumes here a normal background of enough for all. The wise, after all, 'live content with little' (IV App cap 29). Even so, he does not seem entitled to this assumption. Severe food shortages sometimes do arise, for example, in cities under seige, in the case of castaways at sea, and in incidents such as the famous Donner Party in the US, or Uruguayan Air Force Flight 571 in the Andes.

Spinoza explicitly holds in IV p 36 that our highest good, insofar as we pursue virtue, 'is common to all and all can equally enjoy it'.[35] He does not explicitly say that the means to its attainment are in fact available and his meaning, as indicated in the demonstration, may be merely that the possession of the highest good by one does not conflict with its possession by another. This suggests, perhaps, that Spinoza would simply grant the existence of situations in which, because of scarce resources, the continued life of one conflicts with that of others.

Indeed, Spinoza maintains that in certain external situations, a virtuous person will not do what is necessary for the preservation of his or her own life. In IV p 72 he holds that a person who is free never acts deceptively and in the scholium he says this is true even if a lie would save his life.

We can easily imagine that this is a type of situation that Spinoza took very seriously, for it is one that he might very well have had to face. It is certainly one that his ancestors faced, when questioned by the Inquisition about their religious beliefs. Would Spinoza tell the truth to the authorities, if questioned about his own religious views?

Spinoza's answer to this seems puzzling, for the essence and the primary endeavour of each individual, he holds, is the endeavour to persevere in existence and that seems to entail that a person will do anything in order to continue living. Spinoza, however, gets to the point where he thinks that death is not so important.

I think that if there is a solution to this problem, it is to be found by recognizing that Spinoza conceives of people as rational beings, not merely as living things. What we endeavour to do is to persevere as rational beings. It is as if our true or real self consists of our adequate ideas and if we were to lie or steal food to preserve our lives, we would continue to exist, not as rational beings, but as mere animals. More properly put, we, regarded as essentially rational beings, would not be what would continue to exist.

It is certainly not clear that this is Spinoza's view. However, Spinoza does suppose that an individual can cease to exist 'without turning into a corpse', as he puts it in IV p 39s, and he may well think that the transition from infancy to adulthood involves the genesis of a new individual. If that individual is essentially rational, then loss of rationality, as exhibited perhaps in lying, would entail the destruction of the individual.

This is quite like the ideas that Grice outlines in part 3 of his Carus Lectures.[36] We start out as biological beings but we become or can become beings whose primary concern is with understanding. We start out, that is, as members of a biological category, but become essentially rational beings, persons. Unlike Spinoza, however, Grice takes 'metaphysical transubstantiation' as a way of justifying a conception of absolute value.

It may be, but it is not at all clear, that a solution of this sort will work, nor is it clear precisely how it is related to Spinoza's views in Part V of the *Ethics*. More will be said about this in the next chapter. But Spinoza there sets out another perspective from which death is not so important. It is the perspective, not of reason itself of a being in time, but of the third kind of knowledge that arises, or rather 'arises', from reason. But from this perspective we cannot even conceive of ourselves as in time.

CHAPTER 9

THE *ETHICS*, PART V: THE MIND'S POWER AND BLESSEDNESS

BACKGROUND

Main topics of the *Ethics*, Part V

Part V of the *Ethics* is concerned with two topics. The first is the extent to which, and the means by which, reason can destroy or weaken our passive emotions. Spinoza describes this as the way leading to freedom. In dealing with this topic, Spinoza provides a psychotherapy. The second deals with human freedom itself, or blessedness, and with how much stronger the wise are than the ignorant.

Introductory remarks on psychotherapy

Modern psychology originated in the late nineteenth century, primarily with the work of Wilhelm Wundt, William James, and Sigmund Freud.[1] The behaviourist tradition also dates from this period, however, thanks to Edward Lee Thorndike and, somewhat later, Ivan Pavlov and then John Watson. As an academic discipline, psychology did not become independent of philosophy, the 'queen of the sciences', until later.

A variety of relatively new therapies for emotional problems, or treatments for mental disease, was the result, although in the case of Freud, theory and therapy developed hand in hand. In addition, advances in neurophysiology and biochemistry led to the investigation and development of new psychoactive drugs.

We now have a multitude of differently named therapies or special techniques, including art therapy, play therapy, hydrotherapy, and hypnotherapy. The most prevalent general types of therapy are much smaller in number, however, and they include the following.

1. Psychoanalysis. Psychoanalytic therapy originated with Breuer and Freud (1955, first published 1895) and was subsequently developed primarily by Freud. Psychoanalytic theories and therapies were later set out as well as by Jung, Adler, and others. Central to them is the concept of the unconscious, or the id, which contains mental phenomena of which we are not normally aware. These include repressed memories, thoughts, and desires that are unacceptable to the superego (conscience) and that produce mental diseases. Talking with the patient can effect a cure, by bringing repressed memories and desires of the id to consciousness.

2. Behavioural therapies. These arose from the work of Pavlov, Watson, and B. F. Skinner, who conceived of psychology as the science of human behaviour and as confined to the study of observable physical stimuli and responses. Desirable behaviour can be promoted by repeatedly providing a reward ('reinforcement') and undesirable behaviour can be eliminated by providing a penalty ('aversion therapy').

3. Cognitive therapies regard largely conscious thoughts and beliefs as the primary causes of emotions and thus they attempt to change our beliefs and ways of thinking to alleviate emotional problems. They include rational emotive behavioural therapy, developed by Albert Ellis (1962, 1999), and the cognitive therapy developed by Aaron Beck (1967, 1991).

4. Humanistic therapies include the 'person-centred therapy' of Carl Rogers, gestalt therapy, developed by Fritz Perls, and the existential therapy of Rollo May. Existential therapy is based on ideas set out by existential philosophers, primarily Kierkegaard, Nietzsche, Heidegger, and Sartre. It was explicitly discussed by Sartre in his major work, *Being and Nothingness*.[2]

There is also philosophical counselling, which arose with the founding by Gerd Achenbach of the German Society for Philosophical Practice and Counselling. This is now the International Society for Philosophical Practice.

Spinozistic therapy is a form of cognitive therapy, and of philosophical counselling, although Spinoza did not envisage the development of specially trained and licensed professionals who treat patients or consult with clients.

An important difference between Spinozistic therapy and most other forms is that Spinoza's concept of an ideal person diverges quite sharply from the standard norms and ideals of most societies. Spinoza, for example, advocates the eradication of all anger and he advises us to treat those who hate us as if they were friends. He also recommends, with the Stoics, that we love nothing perishable, and no person, very much. Spinoza holds that such love is better replaced with love of what cannot change, namely God. For the love of God cannot turn into hatred, nor can it give rise to other passive emotions such as jealousy and envy. He supposes, in addition, that the passive emotions are harmful primarily because they prevent us from thinking.

The *Ethics*, Part V in a nutshell

Therapy
Spinoza holds that the mind's power over the passive emotions consists in its power:

1. to have knowledge of the emotions;
2. to detach the emotion from the thought of an external cause;
3. to have active emotions, which arise from reason, and which are stronger than emotions that arise from confused thoughts;
4. to relate emotions to the common properties of things or to God;
5. to arrange and associate the emotion in accordance with the order of the intellect.

The primary technique that he advocates is to train ourselves to think differently. We are to develop a habit of thinking of and applying the 'precepts of reason' to the situations we encounter. Thus when someone offends or harms us, for example, we will not just give a 'knee-jerk' reaction, or respond by fuming about it and getting angry. Instead we will actively think of the precepts of reason and will respond with friendliness.

The eternity of the intellect, intuitive knowledge, and blessedness
Spinoza argues in the second division of Part V of the *Ethics* that God has an idea of the essence of the human body, that this idea pertains to the essence of the human mind, and that it is eternal. He thus holds that the mind, or rather 'something of the mind', as he

puts it, is not destroyed with the body, but is eternal. Its eternity consists not in unending temporal existence, but in atemporal existence.

He also holds that insofar as the mind is eternal, or conceives the essence of the body under a kind of eternity (*sub specie aeternitatis*), it has knowledge of the third kind. As we know from II p 40s 2, this proceeds from adequate knowledge of God's essence to knowledge of the essence of individual things. It thus arises from reason.

Since we take pleasure in this knowledge and since this pleasure is accompanied by the idea of God as its cause, we love God. Such love, which arises from the third kind of knowledge and which Spinoza calls 'intellectual love' of God (*amor intellectualis*), is blessedness, and it, too, is eternal.

The more knowledge of this sort that we have, the less we are affected by bad emotions and the less we fear death.

Spinoza concludes the *Ethics* with two claims. (1) What is of primary importance in life, and the right way of living (living in accordance with the precepts of reason), is not dependent on the doctrine of the eternity of the intellect. (2) Blessedness, the highest joy we can attain, is not the reward of virtue. It is virtue.

A RECOMMENDED ORDER OF READINGS FOR PART V OF THE *ETHICS*

Reading	Spinoza's Claim
Pref	Introduction.

Division 1: Therapy (p1–p20s)

p 2	Love, hatred, and emotions arising from them will be destroyed, if we detach from them the idea of an external cause.
p 4,s	We can form a clear and distinct idea of any emotion.
p 6	If we regard each thing as necessary, we have more power over the emotions.
p 7	Emotions that arise from reason are more powerful than emotions toward things we regard as absent.
p 9	An emotion that we regard as having several causes is less harmful than one that we regard as having just one cause.

p 10   We can arrange and associate the emotions in accordance with the order of the intellect.

p 11   An emotion occurs more frequently if it is related to and so caused by more things.

p 16, p 18, p 20   Love of God is the strongest emotion, it cannot be turned into hate, and it cannot produce jealousy or envy.

p 20s   Summary.

Division 2: The eternity of the intellect, intuitive knowledge, and blessedness (p21–p42s)

p 23   The human mind, or 'something of the mind,' is eternal.

p 31,s   Insofar as the mind is eternal it has knowledge of the third kind.

p 32,c   Intellectual love of God arises from the third kind of knowledge.

p 33   Intellectual love is eternal.

p 38,s   The more the mind understands by the second and third kinds of knowledge, the less it is harmed by passive emotions and the less it fears death.

p 40c   The intellect is more perfect than the imagination.

p 41   The eternity of the intellect is not a motive for morality.

p 42   Blessedness is virtue (not the reward of virtue).

DISCUSSION OF THE RECOMMENDED READINGS FOR PART V

Preface

The first paragraph of the Preface is introductory and indicates Spinoza's aims in Part V. They are (1) to establish the extent of reason's power over the emotions and (2) to establish what freedom of mind or blessedness is.

The remainder of the Preface, from the beginning of the second paragraph to the end, is concerned with the views of his opponents.

Spinoza mentions and briefly comments on the Stoics, but his main concern is Descartes. Spinoza describes and criticizes the views of Descartes about the absolute power of reason over the emotions, the union of mind and body, and causal interaction.

Division 1: Therapy (p1–p20s)

This section is concerned with the power of reason over the emotions and with a variety of ways in which negative or passive emotions can be restrained or destroyed by reason. The latter are, if you will, psychotherapeutic techniques or, as he puts it in p 20s, the 'remedies against the emotions'.

Instead of treating each of the recommended readings separately, I will here discuss most of them within the context of a discussion of Spinoza's summary in p 20s.

The power of reason to control the emotions.
p 20s: A summary of p 1–p 20.

This scholium provides a summary of Spinoza's discussion, in p 1–p 20, of the power of the mind over the emotions. It contains five items, but it is evident that much will be missed if we fail to look at the preceding material that Spinoza summarizes here as well as his claims concerned with love of God.

In the second paragraph of p 20s Spinoza remarks that he has now covered (*comprehendi*) all of the remedies against the emotions. 'From this', he says, 'it is apparent that the power of the mind over the emotions' consists in five things, which he sets out in a numbered list.

The list he provides, including his own citation of earlier propositions, is as follows:

1. in knowledge of the emotions (p 4,s);
2. in detaching the emotions from the thought of an external cause (p 2 and p 4,s);
3. 'in the matter of time',[3] where affections we understand are more powerful than those we conceive in a confused way (p 7);
4. in the number of causes by which affections that 'are related to the common properties of things, or to God'[4] are produced (p 9 and p 11);

5. in the order in which the mind can arrange and associate the emotions (p 10s and p 12–p 14).

It is tempting to think that this is itself a list of remedies, taken as practical proposals or maxims, by which we can control or lessen the force of harmful emotions. There is an important difference, however, between a power of the mind and a remedy, conceived as a practical maxim or technique for using that power. You may have the power, for example, to grow vegetables in your garden, but that is different from a technique for growing them, such as planting at the right time, fertilizing the soil, or using certain insecticides.

Despite initial appearances, then, Spinoza's list seems to be a list of powers of the mind, not a list of practical remedies or techniques for controlling the emotions.

In item 1, for example, he simply states that one of the powers of the mind consists in knowledge of the emotions. In item 2, he maintains that one of the powers of the mind consists 'in detaching the emotions from the thought of their external cause'.[5] Although this arguably states both a power of the mind and a remedy, it does not say how we are to detach the emotion from the thought of the cause. It does not, that is, provide a detailed practical maxim or technique. So too, item 5 mentions the order in which the mind can arrange the emotions and their associations, but Spinoza does not here specify what we are to do to arrange them or how we are to change their arrangement.

It is true that for each item on the list Spinoza provides a reference to earlier propositions and scholia. When we examine these, we do find practical remedies mentioned; however, we do not find distinct practical techniques corresponding to each distinct item.

Let us consider each of these items in turn.

1. Knowledge of the emotions (p 4,s)

p 4 itself states, 'There is no affection of the body of which we cannot form some clear and distinct conception.'[6] The argument for this maintains that there is something common to all affections of the body and that what is common can only be adequately (or clearly and distinctly) conceived, by II p 38.

This seems to show, however, not that the affection itself is conceived clearly and distinctly, but that a property of it is so conceived.

Spinoza nevertheless proceeds in V p 4c to maintain on this basis that the affection or emotion (*affectus*) is itself conceived clearly and distinctly.

In reply it might be said that we cannot conceive of a thing without conceiving of some property of it, or that conceiving of a thing is always conceiving of it as having some property. That may be, but it remains true that the common properties of things can only be adequately conceived (II p 38) and they 'constitute the essence' of no singular thing (II p 37). In contrast, the passive emotion itself, that is, the essence of the individual as a passive emotion, cannot in fact be conceived clearly and distinctly at all. For if it were, it would cease to exist (by V p 3).

This may, however, be a purely terminological point. The emotion would cease to exist as a passive emotion, but as V p 3 may suggest, it does not cease to exist. Conceiving of it clearly and distinctly would then not destroy the passive emotion, but rather turn it into an active one.[7]

In the scholium (V p 4s) Spinoza states that if we have clear and distinct knowledge of the emotions, then when we have a passive emotion, we will or may think of something (the definition or a common property) that we clearly and distinctly conceive, thereby detaching the emotion from the thought of its cause. It seems, however, that we may also not think of such a thing.

But does mere possession of this knowledge guarantee that we will not think of the cause? It is difficult to see how that could be, for love of a finite thing that is external to us, for example, would by definition never arise if we did not at least initially think of the cause of our joy. Mere possession of this knowledge also seems insufficient to guarantee a shift from thinking of the cause to thinking of something we clearly and distinctly conceive, unless we have developed an association of ideas or a habit of thinking. Thus this remedy does not seem distinct from the technique alluded to in his fifth item, which we will consider in a moment.

2. Detachment of an emotion from the confused thought of its external cause (p 2 and p 4s)

This detachment, as just noted, apparently consists in a shift from thinking of the cause to thinking of the definition or some common property of the emotion. Love and hatred of perishable things, at least, and all emotions that are either composed of these or arise from them, will then be destroyed, because they all involve confused thought of an external cause. But since this detachment occurs because we focus our attention on clear and distinct ideas, it is not a power of the mind distinct from the power of clear and distinct thinking discussed in item 1. Nor does it provide a technique other than that of shifting our attention from one thing to another.

3. The greater power of emotions that arise from reason in comparison with the power of emotions toward singular things we regard as absent (p 7)

Spinoza states here that an emotion that arises from reason is related to (*refertur*) the common properties of things, by the definition of reason in II p 40s 2, and we always regard these common properties as present. Thus the affect always remains the same and other contrary affects will have to accommodate themselves to it (by V ax1).

Spinoza, however, mentions no special technique by which we can foster emotions that arise from reason, or exploit the greater power they have over other emotions concerning singular things. Whatever we can do to increase our power of reason, or of our actual reasoning, will on his view help us to control emotions that arise regarding singular things.

4. 'In the great number (*multitudo*) of causes by which emotions related to common properties or to God are fostered' (p 20s; see also p 9 and p 11)[8]

Spinoza maintains in p 9d that an emotion that 'determines the mind to think' of many objects is less harmful than an emotion that determines us to think only of one.

In p 11 he expresses the idea that an 'image or emotion' that is 'related to' (*refertur*) many things occurs more frequently, is more often vigorous or effective, and 'occupies the mind' more than one that is related to fewer things. By 'related to' a thing he seems to mean that it is associated in the mind with that thing. So the image or emotion is caused or 'called up' by the idea of the thing (see p 13 and 13d).

Spinoza's main use of p 11 is to show something that may prove too much. For in p 16d he holds that the love of God is joined to all the affections of the body and so by p 11 love of God *must* (*debet*) most occupy the mind. This may prove too much because it seems to show that everyone inevitably experiences love of God all of the time and that we 'automatically', as it were, associate the idea of God with every idea.

What p 11–p 14 themselves suggest, in contrast, is that we must do something to relate or join the idea of God to other ideas. As p 14 puts it, 'The mind can bring it about (*potest efficere*) that all affections of the body, or images of things, are related (*referantur*) to the idea of God.' Such an association or habit of thinking is not just automatically given, but must be created by us.

5. The power to order and connect our emotions (p 10s and p 12–p 14)

p 10s provides a description of Spinoza's primary, and perhaps sole, practical technique for controlling the emotions, that is, for weakening or eliminating bad emotions. It consists in changing the association of our ideas.

> The best course we can adopt (*Optimum . . . quod efficere possumus*), as long as we do not have perfect knowledge of our emotions, is to conceive a right method of living, or fixed rules (*dogmata*) of life, and to commit them to memory and continually apply them to particular situations that are frequently encountered in life, so that our casual thinking is permeated by them and they are always ready to hand.[9]

Spinoza illustrates this with the rule that hatred is to be conquered by love or nobility, rather than reacted to with hatred. Recall that nobility (*generositas*) is the rational desire to help others or to make friends of them. We are to memorize this and often think about the wrongs (*injuria*) that people commonly commit and how best to respond to them. 'For thus we shall associate the image of a wrong with the presentation of this rule of conduct and it will always be ready to hand (II p 18) when we suffer a wrong.'[10]

Consider some common occurrence. Someone tailgates you on the highway or pushes you aside to board a crowded train. Your initial response might normally be to become angry and to pay them back somehow. It would be natural to feel offended and to reflect on their unjustified treatment of you as well as on how inconsiderate they are. You might then step on the brake in order to frustrate them, or push them back or shout something nasty, to repay them for their offence to you.

But if we have trained ourselves to think differently, we will instead recall that the better course is to do one's best to avoid the dangers posed by tailgating, for example by switching to a slower lane to let them pass. We might well think, too, that they could not have acted differently and that it is counterproductive to be upset about it or to regard it as a personal offence when in fact you do not know each other. Anger and hatred are negative emotions, that is, they feel bad. It seems silly to allow others to make us feel bad, and allow what they do to control us, especially when it comes to such inconsequential matters.

If we think along such lines, then, we can proceed cheerfully, more safely, and more independently, instead of fuming about a minor wrong that has been done to us and that could not have been avoided.

Matters seem quite different, however, when it is a question of a serious loss. Suppose, for example, that someone has put a bomb on the train and the explosion kills someone you love. It is then very difficult to repay hatred with love or nobility. Spinoza recognizes this, and replies that

> if the anger that is wont to arise from grievous wrongs be not easily overcome, it will nevertheless be overcome, though not without vacillation, in a far shorter space of time than if we had not previously reflected on these things . . .[11]

This is not to rule out punishment, even capital punishment, but this is to be imposed by the state for its own good and not, as we noted earlier, from anger.[12]

Division 2: The eternity of the intellect, intuitive knowledge, and blessedness (p21–p42s)

Spinoza says at the very end of p 20s that he has finished 'all that concerns the present life' and that he will now turn to 'matters that concern the duration of the mind without respect to the body'.[13]

The major subtopics of this part of the *Ethics* are as follows.

1. The eternity of the intellect (p 21–p 23)
2. The third kind of knowledge (p 24–p 31)
3. The intellectual love of god (p 32–p 37)
4. The motive for morality and blessedness (p 41–p 42)

The eternity of the intellect
p 23: The human mind, or 'something of the mind', is eternal.

Spinoza argues in p 23d that God has an idea of the essence of the human body (by p 22) and that this idea 'pertains to the essence of the human mind' (II p 13). He then reminds us that the human mind endures in time only while the body does, or, as he puts it here, the mind has duration 'only insofar as the mind expresses the actual existence of the body', where this existence is temporal. He proceeds to state, with an appeal to p 22, that, in effect, God's idea of the essence of the body is eternal.

The proof is difficult and the wording seems convoluted, but perhaps the distinction he draws in p 29s will help. Indeed, this is an important key to understanding the whole second division of Part V. For Spinoza explicitly maintains in p 29s that we conceive of things as actual, true, or real in two ways: (1) as existing at a certain time and place and (2) as contained in God and as following from the necessity of his nature.[14]

Thus Spinoza seems to think that the human body is, or can be conceived to be, existent or real in two ways: as contained eternally in God's essence or as enduring in time. The idea of it, or its essence, as eternally contained in God's essence is itself eternal, while the idea of it as actual in time is itself in time. After all, as II p 7s maintains, God's idea of a thing is not distinct from that thing.

In the scholium to p 23 Spinoza makes a number of interesting but problematic claims about the eternal existence of our minds. We cannot remember 'that we existed before the body', since there is no relation between eternity and time. 'Nevertheless', he holds, 'we feel and experience that we are eternal'.[15]

The third kind of knowledge and the intellectual love of God
p 31,s: Insofar as the mind is eternal it has knowledge of the third kind.

p 32,c: Intellectual love of God arises from the third kind of knowledge.

p 33: Intellectual love is eternal.

Spinoza holds that the mind has knowledge of the third kind, insofar as it is eternal, or conceives the essence of the mind 'under a form of eternity' (*sub specie aeternitatis*). He also maintains that the more knowledge we have of this sort the more conscious we are of God and of ourselves (p 31s). Since we also experience pleasure from it along with the idea of God as its cause, this knowledge, according to p 32c, gives rise to intellectual love of God (*amor Dei intellectualis*) and such love is eternal (p 33).

The motive for morality and blessedness
p 41: The eternity of the intellect is not a motive for morality.

p 42: Blessedness is virtue (not the reward of virtue).

In p 41d Spinoza notes that the foundation of virtue and the right way of living, or 'what reason prescribes as advantageous', was established without dependence on, or knowledge of, the doctrine of the eternity of the intellect. So these doctrines still stand, even in ignorance of our eternal existence.

The contrast between his doctrine and that of 'the multitude' is emphasized in the scholium. The multitude regard morality as a burden, and would be slaves to their passion, except for their belief in rewards and punishments in an afterlife.

Spinoza defines blessedness, as well as salvation and freedom, as love of God that arises from the third kind of knowledge (V p 36s), and he infers in p 42d that it is 'related to the mind insofar as the mind is active; and therefore it is virtue itself (IV def8)'.[16] Thus it is because we have blessedness or virtue that we can 'keep our lusts in check', rather than the reverse.

Spinoza ends the *Ethics* with a comparison between the wise and the ignorant. The latter are much weaker: they are driven about by external forces, and they are never really content. In contrast, the wise man, 'being conscious, by a certain eternal necessity, of himself, of God, and of things, never ceases to be, but always possesses true spiritual contentment'.[17]

His very last lines, however, characterize what he has done as pointing out the road that leads to 'spiritual contentment' or 'peace of mind'. No paraphrase or description of these lines seems adequate. He writes,

> If the road I have pointed out as leading to this goal seems very difficult, yet it can be found. Indeed, what is so rarely discovered is bound to be hard. For if salvation were ready to hand and could be discovered without great toil, how could it be that it is almost universally neglected? All things excellent are as difficult as they are rare.[18]

COMPARISON OF SPINOZA WITH OTHERS: SPINOZA'S PHILOSOPHICAL ALLIES AND OPPONENTS

Therapy

Spinoza's primary therapeutic technique is to train ourselves to think differently, that is, to develop different associations of ideas. This is to be accomplished by memorizing the 'rules of life' (V p 10s) and by repeatedly reflecting on the types of situation to which they apply. We will then develop a habit of thought, so that when, for example, someone actually offends or injures us, we will think of the best way to respond and we will reflect, for example, that the person could not have acted otherwise. Thinking in this way will then lead us to respond with courtesy (or even 'nobility') and it will lessen the force of our anger, if it does not wholly prevent it.

Spinoza himself mentions the Stoics, in V Pref, as admitting that 'no little practice' is necessary to control the emotions and it is clear that he agrees. He does not, of course, agree with a strictly behaviourist approach in which only observable stimuli are employed and the 'subjective' or 'inner' thoughts of a person are ignored.

Spinoza's relation to Freud is more complex. Spinoza grants that emotions may be 'accidentally' associated with each other and that we may have an emotion without being aware of its cause.[19] He does not, however, think that such unknown causes must be brought to consciousness to effect a cure or to reduce the power of negative emotions, although, as far as I know, he could accept the utility of this. He also seems much more optimistic than Freud regarding the power of rational thinking to control the emotions. Comparisons with Freud are complicated, however, for as noted earlier, Spinoza does not seem to have a systematic theory of consciousness.[20]

Spinozistic therapy seems most akin to rational emotive therapy. For the leading idea in both types of therapy is that our emotions are to be changed primarily by changing our thoughts.

It should be noted that despite deep differences between them, Spinoza and Sartre are in fundamental agreement in supposing that values are not simply 'given' or 'out there' in the world. They do not exist independently of human choices (Sartre) or desires (Spinoza). What happens in the world is valueless, except in relation to us or, most abstractly, in relation to some being that is in the world. Although Spinoza and Sartre disagree about free will, they are one in thinking that what we most fundamentally want is to be God. According to Sartre, God is the 'in-itself for-itself', but since this is self-contradictory, God cannot exist. According to Spinoza, our most fundamental desire is to understand, that is, to have adequate ideas. A being that had only adequate ideas, however, would never be causally affected by anything outside itself and every action it took would arise from its own essence. It would thus be completely active or self-determining, that is, free. But only God is free in this sense. Spinoza also maintains that a person who was born and remained free would form no concept of evil, and hence no concept of good or evil.

The eternity of the intellect

Spinoza's doctrine of the eternity of the intellect diverges in important ways from standard conceptions of immortality or of an afterlife. For Spinoza does not posit our continued existence in time, after the destruction of the body, and he denies that we can imagine, perceive, or remember anything after death. Our eternal existence consists, not in unending future existence, but in atemporal existence.

Spinoza also explicitly denies that this eternal existence can provide a motive for morality. In V p 41, he maintains that what is of prime importance in life does not depend on the doctrine, or our knowledge of the doctrine, of our eternal existence.

He thus rejects one ordinary type of resolution of the apparent conflict between morality and self-interest. This resolution supposes that morality demands self-sacrifice, perhaps even the sacrifice of your life, and it then provides a self-interested motive for making this sacrifice by positing a reward in another life.[21]

Instead of positing another temporal life, with punishments and rewards to resolve this apparent conflict, Spinoza denies that the conflict is real. He supposes that being moral is the best way for you to live in this world, not because of rewards in a supernatural world, but because morality consists in doing what is best for yourself.

In the process of doing this, however, Spinoza reconceives of us – or of 'our better part', as he puts it in IV App cap 32 – as rational beings, that is, as beings whose primary desire is to understand. We then no longer regard ourselves primarily as biological beings and we recognize that our own death is not so important.

Kant

Spinoza's distinction in V p 29s between two ways of conceiving something as actual is strikingly similar to Kant's distinction between *noumena* and *phenomena*. As noted earlier a *noumenon* is a 'thing in itself', or a thing as it is in itself, independently of us, while a *phenomenon* is an appearance to us of a *noumenon*.

Kant holds that all *phenomena* or appearances are in time and that all physical *phenomena* are locatable in space. Indeed, space and time themselves are '*a priori* forms of intuition', that is, inherent 'features' or structures of the human mind, rather than objective properties of objects as they are in themselves. He also holds that we have *a priori* concepts, which do not arise from sense experiences and which are applicable only to *phenomena*, not *noumena*. These include, for example, the concepts of substance and of causality.

Spinoza, as previously noted, maintains that a thing can be conceived as actual in two ways: insofar as it is related to time and place or insofar as it is contained in God. The distinction is set out in V p 29s. To conceive a thing in the latter way is to conceive it as actual or real, but not, it seems, as temporal or as in time. It is to conceive it 'under a form of eternity' (*sub specie aeternitatis*). To conceive of it in the former way is simply to conceive of it as existing in time (*sub duratione*) and, if it is physical, as in space or as having spatial relations. The distinction between these ways of conceiving a thing is thus quite like Kant's distinction between a *phenomenon* and a *noumenon*.

The most important difference in their views, however, is that Kant holds that we can have no real knowledge of *noumena* and that none of our *a priori* concepts, such as the concepts of substance and of causality, can be applied to *noumena*. Spinoza, on the other hand, maintains that we do have real knowledge of *noumena*, or things as they are in themselves. This includes knowledge of the existence and essence of God, the sole substance, as well as knowledge of God's causality.

It is of more than passing interest to note that Kant locates our inability to know things in themselves in the alleged impossibility of having 'intellectual intuitions'. These would be intuitions of individuals that the intellect has, analogous to the intuitions or experiences we have in sense perception. If there were such intellectual intuitions, according to Kant, they would not be subject to the limiting conditions or *a priori* structures inherent in our sensibility, namely space and time.

It is Spinoza's view, in contrast, that we do have intellectual intuitions, that is, ideas formed by the intellect of individual essences. These ideas, which constitute the third kind of knowledge, are 'clear and distinct' conceptions of individuals as existing, but not as existing in space or time.

PROBLEMS AND DISPUTED ISSUES OF INTERPRETATION

Therapy

Very different assessments of Spinozistic therapy have been made in the past half-century. For example, Hampshire, according to Bennett, presents Spinoza as a 'deep, subtle thinker about psychotherapy',[22] whereas Bennett himself holds that Spinoza had 'a few good intuitive insights . . ., but utterly failed to draw them together into a coherent whole'.[23]

Bennett is the most prominent and the most severe critic of Spinozistic therapy. He holds that many of Spinoza's most important arguments are invalid and that much of what he claims is false. I will comment here, briefly and quite selectively, on only a few of his views.

1. Bennett holds that we cannot form an adequate idea of a passive emotion and hence we cannot turn it into an active one. In addition, since a passive emotion has arisen from an inadequate idea, we cannot make it the case that it arose from an adequate one. The technique recommended in V p 4s thus doesn't work.

Olli Koistinen maintains, in reply, that just as a person may at first believe something on inadequate grounds and later come to have good reasons for the belief, so too an emotion may at first arise from inadequate ideas, but later come to be sustained by adequate ideas. A passive emotion would then turn into an active one.[24]

2. Bennett grants that the force of some emotions can be weakened by regarding what happened as having been necessitated. He adds, however, that this does not hold for all emotions and, in particular, it does not hold for fear. In this I think he is right. It might be noted that Spinoza thinks that hope and fear always occur together and both require doubt about what will or did happen. If the doubt regarding either the past or the future is removed, Spinoza calls it 'despair'.[25]

3. Bennett also maintains that the argument in II p 2d fails, for if we separate joy or sadness from the thought of an external cause, then love or hate will no longer exist, by definition, but the joy or sadness may remain.[26]

Spinoza, however, does not maintain in II p 2d that the joy or sadness is thereby destroyed. He says only that love or hatred, and other 'vacillations' that arise from them, will be destroyed. Jealousy and envy, for example, will no longer arise.[27]

The eternity of the intellect

Difficulties concerning Spinoza's doctrine of the eternity of the intellect are legendary and there is a large and growing body of literature devoted to it.[28]

At issue, most fundamentally, is how or whether Spinoza can consistently hold that the human mind is the idea of the human body and exists just while the body does, and yet also maintain that 'something' of the mind (the human intellect) is eternal.

As with so many of the problems of interpreting Spinoza, resolution of this problem seems to require further explanation of Spinoza's distinction between two ways of conceiving things. In this case, it is the distinction between two ways of conceiving of things as actual, true, or real, which he sets out in V p 29s and uses to establish the eternity of the intellect. But this is the same type of problem that commentators face concerning Spinoza's conception of the relationship between the mind and the body, as well as the closely related problem of the attributes.

My own attempt portrays Spinoza's views in the last half of Part V as a development of his views in KV.[29] In that work, Spinoza accepts a modified form of Cartesian dualism and maintains that the human mind can continue to exist in time after the destruction of the body. In the *Ethics*, however, he abandons 'Spinozistic dualism', but nevertheless attempts to establish a form of immortality or eternity of the intellect.

It is evident that in Part V of the *Ethics* Spinoza wants to show how much stronger the wise man is than the ignorant. On the face of it, he does not do this solely by appealing to the peace of mind that the stronger and wiser experience in this life. Instead, or in addition, he supposes that the wise have an intellect that constitutes a larger part of the mind than does the intellect of the ignorant. His view seems to be that this part of the mind is eternal, that is, atemporally existent, while the other part of the mind, which consists of inadequate ideas of the imagination, exists only in time and lasts only so long as the body does.

The problems that this generates are analogous to those encountered by Kant's famous distinction between *noumena* and *phenomena*. Like Kant, Spinoza may obtain a metaphysical foundation for virtue, but in doing so he winds up ascribing blessedness, and even freedom, only to beings conceived as not in time. It is as if the problem of life can ultimately be solved only by taking a standpoint from which the problem cannot be conceived.

PART III

THE POLITICAL WORKS

CHAPTER 10

THE *TRACTATUS THEOLOGICO-POLITICUS*

INTRODUCTION

Spinoza's *Tractatus Theologico-Politicus* (TTP) appeared in 1670. It was published anonymously and the publisher's name as well as the place of publication was falsified. The title page reads 'Hamburg, from Heinrich Künraht', but in fact it was published in Amsterdam by Jan Rieuwertsz.[1]

It is doubtful whether this deception is consistent with Spinoza's highest ideals, as expressed in E IV p 72. It was unquestionably prudent, however, for there was a very real danger in publishing it. Spinoza's friend, Adriaan Koerbagh, had published Spinozist views in *A Light Shining in Dark Places* in 1668. In the same year he was imprisoned in Amsterdam for this, along with his brother, and he died there in 1669.[2]

Koerbagh's work was in Dutch, which increased its notoriety, and it is probably because of this that Spinoza implored his friend Jarig Jelles to prevent publication of TTP in Dutch.[3]

The full title of the *Tractatus Theologico-Politicus*[4] indicates that one of Spinoza's central interests is in showing that 'freedom of philosophising' is not merely compatible with, but is also required for, 'the piety and peace of the republic'.[5] In fact it advocates freedom of speech quite generally, although this is the explicit concern only of chapter 20, the very last chapter of the book.

The 'several discussions' mentioned on the title page are concerned with a variety of other topics as well, including prophecy, miracles, the divine laws, the interpretation and history of Scripture, the separation of faith and reason, and the foundations of a republic or state (*respublica*).

Spinoza's main aims are set out more fully, and more candidly, in a letter to Oldenburg (Ep 30), written, perhaps, in the autumn of 1665. His goals are to undermine the prejudices of theologians, to refute the charge of atheism, and to promote 'the freedom to philosophise and to say what we think'.[6]

THE OUTLINE OF THE *TRACTATUS THEOLOGICO-POLITICUS*

Prophecy and prophets (chapters 1–2)
The prophets had exceptionally active imaginations, but they did not have exceptional, or even much, knowledge of God.

The divine law (chapter 4)
The divine laws, in one sense, are simply the laws of nature; in another sense, they are human laws, that is, legal rules regarding the state, or rules concerning our highest good, which is knowledge and love of God.

Miracles (chapter 6)
Miracles, taken as events that contravene the laws of nature, do not occur. God's power is not distinct from, nor is it opposed to, the power of nature. It is exhibited in and best established by the existence of universal natural laws, not by alleged exceptions to them. What people call a miracle is merely an event they do not understand.

Biblical interpretation (chapter 7)
The Bible is a book written by people and to understand it we must know who wrote the various parts of it, in what circumstances, and with what intention. We must also know the language they used, who assembled the Bible, and the history of its transmission to later people. In short, the Bible should be investigated, not as a supernatural object, but as a natural one, albeit a creation of human beings. It should be investigated, as we would say, 'scientifically'.[7]

The authors of the Bible (chapters 8–11)
These chapters attempt to answer the various questions raised in chapter 7. Spinoza holds, for example, that Moses did not write the Pentateuch (the first five books of the Bible).

The aim of the Bible (chapter 13)

The Bible has one aim, which is to teach common people 'obedience to the moral law'. It is an attempt to get people to act properly toward each other, not an attempt to inculcate doctrines or knowledge of the real nature of God.

The universal faith (chapter 14)

Spinoza here sets out the 'universal faith' that is taught by the Bible. This requires belief in the existence of a unique, omniscient God who forgives repentant sinners. It also requires the worship of God, but this 'consists solely in justice and charity, or love towards one's neighbour'.[8] Finally, it maintains that a person who believes that God forgives sins, and becomes more inspired by the love of God, 'knows Christ according to the spirit, and Christ is in him'.[9]

The relations between philosophy (science) and theology (religion) (chapter 15)

Spinoza holds that reason (philosophy) and theology do not conflict and that neither is the 'handmaiden' of the other. He takes theology to be the Word of God, which, he says, 'does not consist of a set number of books.[10] Its moral doctrines, he holds, do not conflict with reason, nor does its aim. Doctrines in the Bible that may conflict with reason 'have no bearing on' the Word of God and people may believe what they like about them.[11]

Thus Spinoza rejects the view of Maimonides (which he also discusses in chapter 7). Maimonides holds that passages in the Bible that conflict with reason must be regarded as metaphorical. Spinoza also rejects the view of many of Maimonides' opponents, as set out by Jehuda Alpakhar. On this view, clear biblical teachings that conflict with reason are to be accepted on the authority of the Bible and no passage is to be rejected unless it conflicts with these clear teachings.

The basis of the state and natural right (chapter 16)

Spinoza identifies natural right and natural power and hence holds that we have a natural right to do everything that we can. In nature, then, 'there is no sin'.

It is advantageous to us, however, to join forces and create a state. This occurs when we transfer our natural rights to one, a few, or all, thus forming a monarchy, an aristocracy, or a democracy. This transfer of right or power appears to be accomplished by a covenant or agreement, but 'the validity of an agreement rests on its utility' and the sovereign's right extends just so far as its power.

Justice, injustice, right, and wrong are then possible only in a state. Spinoza holds, as in the *Ethics*,[12] that they consist in actions and dispositions to act that conform to or violate the laws of the state.

The Hebrew state (chapter 17)
Spinoza here holds that no one can transfer all of his rights to the state and he proceeds to consider the history of the Jewish state.

Relations between religion and the state (chapter 18)
Spinoza continues his discussion of the Hebrew state, begun in chapter 17, and draws four conclusions.[13]

1. Religious authorities as such should have no legal powers, including the power to enact laws.

2. Neither the religious authorities nor the state should have the power to dictate what the people should believe. The state should define piety and religious observance as consisting only of works, 'charity and just dealings', and they should allow freedom of judgement in everything.

3. Only the sovereign should determine what is right or wrong.

4. It is disastrous for a people to try to change their form of government to or from a monarchy. Spinoza illustrates this with the example of the English, who executed their monarch (Charles I), but merely replaced him with another (Cromwell) and made things worse. They then replaced Cromwell with the rightful king (Charles II).

Spinoza's view is perhaps being confirmed by the USA's attempt, with the help of the United Kingdom and other countries, to replace an Iraqi tyrant with a democracy.

The sovereign's right over religion (chapter 19)
In this chapter Spinoza maintains that the sovereign has the right to control religion and religious ceremonies.

Freedom of thought and speech (chapter 20)
Spinoza holds that the sovereign does not have the power to prevent people from forming their own judgement, and hence does not have

the right to do so. In addition, people tend to communicate their views to others and sometimes they cannot help doing so even when absolute secrecy is more prudent.

Nevertheless, 'words can be treasonable as well as deeds',[14] and the question is to what extent the sovereign can and should grant freedom of speech.

Spinoza's answer is that the purpose of a state is not to turn people into 'beasts or puppets', but to enable them 'to live in security', to preserve each person's right 'to exist and act, without harm to himself and to others', and 'to develop their abilities in safety'. Thus 'the purpose of the state is, in reality, freedom'.[15]

Spinoza holds that no one may act against the law, but we should be free to express disagreement with it and even to advocate its repeal. We may do both of these, at least, as long as we submit our opinion to the sovereign and defend it with reasons, rather than stirring up hatred and anger or inciting people to break the law.

To punish people for their beliefs and for their honesty in admitting them is also counterproductive. Honourable people are then turned into martyrs and their punishment 'serves not so much to terrorise others as to anger them and move them to compassion, if not to revenge'.[16]

SELECTED ISSUES

Divine laws

Chapter 4 begins with remarks on the meaning of the term 'law':

The word law, taken in its absolute sense, means that according to which each individual thing – either all in general or those of the same kind – act in one and the same fixed and determinate manner, this manner depending either on Nature's necessity or on human will.[17]

Spinoza proceeds to say that although everything is determined by the universal laws of nature to exist and act in a definite manner, it is nevertheless acceptable to speak of laws that depend on human will, for the human mind can be conceived without man-made laws. Laws of this sort he divides into human and divine. The former are rules whose aim is 'to safeguard life and the commonwealth'; the latter are concerned 'only with the supreme good, that is, the true knowledge and love of God'.

It is thus evident that a divine law is not, according to Spinoza, a rule that God, like a ruler, has promulgated. It is not a commandment or imperative issued by God. Instead, it is made by human beings and while it is said to be divine, that, Spinoza emphasizes, is 'because of the nature of the true good', namely, knowledge and love whose object is God.[18]

Spinoza's brief explanation of this begins as follows:

Since our intellect forms the better part of us, it is evident that, if we wish to seek what is definitely to our advantage, we should endeavour above all to perfect it as far as we can, for in its perfection must consist our supreme good. Now since all our knowledge, and the certainty that banishes every possible doubt, depend solely on the knowledge of God . . . it follows that our supreme good and perfection depends solely on the knowledge of God.[19]

Spinoza speaks here of the intellect as 'the better part of us' (*melior pars nostri sit intellectus*), as he does in E IV App cap 32, but here he provides no argument for this and no further discussion of it. Thus far he also maintains merely that our perfection depends on the knowledge of God and this, clearly, is compatible with the view that such knowledge is merely a means to our highest end or perfection. But Spinoza immediately proceeds, as if in reply to this, to argue for the stronger thesis. Knowledge of an effect is knowledge of a property of its cause and God's essence is the cause of everything, 'So the whole of our knowledge, that is our supreme good, not merely depends on the knowledge of God but consists entirely therein'.[20]

We also encounter here a question that arises concerning the *Short Treatise* as well as the *Ethics*. Is it knowledge or love of God that constitutes our perfection or highest good? For while Spinoza explicitly asserts in TTP, as we have just seen, that our perfection consists entirely in knowledge of God, he also immediately proceeds as follows:

This also follows from the principle that man's perfection is the greater, or the reverse, according to the nature and perfection of the thing that he loves above all others. So he who loves above all the intellectual cognition of God, the most perfect Being, and takes especial delight therein, is necessarily most perfect, and partakes most in the highest blessedness.

This, then, is the sum of our supreme good and blessedness, to wit, the knowledge and love of God. . . .

Since the love of God is man's highest happiness and blessedness and the final end and aim of all human action, it follows that only he observes the Divine Law who makes it his object to love God not through fear of punishment nor through love of some other thing . . . but from the mere fact that he knows God, or knows that the knowledge and love of God is the supreme good. . . . For this truth is told us by the idea of God, that God is our supreme good, i.e. that the knowledge and love of God is the final end to which all our actions should be directed.[21]

It is interesting to see that several pages later in chapter 4 Spinoza notes there are two possible translations of Proverbs 2.3–5. He translates the Hebrew text into Latin, whose English meaning, as Shirley renders it, is:

If though criest after knowledge and liftest up thy voice for understanding . . . then shalt thou understand the fear of the Lord and find knowledge of the Lord.[22]

(In the Hebrew original, 'knowledge' may perhaps be 'love', for the Hebrew word *jadah* can have both meanings.)

Chapter 4 also provides a characterization of at least an important part of ethics:

the rules for living a life that has regard to this end [knowledge and love of God] can fitly be called the Divine Law. An enquiry as to what these means are, and what are the rules of conduct required for this end, and how there follow therefrom the fundamental principles of the good commonwealth and social organisation, belongs to a general treatise on ethics.[23]

God as a lawgiver

An important question explicitly raised in chapter 4 is, 'Whether by the natural light of reason we can conceive God as a lawgiver or ruler, ordaining laws for men'.[24] Spinoza's answer here is the same as in all of his other works. Since God's intellect and will are the same thing, his understanding something is the same as his willing it. But his understanding (or his 'affirmations and negations')

> always involve eternal necessity or truth. So if, for example, God said to Adam that he willed that Adam should not eat of the tree of knowledge of good and evil, it would have been a contradiction in terms for Adam to be able to eat of that tree. And so it would have been impossible for Adam to eat of it, because that divine decree must have involved eternal necessity and truth.[25]

Spinoza adds that Adam and other prophets regarded this as a law, and regarded God as 'a kind of lawgiver or ruler', because of their lack of knowledge. Jesus Christ, in contrast, must be regarded as having perceived things adequately, and so if he ever spoke as if God were a ruler, Christ was taking into account the ignorance and obstinacy (*pertinacia*) of the people. Spinoza thus concludes that

> it is only in concession to the understanding of the multitude and the defectiveness of their thought that God is described as a lawgiver or ruler, and is called just, merciful, and so on, and that in reality God acts and governs all things solely from the necessity of his own nature and perfection and his decrees and volitions are eternal truths, always involving necessity.[26]

The foundations of the state

In chapter 16 Spinoza identifies the 'natural right' of a thing with the rules, or rather laws, by which it is naturally determined to exist and act. For example, he says, fish by nature swim and the big ones eat the smaller ones, so it is 'by the highest natural right' (*summo naturali jure*) that they do so. Nature, he says, has the right to do everything it can, for its power is the power of God. But since the power of nature as a whole is the power of all things taken together, 'it follows that each individual thing has the sovereign right to do all that it can do, i. e. the right of the individual is coextensive with its determinate power'.[27]

In this way Spinoza empties the concept of a right of any normative force, at least if the concept of what one has a right to do is taken to rule out something that one is able to do. So the corresponding conception of a wrong, or what is prohibited, has no application to anything actual. As Spinoza puts it, 'Nature's right . . . forbids only those things that no one desires and no one can do; it does not frown on strife, or hatred, or anger, or deceit, or on anything at all urged by appetite'.[28]

Spinoza's argument for this is problematic, however. He argues that God has the highest right over all things, or to do all things (*summum jus ad omnia habet*), and that God's power is the power of nature. More directly, God is nature, but this is *natura naturans*, according to KV I.7 and E I p 29s. Here, however, Spinoza identifies this power with the power of all individual things, that is, *natura naturata*. But *natura naturans* cannot simply be identified with *natura naturata* without identifying what is in itself with what is in another.[29]

It may be that many of Spinoza's contemporaries would assent to the thesis that God has the right to do anything, or anything in his power. But that thesis is not entirely unproblematic. If, on the other hand, the concept of what is right is independent of what God in fact does or wills, and if God has the power to act otherwise than he does, then it is possible for God to do what is not right. On this view, God would not in fact do anything wrong (because of his good will), but God nevertheless has the power to do this.

Spinoza rejects this view, of course, both because God acts only by the necessity of his nature and because there is, so to speak, no legitimate concept of rightness in itself by which God could be judged. But the latter thesis is what is at issue.

An alternative route to Spinoza's conclusion that everything anyone does is right (or is done by 'natural right') would invoke the dictum 'ought implies can'. Spinoza may seem to indicate his acceptance of this quite early in chapter 16: 'Whatever an individual thing does by the laws of its own nature, it does with sovereign right, inasmuch as it acts as determined by Nature, and can do no other.'[30]

This passage, however, appears in the context of a discussion in which Spinoza rejects a conception of natural laws as laws of reason and of natural rights as determined by reason. He states, 'The natural right of every man is determined not by sound reason, but by his desire and his power.'[31]

Spinoza also sets out here a teleological conception of reason and draws attention to an inherent gap between nature and reason. He writes,

Nature's bounds are not set by the laws of human reason which aim only at man's true interest and his preservation, but by infinite other laws which have regard to the eternal order of the whole of Nature, of which man is but a particle. . . . So when something in Nature appears to us as ridiculous, absurd or evil, this is due to the fact that our own knowledge is only partial, that we are largely ignorant of the order and coherence of the whole of Nature and want all things to be arranged to suit our reason. Yet that which our reason declares to be evil is not evil in respect of the order and laws of universal Nature, but only in respect of the laws of our own nature.[32]

Thus Spinoza holds that the world 'is not for us', that is, it does not operate with any concern for our benefit. He also holds that evil and even sin do not exist in nature 'as such' or, if I may so put it, in things considered in themselves. They instead exist only in relation to our reason and so to us, who want things to exist or be arranged for our benefit. Indeed, he ascribes his rejection of wrongdoing conceived independently of law or reason to St Paul, 'who declares that prior to the law – that is, as long as men are considered as living under Nature's rule – there can be no sin'.[33]

Like Hobbes, Spinoza maintains that the state arises with the transfer of natural right, or power, from each individual to a sovereign (one person, many people, or indeed all as a whole) and that such a transfer is necessary in order, as Spinoza says, 'to achieve a secure and good life'.[34]

How such a transfer can be made remains problematic. Spinoza first maintains that it cannot be accomplished if people act only on appetite, and so they must pledge to be guided by reason. But he then emphasizes the universal law that each will choose what he judges to be best, and so promises will not be kept, and in fact need not be kept, if it is more advantageous to break them:

We may thus conclude that the validity of an agreement rests on its utility . . . It is therefore folly to demand from another that he should keep his word for ever, . . .[35]

Nobody can rely on another's good faith unless the promise is backed by something else, for everyone has the natural right to act deceitfully and is not bound to keep his engagements except through hope of greater good or fear of a greater evil.[36]

Spinoza then proceeds to say that since natural right is determined by power, natural right is transferred to the extent that power is transferred and 'the sovereign right over all men is held by him who holds the supreme power whereby he can compel all by force'.[37] Spinoza speaks here as if this solves the problem, but of course this solution, insofar as it supposes that there is a sovereign, assumes what it set out to explain.

The upshot of Spinoza's discussion here seems to be that it is futile to take an agreement or covenant to be the basis of the transfer of natural right. The wise, or those guided by reason, may see the supreme necessity of making and adhering to such an agreement, but others, who constitute the majority, will not.

It may also seem to be Spinoza's intention, in part, to establish the futility of agreement as the basis of any transfer, for he grants that the sovereign will retain a right only so long as the sovereign retains the power: 'nobody who is stronger than he will need to obey him unless he so wishes'.[38]

What undermines this interpretation of Spinoza's intention, however, is the text that immediately follows these quoted words. There he speaks of the original contract as preserved 'in absolute good faith' if all power is transferred to it[39] and he maintains that everyone must obey the sovereign in everything, since this is what everyone must have agreed to when they transferred all of the power.[40]

So Spinoza speaks as if the state arises with a transfer of power (and so of right) and that this transfer is accomplished, at least sometimes, by making a promise. But he himself grants that there is no validity to a contract and no need to keep a promise, if one has the power (and a sufficient motive) to break it with impunity.

In the end, then, it seems that Spinoza's talk of agreement, and even of a transfer of power, is superfluous. The foundation of the state is power (in any form):

Whoever holds sovereign power . . . it is quite clear that to him belongs the sovereign right of commanding what he will. Furthermore, whoever transfers to another his power of self-defence, whether voluntarily or under compulsion, has fully ceded his natural right.[41]

Civil right and wrong; justice and injustice

After establishing, at least to appearances, the basis of the state, Spinoza proceeds in chapter 16 to set out what each of the following are: civil right, wrong, justice and injustice in a state, ally, enemy, and treason. An outline of each of these definitions, with the details of some of them ignored, is as follows.

A civil right is defined as a freedom to act, where this freedom is 'determined by the edicts of the sovereign power and upheld by its authority alone'.[42] In essence, it is acting in accordance with, or in obedience to, the laws. This of course is a conception of a right, or of freedom, as acting in a way that is legally permitted.

A wrong is an act contrary to the law, that is, one that is legally prohibited (impermissible).

Justice is 'a set disposition to render to every man what is his by civil right'.[43] Injustice is depriving someone of what is his by law.

'Right', 'wrong', 'just', and 'unjust' are inapplicable, on this view, in the absence of a legal system, and they are relative to its laws. It also follows from Spinoza's definitions that it is impossible for an act to be just or unjust unless there are laws regarding ownership.

Allies (*confederati*) are people of two states which have agreed to a treaty of non-aggression and mutual aid. The agreement is valid (*erit validus*) just so long as it is advantageous. An enemy is someone who is neither a confederate nor a subject.

Spinoza at this point raises an interesting and important objection to his own views: that those in a state of nature do not have a natural right 'to live by the laws of appetite', for they 'are required by God's command to love their neighbour as themselves'.

Spinoza's reply is that it is only by revelation ('confirmed by signs') that one can know of this duty to God and one can be bound by a law only if one is aware of it. So we must conceive of a state of nature 'as being without religion and without law, and consequently without sin and without wrong.'[44]

The central political problem

At the beginning of chapter 17 Spinoza maintains that his account in chapter 16 is in many respects 'no more than theory'. For people cannot transfer all of their power or right to another. There are laws of human nature (or 'psychological laws', we might say) that cannot be violated even when commanded by the sovereign. We cannot, for example, hate someone to whom we are indebted for helping us nor can we love someone who has harmed us.[45]

The central problem, he holds, is how to organize a state so that people, and especially public administrators, do what they should by law, putting 'public right before private gain', no matter what their character. Despite many attempts to solve it, however, Spinoza holds that every state has been 'in greater danger from its own citizens than from the external enemy'.[46] Although Spinoza raises the problem here, he seems to address it directly only in the *Tractatus Politicus*, to which we now turn.

CHAPTER 11

THE *TRACTATUS POLITICUS*

INTRODUCTION

Spinoza's *Tractatus Politicus* (TP) was probably begun in 1675 or 1676 and it was never completed.[1] Some time in 1676, Spinoza wrote to a friend that he was engaged in the work.[2] In the letter he provides a short description of the topic of each chapter and remarks that the first six chapters are finished. The description he provides is as follows:

1. Introduction
2. Natural right
3. The right of the sovereign powers
4. 'the question of what political matters are under the control of sovereign powers'
5. 'the ultimate and highest aim' of a state
6. The organization of a monarchy (so it will not become a tyranny)

He indicates that he will then proceed to consider aristocracy, democracy, laws, and other political questions.

The first five chapters of the work in its final form correspond to the above description. Chapters 6 and 7 deal respectively with the nature and organization of monarchy. Chapters 8 and 9 deal with two models of aristocracy, while chapter 10 is concerned with the organization of an aristocracy. Chapter 11, which is unfinished, deals with the nature of a democracy.

Chapter 2, on natural right, sets out views that Spinoza had already advanced in the *Tractatus Theologico-Politicus* (TTP). He begins by stating that neither the coming into existence nor the perseverance in existence of a natural thing follows from its essence and hence the power of a thing for either must be the power of God. God's right is his power, however, and he has the right over all things. Hence, since the power of a thing is God's power, everything has as much right as it has power.

Spinoza is quick to add that there is no important difference in this respect between those who are wise, or follow the prescriptions of reason, and those who are ignorant, or between desires that arise from reason and those that do not:

> For in both cases they are the effects of Nature, explicating the natural force whereby man strives to persist in his own being. . . . For whether a man is led by reason or solely by desire, he does nothing that is not in accordance with the laws and rules of Nature, that is . . . he acts by the right of Nature.[3]

Spinoza notes, as he had in TTP, that a promise, or pledge (*fides*),

> remains valid for as long as he who made it has not changed his mind. For he who has the power to break faith has in reality not given up his right; he has given no more than words.[4]

Unlike some passages in TTP, however, TP does not take the foundation of a state to rest on agreement. In TP Spinoza clearly abandons the notion of a transfer of right or power by means of a promise. He states merely that if two people 'come together and join forces,' or 'form a union', they have more power and hence more right than either one alone.[5] Also quite significantly, he holds that the power and right of a solitary individual is 'notional rather than factual'.[6] Indeed, without helping each other, people can hardly live. Spinoza therefore concludes that

> the natural right specific to human beings can scarcely be conceived except where men have their rights in common and can defend the territories which they can inhabit . . . and live in accordance with the judgment of the entire community.[7]

Spinoza also reiterates his view in TTP that sin 'cannot be conceived except in a state'. Although he grants that the term 'sin' (*peccatum*) is often used for violations of the dictates of reason, and 'obedience' (*obsequium*) for the constant will to follow them, he objects to this usage. For 'the life of reason' is really freedom, not obedience, and in this sense sin is really a 'weakness of the mind' (*mentis impotentia*).[8]

Spinoza concedes, however, that such a usage of 'sin' is not so improper, 'For the laws of a good state . . . ought to be established in accordance with the dictates of reason.'[9]

The purpose of a state, according to Spinoza, is 'peace and security of life'.[10] The best state, he says, is one where men live in harmony and adhere to the laws. Where this is not the case, it is not so much because people are 'wicked', but because the state is poorly organized.

MONARCHY

Chapter 6 primarily describes, and chapter 7 explains and justifies, the features of a Spinozistic monarchy.

The people of each fortified city are to be divided into clans and each clan is to select, from among the male citizens, potential counsellors to advise the king. The king himself selects a large number from among them, thus forming the Great Council. This council will propose and vote on laws to present to the king or, if there is disagreement, they will submit their major proposals and reasons for them. Another council, composed of lawyers, will be judges, but their decisions are overseen by members of the Great Council. Part of the composition of each council will vary every year.

The initial king is elected. Thereafter sovereignty passes to his oldest son or near male relative, but the king is forbidden to marry a foreigner. The people will not own land or houses; they will instead rent them from the king and there will be no other taxes in peacetime. The army will be composed only of citizens.

The king may worship as he will and may build a private chapel. No other church is to be built at public expense, but approved religious groups may build churches out of their own funds.

It is clear that a Spinozistic monarch, very much by design, has quite limited power on his own. Spinoza's aim, he says, is to establish 'security for the monarch and peace for his people, thus ensuring that the king is most fully in control of his own right when he is most concerned for the welfare of his people'.[11]

The structure that Spinoza proposes is one form of constitutional monarchy, the seeds of which were planted, in England, at least as far back as Magna Carta (1215). It is certainly similar, in some important respects, to the scheme even now in place in England or even the US. For in England the sovereign has, at least in theory, the power to approve or disapprove of laws proposed by Parliament, as, in the US, the President may sign or veto laws passed by Congress.

ARISTOCRACY

In chapters 8 and 9 Spinoza describes two forms or models of aristocracy. The first, which is discussed in chapter 8, has a capital city and a supreme council is composed only of citizens of this city. The class of 'patricians', as they are called, is very large, about 5,000 for a medium-sized city, and this, Spinoza supposes, ensures that at least 100 of them are 'singularly gifted with skill and understanding'.[12] The people, he says, have nothing to fear, because the council is so large that 'its will is determined by reason, rather than mere caprice'.[13]

Patricians are elected for life and when one of them dies the council elects a replacement. This council enacts the laws and repeals them, and also appoints ministers of state. In addition it selects the members of another council, which ensures that the laws are not violated. Spinoza mentions several other differences between this form of aristocracy and a monarchy, but I will not discuss them in detail here. One interesting difference, however, is that the citizens do not rent their land or houses from the state; unlike a monarchy they buy them.

The second form of aristocracy, discussed in chapter 9, differs from the first in having no capital city. Each city selects the members of the supreme council and there are patricians and judges for each city. The patricians, Spinoza maintains, should all be of the same religion. Here, as in chapter 8, Spinoza sets out additional rules and arrangements as well, often in some detail.

DEMOCRACY

Chapter 11, on democracy, is unfinished and it is very short. Spinoza, however, does manage to say that a democracy is most 'natural' and is the best form of government because each citizen, or rather most adult males, retain a say in the decisions of the state.

Spinoza begins by distinguishing a democracy from an aristocracy. In a democracy, he maintains, general laws determine who has the right to vote and be considered for public office. In an aristocracy, those with such rights (the patricians) are instead selected by the supreme council. Spinoza does not consider how the general laws of a democracy are established, nor does he note that the citizens of an aristocracy select the initial patricians who are to determine the laws.

He also maintains that there are different kinds of democracy (as indicated in TP 11.3), such as one that confers decision-making power on all men of a certain age or on those with wealth. The type of democracy that he will discuss, he says, is one in which 'all without exception who owe allegiance only to their country's laws and are in other respects in control of their own right' have a vote in the supreme council.[14]

Those who are not in control of their own right are women, servants, children, and wards.

Spinoza then immediately turns to the question whether it is 'by nature or by convention that women are subject to the authority of men'.[15] He argues that it is by nature, on the grounds that if women were the equal of men 'in strength of mind and ability',[16] then there would be examples of states where women ruled men or where women and men both ruled. But there are none, he claims. The legendary Amazons are evidently excluded from consideration because the Amazons did not allow men to live with them. Spinoza does not mention women rulers such as Elizabeth I.

He proceeds, however, to note 'that men generally love women from mere lust, assessing their ability and their wisdom by their beauty',[17] and that men resent it when a woman they love shows favour to another man. Equality will thus 'involve much damage to peace.'[18]

It is here that the unfinished *TP* comes to an end and Spinoza's last words of the treatise are 'But I have said enough.'[19] Indeed, he seems to us to have said too much.[20]

SOME REMARKS ON SPINOZA'S POLITICAL PHILOSOPHY

Spinoza's political philosophy exhibits, or in outline is, a kind of realism, in which the fundamental question is how to organize a state so that there is a balance of power. The object is to achieve stability while still fulfilling the goal of the state, which is to enable people to live in harmony, to develop their abilities, and, in short, to be free. The central technique is to tie the self-interest of the rulers to the self-interest or good of the ruled.

It is realistic because it conceives of the problem primarily as a problem of co-ordinating the self-interests of diverse people. Thus it is mainly a question of power rather than of morality, although it must be granted that a moral ideal, the good of the people, underlies it.

In this respect, Spinoza seems to jettison the idea of a social contract, in which legitimacy is achieved by voluntary agreement. We may think that promises create moral obligations, but the more important question is whether promises will be kept. The central question thus becomes how to get people to fulfil their duty, despite their inclinations and passions, so the state will be stable. 'This is the task, this the toil.'[21]

The ordinary normative foundation of the state is thus abandoned by Spinoza. It is retained, however, by Locke.

Locke's conception of the foundation of legitimate government diverges in crucial ways from Spinoza's. For Locke holds that God, like a human ruler, issues commands. We have a God-given duty, for example, to preserve ourselves. In addition, we have natural rights, understood normatively, and to each right that we have, there is a corresponding duty on others not to violate it. Thus we have natural rights, created by God, to life, liberty and property or, equivalently, we all have a moral obligation, prior to the state, not to deprive others of their lives, liberty or property.

Unlike Spinoza, Locke holds that ownership is a natural relation, not one that exists only in virtue of human laws. When we mix our labour with something, it becomes ours and it is on this basis that we 'own' our bodies. We also own things that we ourselves make as well as the land that we fence off or otherwise improve. This, not incidentally, proves useful in colonial expansion, but Spinoza's equation of right with power may well yield the same result. Whether it does seems to depend on the extent to which we can unite ourselves in friendship with those beyond our borders or those who, while within them, belong to a different culture.[22]

Like Spinoza, however, Locke argues that the state does not have the power to control what people think and so he, too, is an early advocate of free speech, as is John Milton, who advocates freedom of the press.[23]

POSTSCRIPT: A NOTE ON SPINOZA'S INFLUENCE

Initial reactions to Spinoza's 'atheistic' thought were vehemently hostile and this attitude persisted unabated until the early nineteenth century. The *Tractatus Theologico-Politicus* was immediately denounced as blasphemous, removed from bookstores, and after Jan de Witt's murder, banned.[1] The *Opera Posthuma* and the *Nagelate Schriften*, as well as future translations and extracts, were also banned not long after their publication.[2]

Bayle's article on Spinoza in his *Historical and Critical Dictionary*[3] appeared in 1697 and was a major source of information on Spinoza in the early eighteenth century.[4]

With the exception of Spinoza's friends and those writing 'underground militant literature',[5] almost no one seems to have had anything good to say about him for more than a century after his death. Hobbes, however, comes close. He merely commented, in reaction to the *Tractatus Theologico-Politicus*, 'I durst not write so boldly'.[6]

Hume famously referred to Spinoza's 'hideous hypothesis' in his *Treatise*,[7] by which he meant the doctrine that there is a single substance (God) in which everything inheres. However, Hume cast so much doubt on the arguments for a traditional God that he himself was suspected of atheism.

In the late eighteenth century a dispute arose and became so famous it was given a name, the 'Pantheismusstreit', or 'Pantheism Conflict'. This began with a report by Jacobi that Lessing had admitted before his death to being a Spinozist. Moses Mendelssohn replied on behalf of Lessing, his close friend, and almost everyone entered the fray.[8] According to Moreau, the issue concerned both Lessing's belief in Spinozism and its truth, where 'Spinozism' is taken to accept 'the world's unity of principle, and to reject 'all revealed theology'.[9] On Moreau's view, 'the conflict terminated the Enlightenment'[10] and helped to create Romanticism.[11]

The apparent partial result, at least, was that Spinozism, as Moreau puts it, 'gained metaphysical respectability'. Indeed, it was even proclaimed by Hegel to be the starting point of any philosophy,[12] and in Spinoza, Nietzsche found a predecessor.[13]

Things had no doubt changed by the nineteenth century. Marx admitted that he was an atheist, but the penalty was not imprisonment or burning at the stake. It was inability to get a government job.

In the twentieth century, Freud spoke of his 'high respect' for Spinoza as well as for his work,[14] and Russell seems to have accepted a broadly Spinozist ethics.[15] Einstein also thought highly of Spinoza. Indeed, he went so far as to say, when pressed by a rabbi, 'I believe in Spinoza's God, Who reveals Himself in the lawful harmony of the world, not in a God Who concerns Himself with the fate and the doings of mankind.'[16]

The later twentieth century experienced a resurgence of interest in Spinoza and it is indebted to earlier historical and textual studies by Freudenthal, Gebhardt, Meinsma, and Wolfson. A few of the very many authors who have contributed are Gueroult and Matheron, as well as Bennett, Curley, Hampshire, and Yovel. See the Bibliography for these and other authors, such as Balibar, Negri, and Deleuze.

Interest in Spinoza is perhaps stronger now than it has ever been[17] and historical, textual, and philosophical work on Spinoza continues to appear at a rapid rate.[18]

NOTES

PREFACE

1 I am indebted to Ed Pollitt, Amy Jarrett, and John Wall for their comments on an earlier draft of this work.

1: THE NETHERLANDS IN THE SEVENTEENTH CENTURY

1 Israel (1995: 135); Nadler (1999: 7–8).
2 Parker (1977: 15).
3 Parker (1977: 194).
4 Parker (1977: 199, 304).
5 Parker (1977: 265–66).
6 Nadler (1999: 7).
7 Israel (1995: 292–93).
8 Israel (1995: 302).
9 Price (1998: 21, 65).
10 Price (1998: 70).
11 Price (1998: 13, 89).
12 Price (1998: 93).
13 Nadler (1999: 6).
14 Israel (1995: 376–77).
15 Price (1998: 81).
16 Israel (1995: 796–800).
17 Israel (1995: 803).
18 Israel (1995: 803).
19 Nadler (1999: 306).
20 Nadler (1999: 306).
21 Israel (1995: 813).
22 Price (1998: 39).
23 Price (1998: 57–58).
24 They are described as committing 'quasi-genocide' by Price (1998: 21).
25 Price (1998: 58).

26 Israel (1995: 548).
27 Two other celebrated artists of the period, Peter Paul Rubens (1577–1640) and Sir Anthony van Dyck (1599–1641), were Flemish.
28 Nadler (1999: 45).
29 Nadler (1999: 76–79).
30 See the website of the Royal Society at <www.royalsoc.ac.uk/page.asp?id=2176> (accessed 7 September 2006).

2: SPINOZA'S LIFE AND THOUGHT

1 Nadler (1999: 19–21). Ashkenazi Jews are descended from those living along the river Rhine in Germany.
2 Nadler (1999: 36).
3 Nadler (1999: 31). Klever (1996: 14) maintains that it was 1587.
4 Nadler (1999: 4).
5 Gullan-Whur (1998: 4–5).
6 Nadler (1999: 36) supposes that Isaac is Hanna's son, not Rachel's, but does not regard this as certain. Klever (1996: 14) maintains that Isaac is Rachel's son.
7 Nadler (1999: 45). Gullan-Whur (1998: 17) holds that Gabriel is merely 'assumed to be younger than Bento'.
8 See Nadler (1999: 45). Klever (1996: 14) maintains that Rachel was the mother of Rebecca and Isaac.
9 Nadler (1999: 45) regards it as unclear whether Rebecca's mother was Hanna or Esther. Klever (1996: 14) holds that her mother was Hanna. Gullan-Whur (1998: 16) agrees with Klever, but grants that her mother could have been Rachel, Esther, or Hanna.
10 Nadler (1999: 34).
11 Nadler (1999: 64–65, 80–81) and Klever (1996: 15).
12 Nadler (1999: 106).
13 See Moreau (n.d.).
14 Klever (1996: 26).
15 Nadler (1999: 108–09).
16 Nadler (1999: 108–09).
17 Nadler (1999: 105–06).
18 Wolf (ed. and trans.) (1927: 47).
19 See Spinoza (1966: 48–49).
20 Nadler (1999: 130). Moreau (n.d.) explicitly recounts that Spinoza and Prado declared: 'Dieu n'existe que philosophiquement parlant; l'âme meurt avec le corps; la loi juive est fausse' (God exists only philosophically speaking; the soul dies with the body; the Jewish law is false).
21 Nadler (1999: 163).
22 Nadler (1999: 155).
23 Nadler (1999: 158–62); Gullan-Whur (1998: 81–83). Margaret Fell Fox is generally known as 'the mother of the Quakers'.
24 All information and dates in this paragraph are from Wolf in Spinoza (1966: 49–53).

25 Wolf, in Spinoza (1966: 52).
26 See their website at <www.spinozahuis.nl>.
27 Moreau (n.d.).
28 Nadler (1999: 288).
29 Nadler (1999: 295–97).
30 Moreau (n.d.).
31 Gullan-Whur (1998: 317–18).
32 See Steenbakkers (1994) on the creation of the *Opera Posthuma*. See also Akkerman and Steenbakkers (2005).
33 See Nadler (1999: 163).
34 Spinoza certainly had very strong interests in what we call 'science', and, indeed, Klever (1996: 33) characterizes him as 'a man of science rather than a twentieth century kind of philosopher'. For more on Spinoza and science, see Grene and Nails (1986).
35 Descartes, *Principles of Philosophy*, Preface (Descartes 2000: 23).
36 Newton (1972, 1999).

3: THE *TREATISE ON THE EMENDATION OF THE INTELLECT*

1 There is a dispute about whether this is Spinoza's earliest work. Mignini has argued that it is, but the traditional view is that KV predates it. See Spinoza (1985: 3–4), Mignini (1979, 1986), and Nadler (1999: 175–76 with n. 61, 62).
2 In the original Latin, *Tractatus de Intellectus Emendatione, Et de via, qua optime in verum rerum Cognitionem dirigitur*.
3 These section numbers are the same as Bruder's paragraph numbers, and are retained, for example, in C and S.
4 C 7.
5 C 10; G II.8.12–27. Note that Curley translates 'homo . . . nihil obstare videat, quominus talem naturam acquirat' as 'man . . . sees that nothing prevents his acquiring such a nature'. This, however, seems to imply that we do have a good deal of knowledge of the causal order of nature. So Shirley's translation, 'man . . . sees no reason why he cannot acquire such a nature' (S 5), seems better on this count. For seeing no reason does not entail that there is no reason. Even better, however, might be, 'man . . . sees nothing [or: does not see anything] to prevent his acquiring such a nature'.
6 See E IV Pref.
7 See, for example, TdIE §100 (S 27).
8 C 13; S 7.
9 C 15; G II.12.22–24: 'Et ex istis facile apparebit summa, ad quam homo potest pervenire, perfectio.' Shirley translates, 'From this the highest degree of perfection that man can attain will readily be made manifest' (S 8).
10 More recent authors who have usefully discussed these questions include Rawls (1971, 2001) and Grice (1991).

11 Shirley translates *laetitia* and *tristitia* in the *Ethics* as 'pleasure' and 'pain'. Curley's 'joy' and 'sadness' seem to me generally preferable, however. See chapter 7.

12 Bentham (1982: 38–39) proposes that the value of pleasures and pains, considered by themselves, varies with their intensity, duration, certainty, and propinquity (to the present time). Relevant as well, in his view, is their fecundity, purity, and extent ('that is, the number of persons to whom it extends').

13 C 9 (see also C 9 n. 5). Shirley renders this 'unmixed with any sadness' (S 5). The original reads, 'Sed amor erga rem aeternam, & infinitam sola laetitia pascit animum, ipsaque omnis tristitiae est expers.'

14 This is my translation of 'Haec fusius suo loco explicantur' at G II.8.33 (footnote c).

15 See, for example, E IV Pref: 'when I say that some pass to a lesser or greater perfection, and the contrary, I do not understand that it changes from one essence or form into another. For a horse, for example, would be as much destroyed if it changed into a man, as into an insect' (my translation).

16 Spinoza here provides a general description of our goal as the perfection of our nature. What will become apparent after we compare our power with that of nature is just the 'highest perfection' that we can attain: 'summa, ad quam homo potest pervenire, perfectio' (G II.12.22–24).

17 See, for example, E IV App cap 6.

18 Cf. Sartre (1956: 724), who holds that our fundamental project is to be God.

19 In the *Ethics*, this is supplanted by knowledge of God, which increases with every increase in our knowledge of things.

20 'Felicity is a continual progress of the desire from one object to another, the attaining of the former being still but the way to the latter' (Hobbes, *Leviathan* XI.1; 1994: 57); 'Continual success in obtaining those things which a man from time to time desireth, that is to say, continual prospering, is that men call felicity; I mean the felicity of this life. For there is no such thing as perpetual tranquillity of mind, while we live here; because life itself is but motion, and can never be without desire, nor without fear, no more than without sense' (*Leviathan* VI. 58; 1994: 34–35).

21 If they were distinct, achieving A would be done for the sake of achieving B, since achieving B is a highest good. Hence achieving A could not be a highest good.

22 Tolstoy (1995).

23 This is based solely on anecdotal evidence, such as what students have said in my classes.

24 He mentions marriage and raising children in E IV App cap 20 (G II.271.25–272.4).

25 See Nadler (1999: 108).

26 Notable exceptions are found in literature, such as Franz Kafka, 'The Metamorphosis'.

27 Cf. Rawls (1971: 440), where he states, 'perhaps the most important primary good is that of self-respect'.

4: INTRODUCTION TO THE *ETHICS*

1 See Ep 2 (S 761), written, perhaps, in September 1661.
2 As do the editors of the *Opera Posthuma*, who include this note regarding the enclosure he sent to Oldenburg: 'See E I from the beginning to Prop. 4'. (S 762).

5: THE *ETHICS*, PART I: GOD

1 For more on folk psychology, see Greenwood (1991), Stich and Ravenscroft (1994), and Davies and Stone (1995).
2 G. IV.260.5–8 (my translation). For the whole letter, see S 903–06.
3 See Spinoza (1963: 451).
4 See, for example, Ep 21 and 23 to Blyenbergh.
5 Nadler (1999: 136).
6 Anselm (2001).
7 Kant, *Critique of Pure Reason*, A598/B626 (Kant 1984).
8 Moore (1936).
9 See Hartshorne (1962) and Jarrett (1976b). More difficult discussions are found in Plantinga (1975: 213–21), Sobel (1987, 2001), Anderson (1990), and Gödel (1995).
10 See Frege (1974) for a criticism of Spinoza's view about this.
11 S 228.
12 S 217.
13 White and Stirling, in Spinoza (1923) translate 'Deo aliam libertatem assueti sunt tribuere, longe diversam ab illa, quae a nobis (Defin. 7.) tradita est; videlicet, absolutam voluntatem' (G II.74.30–33) as 'they have been in the habit of assigning to God another liberty widely different from that absolute will which (Def. 7) we have taught'. The passage should instead read, 'they are in the habit of attributing to God another liberty, namely an absolute will, very different from that which (Def. 7) we have taught'. There is no absolute will, according to Spinoza, since such a will is free (in his usage). On this see II p 48 and p 48d.
14 For more on Spinoza's relations to other thinkers, see, for example, Yovel (1989) and Curley (1992).
15 S 921.
16 See Jarrett (1977c, 2001).
17 Some of the material in this section is drawn from Jarrett (1977a).
18 G II.59.27–35 (my translation).
19 G III.83.34–35.
20 Curley (1969).
21 Bennett (1984).
22 See, for example, S 445.
23 Bennett (1984: 89).
24 Bennett (1984: 92); originally from Zukav (1979: 200).
25 See, for example, de Deugd (1966: 146), Hampshire (1967: 16,18–41), and Mark (1972: 9, 12).

26 Spinoza (1966: 21).
27 Spinoza (1966: 19).
28 Spinoza (1966: 344).
29 G II.29.16–18 (my translation).
30 C 462. (G II.102.10–13).
31 But see the end of chapter 7 for further discussion of Spinoza's views on teleology.
32 See Bennett (1996) for more on this issue.
33 This view is set out by Curley (1969) and Curley and Walski (1999).
34 See Carriero (1991), Garrett (1991), Huenemann (1999), Koistinen (2003), and Jarrett (forthcoming).
35 For discussion of Spinoza's view on teleology, see Bennett (1984, 1990), Curley (1990), Garrett (1999), Jarrett (1999), and Carriero (2005).

6: THE *ETHICS*, PART II: MIND AND KNOWLEDGE

1 See, for example, Descartes' remarks to Princess Elisabeth (21 May and 28 June 1643) in Descartes (2000: 215–16).
2 Matson (2000: 331).
3 Locke, *Essay Concerning Human Understanding*, II.viii.8 (Locke 1996: 48).
4 For more on Spinoza's identity theory, see Della Rocca (1993, 1996).
5 See, for example, Loeb (1981).
6 Koistinen (1996); Davidson (1999).
7 Davidson (1999: 104).
8 See Della Rocca (1991), Jarrett (1991), Koistinen (1996), and Davidson (1999).

7: THE *ETHICS*, PART III: EMOTIONS

1 See Damasio (2003) for more on neurology and Spinoza's account of emotions.
2 For more on the emotions see Rorty (1980), Frijda (1986, 1999), Yovel (1999), Alanen (2003), and Solomon (2003). For more on Spinoza on emotions, see Frijda (1999), Steenbakkers (1999), and Ravven (2003).
3 Darwin (1998).
4 Nozick (1974: 42–45).
5 Epictetus, *Enchiridion* 3 (Epictetus 1983)
6 T. W. Bartel notes, 'This doctrine has always been rejected by orthodox Christian teachers. For example, the highly influential French Catholic bishop Francis de Sales, a near-contemporary of Spinoza, condemns those who deny recreation to themselves and others as 'austere and unsociable', and approves as legitimate amusements such pastimes as 'cheerful and friendly conversation', hunting, and games in which success depends largely on skill rather than chance – including games played for moderate stakes. See Francis de Sales, *Introduction to the*

Devout Life, part III, ch. 31 (Francis de Sales 1956: 172–73).' I am grateful to T. W. Bartel for this note.
7 G II.146.17: 'in suo esse perseverare conatur' (my translation).
8 G II.248.10–12 (my translation).
9 See Hobbes (1994: 27–35).
10 See, for example, Descartes (1985).
11 E III def.aff.4exp.
12 Descartes, *The Passions of the Soul*, §37 (Descartes 1985: 342).
13 Descartes, *The Passions of the Soul*, §40 (Descartes 1985: 343).
14 See *Meditations* VI.
15 Descartes, *The Principles of Philosophy*, IV. 190 (Descartes 1985: 281).
16 See Steenbakkers (1999) for more on Spinoza's account of emotions in relation to Descartes and to Spinoza's close friend, Lodewijk Meyer.
17 G II.80.3–4: 'omnes causas finales nihil, nisi humana esse figmenta'.

8: THE *ETHICS*, PART IV: ETHICS

1 See Mackie (1977: 106–07).
2 Mill (2002).
3 Kant (1993).
4 Frankena (1973: 14–16, 62–67). For Frankena's views on Spinoza's ethics, see Frankena (1975).
5 See Frankena (1973: 65) for more on this.
6 See Watson (1990). I am indebted to T. W. Bartel for this reference and for other helpful remarks.
7 A now classic paper on this is Anscombe (1958).
8 S 311.
9 For more on Spinoza and suicide, see, for example, Bennett (1984: esp. 237–40) and Barbone and Rice (1994).
10 See, for example, the first sentence of III p 1d as well as the first sentence of III p 3d.
11 S 338.
12 For work on Spinoza and ecology see Naess (1977, 1980, 1993) and Lloyd (1980).
13 See Curley, in Spinoza (1985: 569), and his reference to G I.170. The Spanish poet may be Góngora, that is, Luis de Góngora y Argote (1561–1627).
14 See IV p 23 and p 24, for example.
15 This is my translation, which is very similar to Shirley's, of 'Hominem, quem odimus, destruere conamur (*per Prop. 39. p.3.*), hoc est (*per Prop. 37.* hujus), aliquid conamur, quod malum est. Ergo &c. Q.E.D.' (G II.243.30–32).
16 See IV p 63cs.
17 'He who goes mad from the bite of a dog is indeed to be excused; still, it is right that he should die of suffocation', Ep 78 (S 952).
18 See, for example, TP 6.9.

19 The term 'superhuman' suggests a connection with Nietzsche. See Yovel (1989: vol. II, ch. 5) and Schacht (1999) for excellent discussions of the relations between Spinoza and Nietzsche.
20 C 576; 'terret vulgus, nisi metuat'.
21 C 587.
22 S 357.
23 S 358.
24 S 243.
25 This is evidently a suggestion made by Foot (1978), as described by Grice (1991: 57).
26 Curley (1973).
27 Curley (1973).
28 See TP 2.19, but compare TP 2.20–21 as well.
29 See S 834.
30 KV II.16.
31 See KV II.25 ('On Devils'), S 98–99.
32 IV p 63cs.
33 Broad (1930: 43); Steinberg (2000: 75).
34 Steinberg (1984, 2000: 74–79).
35 S 338.
36 Grice (1991: 69–91).

9: THE *ETHICS*, PART V: THE MIND'S POWER AND BLESSEDNESS

1 See Kassim (2001: 6–7).
2 See *Being and Nothingness* (Sartre 1956), part IV, ch. 2, sect. 1 ('Existential Psychoanalysis').
3 S 372 (translating 'in tempore').
4 S 372.
5 S 372.
6 S 366.
7 See Koistinen (1998).
8 G II.293.13–15 (my translation).
9 S 369. The parenthetical expressions are my addition.
10 S 369.
11 S 369.
12 See the scholium following IV p 63c.
13 S 373.
14 Relevant to this distinction are II p 45,d,s and II p 8,d,c,s.
15 S 374.
16 S 382.
17 S 382. 'Spiritual contentment' is 'animi acquiescentia', which Curley translates as 'peace of mind'.
18 S 382.
19 See III p 15s and also I App, where the common belief in free will is said to be caused, in part, by our being unaware of the causes of our desires.
20 For more on Spinoza and Freud, see Yovel (1989, vol. II, ch. 6).

21 What I call here an 'ordinary type of resolution' of the conflict is perhaps a popular one, but it is contrary to orthodox theology. For the rewards of an afterlife are not to be bestowed on those who act solely for their own gain.
22 Bennett (1984: 347).
23 Bennett (1984: 347).
24 See Koistinen (1998).
25 See Spinoza's definitions of hope, fear, and despair in III def.aff12, 13, and 15, along with his explication of these (S 313–14).
26 Bennett (1984: 333–34).
27 On envy and jealousy, see, for example, III p 35,s.
28 See Rousset (1968), Donagan (1973), Kneale (1973), Harris (1975), Curley (1977), Bennett (1984: 357–75), Lloyd (1986), Matheron (1986c), Hardin (1987), Matson (1990), Macherey (1997), Parchment (2000), Nadler (2001).
29 See Jarrett (1990).

10: THE *TRACTATUS THEOLOGICO-POLITICUS*

1 Klever (1996: 39 with n. 43). See also S 387.
2 See Klever (1996: 38–39), Nadler (1999: 266–67), and Michael L. Morgan's discussion in S 383–84. Klever relates that Koerbagh's sentence was ten years in prison, ten years in exile, and a fine of 6,000 guilders.
3 See Morgan's remarks in S 384.
4 The full title is, 'The Theological-Political Tractate, containing Several Discussions, by which it is shown not only that Freedom of Philosophising can be granted without harm to the Piety and Peace of the Republic, but that the same cannot be destroyed except with the Peace of the Republic and Piety itself'. (S 387).
5 S 387.
6 S 843–44.
7 See Popkin (1986, 1996) for more on Spinoza and biblical scholarship.
8 S 518.
9 S 518.
10 S 523.
11 S 523.
12 See E IV p 37s 2.
13 S 555.
14 S 567.
15 S 567.
16 S 572.
17 S 426.
18 S 427–28.
19 S 427.
20 S 428.
21 S 428.
22 S 433.
23 S 428.

24 S 429.
25 S 430.
26 S 432.
27 S 527.
28 S 528.
29 But see Mason (1997: 33), who holds that *natura naturans* and *natura naturata* are two ways of conceiving 'the same reality'.
30 S 527.
31 S 527.
32 S 528.
33 S 527.
34 S 528. Spinoza also speaks as if mutual help were impossible without a transfer of natural right, and that without it, life would be 'most wretched and must lack the cultivation of reason (miserrime, & absque rationis cultu)'.
35 S 529.
36 S 529–30.
37 S 530.
38 S 530.
39 See S 530, where he states that 'a community can be formed and a contract be always preserved in its entirety in absolute good faith on these terms, that everyone transfers all the power that he possesses to the community'.
40 See S 530: 'all must obey it in all matters; for this is what all must have covenanted tacitly or expressly when they transferred to it all their power of self-defence'.
41 S 532. It must be granted, however, that this interpretation is difficult to reconcile with the opening paragraphs of chapter 17, where Spinoza maintains that no one can transfer all of his or her power (S 536), and a passage later in the same chapter, where he holds that preservation of the state depends mainly on the subjects' loyalty, virtue, and steadfastness in carrying out orders (S 537). The main task of the state is to set up its constitution and organization in a way that motivates each to do his or her duty despite private advantage (S 538).
42 S 532.
43 S 532.
44 S 534.
45 Spinoza does not note the fact that in the *Ethics*, he advocates love of those who have harmed us (IV p 46).
46 S 538.

11: THE *TRACTATUS POLITICUS*

1 See Michael L. Morgan's remarks at S 676.
2 See Ep 84 (S 959), dated simply 1676. This is the last surviving letter of Spinoza's.
3 TP 2.5 (S 683–84).
4 TP 2.12 (S 686).

5 TP 2.13 (S 686).
6 TP 2.15 (S 687); G III. 28.18. 'magis opinione, quam re constare'.
7 TP 2.15 (S 687).
8 TP 2.20 (S 688).
9 TP 2.21 (S 688).
10. TP 5.2 (S 699).
11 TP 6.8 (S 702).
12 TP 8.2 (S 723).
13 TP 8.6 (S 725).
14 TP 11.3 (S 753).
15 TP 11.4 (S 753).
16 TP 11.4 (S 753).
17 TP 11.4 (S 754).
18 TP 11.4 (S 754).
19 TP 11.4 (S 754).
20 For more on Spinoza's views on women, see Gullan-Whur (1998). See also Matheron (1986b).
21 TTP 17 (S 538).
22 A small sample of works on Spinoza's social and political philosophy is Montag and Stolz (1997) and Gatens and Lloyd (1999).
23 Milton (1644).

12: POSTSCRIPT: A NOTE ON SPINOZA'S INFLUENCE

1 Israel (1995: 920–21).
2 Israel (1995: 921).
3 Bayle (1697, 1965).
4 Moreau (1996: 410, 413).
5 Moreau (1996: 414). See also Israel (1995: 922–31), who discusses literature concerning 'The Death of the Devil'.
6 Clark (1898: 357). This is quoted and discussed in Curley (1992).
7 Hume, *A Treatise of Human Nature* I.iv.5. (Hume 1951: 241.) For more on this, see Popkin (1979).
8 Moreau (1996: 420).
9 Moreau (1996: 420).
10 Moreau (1996: 420).
11 Moreau (1996: 420–21).
12 Moreau (1996: 423–24).
13 See Yovel (1989: vol. II, ch. 5) and Schacht (1999).
14 Yovel (1989: vol. II, p. 139).
15 See Blackwell (1985).
16 Quoted in Horton (2003: 31).
17 There are, for example, Spinoza associations or institutes in many different countries, including France, Germany, Israel, Italy, Japan, The Netherlands, and Spain.
18 Topics of recent interest include Judaism and Jewish identity as well as feminism. For the former, see, for example, Nadler, Walther, and Yakira

(1997), Smith (1997), and Ravven and Goodman (2002). For the latter, see, for example, Gatens, Lloyd and James (1998), Ribeiro Ferreira (1999), and Gatens (2002).

An excellent bibliography of work since 1978 is provided by the Index du Bulletin de Bibliographie Spinoziste. It can be accessed online at <www.cerphi.net/bbs/bbs.htm>.

BIBLIOGRAPHY

Akkerman, Fokke and Piet Steenbakkers (2005), *Spinoza to the Letter: Studies in Words, Texts and Books*, Brill's Studies in Intellectual History 137 (Leiden: Brill).

Alanen, Lilli (2003), 'What are Emotions About?', *Philosophy and Phenomenological Research*, 67.2: 311–34.

Anderson, C. Anthony (1990), 'Some Emendations of Gödel's Ontological Proof', *Faith and Philosophy*, 7: 291–303.

Anscombe, G. E. M. (1958), 'Modern Moral Philosophy', *Philosophy*, 33: 1–19.

Anselm (2001), *Proslogion*, ed. and trans. Thomas Williams (Indianapolis: Hackett Publishing Company; 1st publ. 1077–78).

Aristotle (1941), *The Basic Works of Aristotle*, ed. W. D. Ross (New York: Random House).

——(1949), *Categoriae*, ed. L. Minio-Paluello (Oxford: Oxford University Press).

Armstrong, D. M. (1968), *A Materialist Theory of the Mind* (London: Routlege & Kegan Paul).

Arnauld, Antoine and Pierre Nicole (1683), *Logique de Port-Royal*, 5th edn, Desprez (repr. Lille: Librairie R. Giard, 1964, with introd. by P. Roubinet).

Balibar, Étienne (1985), *Spinoza et la politique* (Paris: Presses Universitaires de France).

——(1996), *Spinoza and Politics*, trans. Peter Snowden (London and New York: Verso; English trans. of Balibar 1985).

Barbone, Steven and Lee C. Rice (1994), 'Spinoza and the Problem of Suicide', *International Philosophical Quarterly*, 34.2: 229–41.

Bayle, Pierre (1697), *Dictionnaire historique et critique* (Rotterdam: Chez Reinier Leers).

——(1965), *Historical and Critical Dictionary: Selections*, ed. and trans. Richard H. Popkin (Indianapolis: Bobbs-Merrill).

Beck, Aaron (1967), *Cognitive Therapy and the Emotional Disorders* (New York: International University Press).

——(1991), 'Cognitive Therapy: A 30-Year Respective', *American Psychologist*, 46: 368–75.

Bennett, Jonathan (1984), *A Study of Spinoza's Ethics* (Indianapolis: Hackett Publishing Company).

——(1990), 'Spinoza and Teleology: A Reply to Curley', in Curley and Moreau (1990): 49–52.

——(1996), 'Spinoza's Metaphysics', in Garrett (1996): 61–88.

Bentham, Jeremy (1982), *An Introduction to the Principles of Morals and Legislation*, ed. J. H. Burns and H. L. A. Hart (London and New York: Methuen; 1st publ. 1789).

Blackwell, Kenneth (1985), *The Spinozistic Ethics of Bertrand Russell* (London: George Allen and Unwin).

Boscherini, E. G. (1970), *Lexicon Spinozanum*, 2 vols (The Hague: Martinus Nijhoff).

Broad, C. D. (1930), *Five Types of Ethical Theory* (London: Routledge & Kegan Paul).

Breuer, Josef and Sigmund Freud (1955), *Studies in Hysteria*, in J. Strachey (ed.), *The Standard Edition of the Complete Works of Sigmund Freud* (London: Hogarth Press, 1st publ. 1895).

Burgersdijck, F. (1653), *Institutionum Metaphysicarum Libri Duo* (London).

Carriero, John (1991), 'Spinoza's Views on Necessity in Historical Perspective', *Philosophical Topics*, 19: 47–96.

——(2005), 'Spinoza on Final Causality', in Garber and Nadler (2005): 105–47.

Churchland, P. (1981), 'Eliminative Materialism and the Propositional Attitudes', *Journal of Philosophy*, 78: 67–90.

Clark, Andrew (ed.) (1898), *Brief Lives, Chiefly of Contemporaries, Set Down by John Aubrey, Between the Years 1669 and 1696*, vol. 1 (Oxford: Clarendon Press).

Copernicus, Nicholaus (1976), *On the Revolutions of the Heavenly Spheres*, introd. and notes by A. M. Duncan (Newton Abbot: David and Charles; New York: Barnes and Noble; 1st publ. 1543).

Curley, Edwin M. (1969), *Spinoza's Metaphysics: An Essay in Interpretation* (Cambridge, Mass.: Harvard University Press).

——(1973), 'Spinoza's Moral Philosophy', in Grene (1973): 354–75.

——(1977), 'Notes on the Immortality of the Soul in Spinoza's *Short Treatise*', *Giornale critico della filosofia italiana*, 56. 3–4: 327–36.

——(1986), *Behind the Geometrical Method: A Reading of Spinoza's Ethics* (Princeton, N.J.: Princeton University Press).

——(1990), 'On Bennett's Spinoza: The Issue of Teleology', in Curley and Moreau (1990): 37–48.

——(1992), 'I durst not write so boldly: or How to Read Hobbes' Theologico-Political Treatise', in Daniela Bostrenghi (ed.) (1992), *Hobbes e Spinoza* (Naples: Bibliopolis), 497–593.

——and Pierre-François Moreau (eds) (1990), *Spinoza: Issues and Directions* (Leiden: Brill).

——and Gregory Walski (1999), 'Spinoza's Necessitarianism Revisited', in Gennaro and Huenemann (1999): 224–40.

Damasio, Antonio (2003), *Looking for Spinoza: Joy, Sorrow, and the Feeling Brain* (Orlando, Fla.: Harcourt, Inc.).

Darwin, Charles (1998), *The Expression of the Emotions in Man and Animals*, introd. and commentaries by Paul Ekman, 3rd edn (Oxford and New York: Oxford University Press; 1st publ. 1872).

Davidson, Donald (1999), 'Spinoza's Causal Theory of the Affects', in Yovel (1999): 95–111.

Davies, Martin and Tony Stone (1995), *Folk Psychology: The Theory of Mind Debate* (Oxford: Blackwell).

de Deugd, C. (1966), *The Significance of Spinoza's First Kind of Knowledge* (Assen, The Netherlands: Van Gorcum).

Deleuze, Gilles (1968), *Spinoza et le problème de l'expression* (Paris: Éditions de Minuit).

——(1981), *Spinoza: Philosophie pratique* (Paris: Éditions de Minuit).

——(1988), *Spinoza: Practical Philosophy* trans. Robert Hurley (San Francisco: City Lights; English trans. of Deleuze 1981).

——(1990), *Expressionism in Philosophy: Spinoza*, trans. Martin Joughin (New York: Zone Books; English trans. of Deleuze 1968).

Della Rocca, Michael (1991), 'Causation and Spinoza's Claim of Identity', *History of Philosophy Quarterly*, 8: 265–76.

——(1993), 'Spinoza's Argument for the Identity Theory', *Philosophical Review*, 102: 183–213.

——(1996), *Representation and the Mind–Body Problem in Spinoza* (New York: Oxford University Press).

Descartes, René (1897–1910), *Œuvres de Descartes*, 12 vols, ed. Charles Adam and Paul Tannery (Paris: Cerf).

——(1967), *Philosophical Works*, vol. 1, trans. E. S. Haldane and G. T. R. Ross (Cambridge: Cambridge University Press).

——(1985), *The Philosophical Writings of Descartes*, trans. John Cottingham, Robert Stoothoff and Dugald Murdoch, vol. 1 (Cambridge: Cambridge University Press).

——(2000), *René Descartes: Philosophical Essays and Correspondence*, ed. and introd. Roger Ariew (Indianapolis and Cambridge: Hackett Publishing Company).

Donagan, Alan (1973), 'Spinoza's Proof of Immortality', in Grene (1973): 241–58.

——(1988), *Spinoza*. (Chicago: University of Chicago Press).

——(1996), 'Spinoza's Theology', in Garrett (1996): 343–82.

Ellis, Albert (1962), *Reason and Emotion in Psychotherapy* (New York: Lyle Stuart).

——(1999), 'Why Rational Emotive Therapy to Rational Emotive Behavior Therapy?', *Psychotherapy*, 36: 154–59.

Epictetus (1983), *The Handbook (The Enchiridion)*, trans. N. P. White (Indianapolis: Hackett Publishing Company).

Euclid (1956), *The Thirteen Books of Euclid's Elements*, vol. 1, 2nd edn, trans., introd., and commentary by Thomas L. Heath (New York: Dover Publications).

Flanagan, Owen and Amélie Rorty (eds) (1990), *Identity, Character, and Morality: Essays in Moral Psychology* (Cambridge, Mass.: MIT Press).

Fox, Margaret Askew Fell (1656), *A Loving Salutation to the Seed of Abraham among the Jewes* (London).

Foot, Philippa (1978), *Virtues and Vices and Other Essays in Moral Philosophy* (Berkeley, Calif. and Los Angeles: University of California Press).

Francis de Sales (1956), *Introduction to the Devout Life*, trans. Michael Day (London: Burns and Oates; 1st definitive edn 1619).

Frankena, William (1973), *Ethics*, 2nd edn (Upper Saddle River, N.J.: Prentice Hall; 1st edn 1963).

——(1975), 'Spinoza's "New Morality": Notes on Book IV', in Freeman and Mandelbaum (1975): 85–100.

Freeman, Eugene and Maurice Mandelbaum (eds) (1975), *Spinoza: Essays in Interpretation* (LaSalle, Ill.: Open Court).

Frege, Gottlob (1974), *The Foundations of Arithmetic: A Logico-Mathematical Enquiry into the Concept of Number*, trans. J. L. Austin, 2nd revd edn (Oxford: Blackwell).

Freudenthal, Jacob (1904), *Spinoza: seine Leben und seine Lehre, vol. 1, Das Leben Spinozas* (Stuttgart: F. Frommann).

——(1927), *Spinoza, Leben und Lehre*, 2 vols in one (Heidelberg: Carl Winter Verlag).

——(ed.) (1899), *Die Lebensgeschichte Spinoza's in Quellenschriften, Urkunden und nichtamlichen Nachrichten* (Leipzig: n. p.).

Friedman, Joel (1978), 'An Overview of Spinoza's *Ethics*', *Synthese* 37: 67–106.

Frijda, Nico H. (1986), *The Emotions* (Cambridge: Cambridge University Press).

——(1999), 'Spinoza and Current Theory of Emotion', in Yovel (1999): 235–61.

Galilei, Galileo (1953), *Dialogue Concerning the Two Chief World Systems, Ptolemaic and Copernican*, trans. Stillman Drake (Berkeley, Calif.: University of California Press; 1st publ. 1632).

Garber, Daniel and Steven Nadler (eds) (2005), *Oxford Studies in Early Modern Philosophy*, vol. 2 (New York: Oxford University Press).

Garrett, Don (1991), 'Spinoza's Necessitarianism', in Yovel (1991): 191–218.

——(1999), 'Teleology in Spinoza and Early Modern Rationalism', in Gennaro and Huenemann (1999): 310–55.

——(ed.) (1996), *The Cambridge Companion to Spinoza* (Cambridge: Cambridge University Press).

Gatens, Moira (2002), 'Feminism as "Password": Rethinking "Possible" with Spinoza and Deleuze', *Hypatia*, 15.2: 59–75.

—— and Genevieve Lloyd (1999), *Collective Imaginings: Spinoza, Past and Present* (London and New York: Routledge).

—— —— and Susan James (1998), 'The Power of Spinoza: Feminist Conjunctions', *Women's Philosophy Review*, 19: 6–28; repr. in *Hypatia* 15.2: 40–58.

Gebhardt, Carl (1905), *Abhandlung über die Verbesserung des Verstandes: Eine Entwicklungsgeschichtliche Unterstuchung* (Heidelberg: n. p.).

Gennaro, Rocco J. and Charles H. Huenemann (eds) (1999), *New Essays on the Rationalists* (New York and Oxford: Oxford University Press).

Giancotti, Emilia (1970), *Lexicon Spinozanum* (The Hague: Martinus Nijhoff).

—— (ed.) (1992), *Hobbes e Spinoza* (Naples: Bibliopolis).

Gödel, Kurt (1995), *Collected Works*, vol. 3, *Unpublished Essays and Lectures* (Oxford: Oxford University Press).

Greenwood, John D. (ed.) (1991), *The Future of Folk Psychology: Intentionality and Cognitive Science* (Cambridge: Cambridge University Press).

Grene, Marjorie (ed.) (1973), *Spinoza: A Collection of Critical Essays* (Garden City, N.Y.: Anchor-Doubleday).

—— and Debra Nails (eds) (1986), *Spinoza and the Sciences* (Dordrecht: D. Reidel).

Grice, Paul (1991), *The Conception of Value*, introd. Judith Baker (Oxford: Clarendon Press).

Gueroult, Martial (1968–74), *Spinoza*, 2 vols (Paris: Aubier).

Gullan-Whur, Margaret (1998), *Within Reason: A Life of Spinoza* (New York: St Martin's Press).

Hampshire, Stuart (1967), *Spinoza* (Baltimore: Penguin).

—— (1977), *Two Theories of Morality* (Oxford: Oxford University Press).

—— (2005), *Spinoza and Spinozism* (Oxford: Oxford University Press).

Hardin, C. L. (1987), 'Spinoza on Immortality and Time', in Shahan and Biro (1987): 129–38.

Harris, Errol (1975), 'Spinoza's Theory of Immortality', in Freeman and Mandelbaum (1975): 245–62.

Hartshorne, Charles (1962), *The Logic of Perfection* (La Salle, Ill.: Open Court).

Heerboord, Adrianus (1650), *Disputationes ex Philosophia Selectae* (Leiden).

—— (1680), *Meletemata Philosophica* (Amsterdam).

Hobbes, Thomas (1994), *Leviathan*, ed. and trans. Edwin Curley (Indianapolis and Cambridge: Hackett Publishing Company; 1st publ. 1651).

Horton, Gerald (2003), 'Einstein's Third Paradise', *Daedalus*, Fall 2003: 26–34.

Hubbeling, H. G. (1967), *Spinoza's Methodology* (Assen, The Netherlands: Van Gorcum).

—— (1977), 'The Development of Spinoza's Axiomatic Method', *Revue Internationale de Philosophie*, 31: 53–68.

Huenemann, Charles (1999), 'The Necessity of Finite Modes and Geometrical Containment in Spinoza's Metaphysics', in Gennaro and Huenemann (1999): 224–40.

Hume, David (1951), *A Treatise of Human Nature* ed. L. A. Selby-Bigge (Oxford: Clarendon Press; 1st publ. 1739–40).

Huxley, T. H. (1874), 'On the Hypothesis that Animals are Automata, and its History', *Nature*, 3 September: 362–66.

—— (1893), *Collected Essays*, vol. 1, *Method and Results* (London: Macmillan and Company).

Israel, Jonathan (1995), *The Dutch Republic: Its Rise, Greatness, and Fall. 1477–1806* (Oxford: Clarendon Press).

Jarrett, Charles (1976a), 'A Note on Spinoza's Ontology', *Philosophical Studies*, 29.6: 415–18.

——(1976b), 'Spinoza's Ontological Argument', *Canadian Journal of Philosophy*, 6: 685–92.

——(1977a), 'The Concepts of Substance and Mode in Spinoza', *Philosophia*, 7: 83–105.

——(1977b), 'Leibniz on Truth and Contingency', *Canadian Journal of Philosophy*, suppl. vol. 4: 83–100.

——(1977c), 'Some Remarks on the "Objective" and "Subjective" Interpretations of the Attributes', *Inquiry*, 20: 447–56.

——(1978), 'The Logical Structure of Spinoza's *Ethics*. Part I', *Synthese*, 37: 15–65.

——(1981), 'Cartesian Pluralism and the Real Distinction', *Southern Journal of Philosophy*, 19.3: 347–60.

——(1982), 'On the Rejection of Spinozistic Dualism in the *Ethics*', *Southern Journal of Philosophy*, 20.2: 153–75.

——(1990), 'The Development of Spinoza's Conception of Immortality', in Mignini (1990): 147–88.

——(1991), 'Spinoza's Denial of Mind–Body Interaction and the Explanation of Human Action', *Southern Journal of Philosophy*, 29.4: 465–85.

——(1999), 'Teleology and Spinoza's Doctrine of Final Causes', in Yovel (1999): 3–23.

——(2001), 'Spinoza's Distinction between Essence and Existence', *Iyyun: The Jerusalem Philosophical Quarterly*, 50: 245–52.

——(2002), 'Spinoza on the Relativity of Good and Evil', in Koistinen and Biro (eds) (2002): 159–81.

——(forthcoming), 'Spinoza on Necessity', in Koistinen (ed.) (forthcoming).

Joachim, H. H. (1901), *A Study of the Ethics of Spinoza* (Oxford: Clarendon Press).

Kant, Immanuel (1984), *Critique of Pure Reason*, introd. A. D. Lindsay; trans. J. M. D. Meiklejohn (London: Dent; 1st publ. 1781).

——(1993), *Grounding for the Metaphysics of Morals*, trans. James W. Ellington, 3rd edn (Indianapolis: Hackett Publishing Company; 1st publ. 1785).

Kashap, S. Paul (ed.) (1972), *Studies in Spinoza: Critical and Interpretive Essays* (Berkeley, Calif.: University of California Press).

Kassim, Saul (2001), *Psychology*, 3rd edn (Upper Saddle River, N.J.: Prentice Hall).

Kennington, Richard (ed.) (1980), *The Philosophy of Baruch Spinoza* (Washington, D.C.: Catholic University of America Press).

Klever, Wim (1996), 'Spinoza's Life and Works', in Garrett (1996): 3–60.

Kneale, Martha (1973), 'Eternity and Sempiternity', in Grene (1973): 227–40.

Koistinen, Olli (1996), 'Causality, Intensionality and Identity: Spinoza's Denial of Mind–Body Interaction', *Ratio*, 9.1: 23–38.

——(1998), 'Bennett on Spinoza's Philosophical Psychotherapy', paper presented at the 20th World Congress of Philosophy; available online from Paideia Project On-Line at <www.bu.edu/wcp/Papers/Mode/ModeKois.htm> (accessed 25 August 2006).

Koistinen, Olli (2003), 'Spinoza's Proof of Necessitarianism', *Philosophy and Phenomenological Research*, 67.2: 283–310.
——(ed.) (forthcoming), *Cambridge Companion to Spinoza's 'Ethics'* (Cambridge: Cambridge University Press).
——and John Biro (eds) (2002), *Spinoza: Metaphysical Themes* (Oxford: Oxford University Press).
La Mettrie, Julian Offray de (1974), *Man a Machine* (Chicago: Open Court Publishing Company; 1st publ. 1748).
Leibniz, Gottfried Wilhelm (1969), *Gottfried Wilhelm Leibniz: Philosophical Papers and Letters*, ed. and trans. L. E. Loemker, 2nd edn (Dordrecht: D. Reidel).
——(1989), *Leibniz: Philosophical Essays*, ed. and trans. Roger Ariew and Daniel Garber (Indianapolis: Hackett Publishing Company).
Lloyd, Genevieve (1980), 'Spinoza's Environmental Ethics', *Inquiry*, 23: 293–311.
——(1986), 'Spinoza's Version of the Eternity of the Mind', in Grene and Nails (1986): 211–33.
——(1994), *Part of Nature: Self-Knowledge in Spinoza's Ethics* (Ithaca, N.Y.: Cornell University Press).
——(1996), *Spinoza and the 'Ethics'* (London: Routledge).
Locke, John (1996), *An Essay Concerning Human Understanding*, ed. Kenneth P. Winkler (Indianapolis and Cambridge: Hackett Publishing Company; 1st publ. 1689).
Loeb, Louis E. (1981), *From Descartes to Hume: Continental Metaphysics and the Development of Modern Philosophy* (Ithaca, N.Y. and London: Cornell University Press).
Machado de Abreu, Luís (1999), *Sob o Olhar de Spinoza: Actes du Séminaire Portugais et Hispanique sur Spinoza tenu à l'Université de Aveiro (Portugal), les 13 et 14 novembre 1998* (Aveiro, Portugal: Departamento de Linguas e Culturas).
Macherey, Pierre (1997), *Introduction à "L'Éthique" de Spinoza*, part 5, 2nd edn (Paris: Presses Universitaires de France).
Mackie, J. L. (1977), *Ethics: Inventing Right and Wrong* (London: Penguin Books).
Mark, Thomas Carson (1972), *Spinoza's Theory of Truth* (New York and London: Columbia University Press).
Mason, Richard (1997), *The God of Spinoza: A Philosophical Study* (Cambridge: Cambridge University Press; repr. 2001).
Matheron, Alexandre (1969), *Individu et communauté chez Spinoza* (Paris: Les Éditions de Minuit).
——(1971), *Le Christ et le salut des ignorants chez Spinoza* (Paris: Aubier).
——(1986a), *Anthropologie et Politique au XVIIe Siecle (Études sur Spinoza)* (Paris: J. Vrin).
——(1986b), 'Femmes et serviteurs dans la démocratie spinoziste', 1st publ. 1977, repr. in Matheron (1986a): 189–208.
——(1986c), 'Remarques sur l'lmmortalité de l'âme chez Spinoza', 1st publ. 1972, repr. in Matheron (1986a): 7–16.

Matson, Wallace I. (1977), 'Death and Destruction in Spinoza's Ethics', *Inquiry*, 20: 403–17, repr. in Matson (2006): 300–14.

——(1990), 'Body Essence and Mind Eternity in Spinoza', 1st publ. in Curley and Moreau (1990), repr. in Matson (2006): 315–33.

——(2000), *A New History of Philosophy, vol. 2, From Descartes to Searle* (Fort Worth, Tex.: Harcourt, Inc.).

——(2006), *Uncorrected Papers: Diverse Philosophical Dissents* (Amherst, N.Y.: Humanity Books).

Meinsma, K. O. (1980), *Spinoza en zijn kring: Historisch-kritische studiën over Hollandsche vrijgeesten* (repr. Utrecht: Martinus Nijhoff; 1st publ. 1896).

——(1983), *Spinoza et son circle*, ed. Henri Mechoulan and Pierre-François Moreau (Paris: Vrin; edited repr. of Meinsma 1980).

Mignini, Filippo (1979), 'Per la datazione e l'interpretazione del *Tractatus de intellectus emendatione* di B. Spinoza', *La Cultura*, 17: 87–160.

——(ed. and trans.) (1986), *Benedictus de Spinoza: Breve trattato su Dio, l'uomo e il suo bene* (L'Aquila: L. U. Japadre).

——(ed.) (1990), *Dio, l'uomo, la liberta: Studia sul 'Breve Trattato' di Spinoza* (L'Aquila: L. U. Japadre).

Mill, John Stuart (2002), *Utilitarianism*, ed. George Sher (Indianapolis: Hackett Publishing Company; 1st publ. 1863).

Milton, John (1644), *Areopagitica* (London).

Montag, Warren and Ted Stolz (1997), *The New Spinoza: Theory Out of Bounds* (Minneapolis: University of Minnesota Press).

Moore, G. E. (1936), 'Is Existence a Predicate?', *Aristotelian Society*, suppl. vol. 15: 154–88.

Moreau, Pierre-François (1994), *Spinoza: L'expérience et l'éternité* (Paris: Presses Universitaires de France).

——(1996), 'Spinoza's Reception and Influence', in Garrett (1996): 408–33.

——(n.d.), 'Spinoza: Eléments de Biographie', <www.cerphi.net/public/biospino.htm> (accessed 27 August 2006).

Nadler, Steven (1999), *Spinoza: A Life* (Cambridge: Cambridge University Press).

——(2001), *Spinoza's Heresy: Immortality and the Jewish Mind* (Oxford: Oxford University Press).

——Manfred Walther, and Elhanan Yakira (eds) (1997), *Spinoza and Jewish Identity*, Studia Spinozana 13 (Würzburg: Verlag Königshausen and Neumann GmbH).

Naess, Arne (1977), 'Spinoza and Ecology', *Philosophia*, 7: 45–54.

——(1980), 'Environmental Ethics and Spinoza's Ethics: Comments on Genevieve Lloyd's Article', *Inquiry*, 23: 313–35.

——(1993), *Spinoza and the Deep Ecology Movement* (Delft: Eburon).

Negri, Antonio (1981), *L'anomalia selvaggia: Saggio su potere e potenza in Baruch Spinoza* (Milan: Felltrinelli).

——(1982), *L'anomalie sauvage: Puissance et pouvoir chez Spinoza* (Paris: Presses Universitaires de France; French trans. of Negri 1981).

——(1991), *The Savage Anomaly: The Power of Spinoza's Metaphysics and Politics*, trans. Michael Hardt (Minneapolis: University of Minnesota Press; English trans. of Negri 1981).

Newton, Isaac (1972), *Philosophiae Naturalis Principia Mathematica*, 3rd edn, 2 vols, ed. Alexandre Koyré and I. Bernard Cohen, with the assistance of Anne Whitman (London: Cambridge University Press; this edn 1st publ. 1726).

—— (1999), *The Principia: Mathematical Principles of Natural Philosophy*, trans. I. Bernard Cohen and Anne Whitman, assisted by Julia Budenz (Berkeley, Calif.: University of California Press).

Nozick, Robert (1974), *Anarchy, State and Utopia* (New York: Basic Books).

Parchment, Steven (2000), 'The Mind's Eternity in Spinoza's *Ethics*', *Journal of the History of Philosophy*, 38.3: 349–82.

Parker, Geoffrey (1977), *The Dutch Revolt* (Ithaca, N.Y.: Cornell University Press).

—— (1984), *The Thirty Years War* (London: Routledge & Kegan Paul).

Parkinson, G. H. R. (1964), *Spinoza's Theory of Knowledge* (Oxford: Oxford University Press).

Perzanowski, Jerzy (1991), 'Ontological Arguments II: Cartesian and Leibnizian', in Hans Burkhardt and Barry Smith (eds), *Handbook of Metaphysics and Ontology*, vol. 2 (Munich: Philosophia), 625–33.

Plantinga, Alvin (1975), *The Nature of Necessity* (Oxford: Clarendon Press).

Plato (2004), *The Republic*, trans. C. D. C. Reeve (Indianapolis: Hackett Publishing Company).

Popkin, Richard (1979), 'Hume and Spinoza', *Hume Studies*, 5.2: 65–93.

—— (1986), 'Some New Light on the Roots of Spinoza's Science of Bible Study', in Grene and Nails (1986): 171–88.

—— (1987), *Spinoza's Earliest Publication? The Hebrew Translation of Margaret Fell's 'A Loving Salutation to the Seed of Abraham among the Jewes, Wherever They Are Scattered Up and Down Upon the Face of the Earth'* (Assen, The Netherlands: Van Gorcum).

—— (1996), 'Spinoza and Bible Scholarship', in Garrett (1996): 383–407.

Price, J. L. (1998), *The Dutch Republic in the Seventeenth Century* (New York: St Martin's Press).

Prior, A.N. (1968), *Time and Modality* (Oxford: Oxford University Press; 1st publ. 1957).

Ptolemy (1997), *Ptolemy's Almagest*, trans. G. J. Toomer (Princeton, N.J.: Princeton University Press; 1st publ. 1984, orig. c. 150 AD).

Ravven, Heidi Morrison (2003), 'Spinoza's Anticipation of Contemporary Affective Neuroscience', *Consciousness and Emotion*, 4.2: 257–90.

—— and L. E. Goodman (eds) (2002), *Jewish Themes in Spinoza's Philosophy* (Albany, N.Y.: State University of New York Press).

Rawls, John (1971), *A Theory of Justice,* revd edn (Cambridge, Mass.: Harvard University Press).

—— (2001), *Justice as Fairness: A Restatement*, ed. Erin Kelly (Cambridge, Mass. and London: Harvard University Press).

Ribeiro Ferreira, Maria Luisa (1999), 'Spinoza, Hobbes et la condition féminine', in Machado de Abreu (1999).

Rice, Lee (1991), 'Tanquam Naturae Humanae Exemplar: Spinoza on Human Nature', *Modern Schoolman*, 68: 291–303.

Rorty, Amélie Oksenberg (1980), *Explaining Emotions* (Berkeley, Calif.: University of California Press).

Rousset, B. (1968), *La perspective finale de l'Éthique et le problème de la cohérence du spinozisme* (Paris: Vrin).

Sartre, Jean-Paul (1956), *Being and Nothingness*, trans. Hazel E. Barnes (New York: Washington Square Press).

Schacht, Richard (1999), 'The Spinoza–Nietzsche Problem', in Yovel (1999): 211–32.

Shahan, Robert W. and J. I. Biro (eds) (1987), *Spinoza: New Perspectives* (Norman, Okla.: University of Oklahoma Press).

Smart, J. J. C. (1959), 'Sensations and Brain Processes', *Philosophical Review*, 68: 141–56.

Smith, Steven (1997), *Spinoza, Liberalism, and the Question of Jewish Identity* (New Haven, Conn.: Yale University Press).

Sobel, Jordan Howard (1987), 'Gödel's Ontological Proof', in Thompson (1987): 241–61.

——(2004), *Logic and Theism: Arguments For and Against Beliefs in God* (Cambridge: Cambridge University Press).

Solomon, Robert C. (ed.) (2003), *What is an Emotion? Classic and Contemporary Readings*, 2nd edn (Oxford: Oxford University Press).

Spinoza, Benedictus de (1910), *Spinoza's Short Treatise on God, Man, and his Well-Being*, ed. and trans. A. Wolf (London: Adam and Charles Black).

——(1923), *Ethic: Demonstrated in Geometrical Order and Divided into Five Parts*, trans. W. Hale White and Amelia Hutchinson Stirling, 4th edn (London: Oxford University Press).

——(1962), *Baruch Spinoza: Hebrew Grammar*, ed. and trans. Maurice J. Bloom (New York: Vision Library).

——(1963), *Spinoza's Short Treatise on God, Man, and His Well-Being*, ed. and trans. A. Wolf (New York: Russell and Russell).

——(1966), *The Correspondence of Spinoza*, ed. and trans. A. Wolf (New York: Dial Press; 1st publ. 1927).

——(1972), *Spinoza Opera*, ed. Carl Gebhardt, 4 vols (Heidelberg: Carl Winter; repr. of 1st edn, 1925).

——(1985), *The Collected Works of Spinoza*, vol. 1, ed. and trans. Edwin Curley (Princeton, N.J.: Princeton University Press).

——(1986), *Korte Verhandeling van God, de Mensch en deszelvs Welstand*, ed. and trans. Filippo Mignini (L'Aquila: L. U. Japadre).

——(2002), *Spinoza: Complete Works*, ed. Michael L. Morgan, trans. Samuel Shirley (Indianapolis and Cambridge: Hackett Publishing Company).

Statman, Daniel (ed.) (1997), *Virtue Ethics: A Critical Reader* (Washington, D.C.: Georgetown University Press; Edinburgh: Edinburgh University Press).

Steenbakkers, Piet (1994), *Spinoza's Ethica from Manuscript to Print: Studies on Text, Form and Related Topics* (Assen: Van Gorcum).

——(1999), 'The Passions According to Lodewijk Meyer: Between Descartes and Spinoza', in Yovel (1999): 193–209.

Steinberg, Diane (1981), 'Spinoza's Theory of the Eternity of the Human Mind', *Canadian Journal of Philosophy*, 11: 35–68.

——(1984), 'Spinoza's Ethical Doctrine and the Unity of Human Nature', *Journal of the History of Philosophy*, 22: 303–24.

——(2000), *On Spinoza* (Belmont, Calif.: Wadsworth).

Stich, Stephen and Ian P. Ravenscroft (1994), 'What is Folk Psychology?', *Cognition*, 50: 447–68.

Strauss, Leo (1997), *Spinoza's Critique of Religion*, trans. E. M. Sinclair (Chicago: University of Chicago Press; 1st publ. 1930).

Strawson, Peter (1959), *Individuals: An Essay in Descriptive Metaphysics* (London: Methuen).

Suárez, Francisco (1965), *Disputationes Metaphysicae* (Hildesheim: G. Olms; 1st publ. 1597).

Thompson, J. J. (ed.) (1987), *On Being and Saying: Essays for R. L. Cartwright* (Cambridge, Mass.: MIT Press).

Tolstoy, Leo (1995), *My Confession* (London: Fount; 1st publ. 1882).

van der Bend, J. G. (ed.) (1974), *Spinoza on Knowing, Being, and Freedom* (Assen: Van Gorcum).

Watson, Gary (1990), 'On the Primacy of Character', in Flanagan and Rorty (1990); repr. in Statman (1997): 56–81.

Wilson, Margaret (1980), 'Objects, Ideas, and "Minds": Comments on Spinoza's Theory of Mind', in Kennington (1980): 103–20.

Wolf, A. (1927), 'Spinoza's Conception of the Attributes of Substance', *Proceedings of the Aristotelian Society*, n. s., 27: 177–92; repr. in Kashap (1972).

——(ed. and trans.) (1927), *The Oldest Biography of Spinoza* (London: George Allen and Unwin).

Wolfson, Harry Austryn (1969), *The Philosophy of Spinoza: Unfolding the Latent Processes of his Reasoning*, 2 vols (New York: Schocken; repr. of 1st edn, 1934).

Yovel, Yirmiyahu (1989), *Spinoza and Other Heretics*, 2 vols (Princeton, N.J.: Princeton University Press).

——(ed.) (1991), *God and Nature: Spinoza's Metaphysics. Papers Presented at the First Jerusalem Conference (Ethica I)* (Leiden: E. J. Brill).

——(ed.) (1999), *Desire and Affect: Spinoza as Psychologist. Papers Presented at the Third Jerusalem Conference (Ethica III)* (New York: Little Room Press).

Zukav, Gary (1979), *The Dancing Wu Li Masters* (New York: William Morrow and Company).

INDEX

Achenbach, Gerd 156
actions and passions 28, 99, 100,
    102, 103–4, 107, 112, 115, 123,
    127, 131, 145, 157, 162, 167,
    169, 171–2, 173
Adam 103, 184
Adler, Alfred 156
affectio (affection) 71, 78, 79, 80,
    81, 82, 93, 99, 103, 108, 128–9,
    131, 160–2, 163–4 *see also*
    mode
affectus (affect) *see* emotion
akrasia *see* weakness of will
amor intellectualis *see* intellectual
    love
anger 32, 37, 96, 98, 108, 112, 126,
    142, 145, 147, 150, 157, 164,
    165, 168, 181, 185
animals 28, 102, 111–112, 125, 137,
    153, 181
Anselm, Saint 45
appetite 93, 101, 104, 105–6, 113,
    117, 132, 185 *see also* desire
Aquinas, Saint Thomas 6, 27, 40,
    50, 61
Aristotle 6, 14, 28, 33, 35, 46
    on causality 53, 60
    on ethics 146–7
    on God 52
    on knowledge 54, 66
    on mind 61
    on substance 53–4
Armstrong, D.M. 64

atheism 39–40, 178, 196, 197
attribute 36, 39, 40, 41, 42, 45, 46,
    47–8, 49, 54–6, 57, 63, 67, 68,
    70, 72, 73, 75, 81, 82, 88, 90–1,
    106, 114, 172
Augustine, Saint 6

Balibar, Étienne 197
Bayle, Pierre 196
Beck, Aaron 156
Bennett, Jonathan 60, 116, 151,
    171–2, 197
Berkeley, George 54, 64, 86
Bible 4, 178–9
blessedness 22, 40, 122, 135, 148,
    151, 155, 158–9, 167–8, 183
Boyle, Robert 7, 14
Breuer, Josef 156
Broad, C.D. 151
Bruno, Giordano 50

Calvin, John 4
Cartesian dualism 62, 63, 173
categorical imperative 120, 147–8
causality 6, 19, 22, 36, 37, 45, 47,
    48–9, 50, 59–60, 62–4, 70–1,
    73–4, 87, 91–2, 100, 104, 115
    see also teleology
certainty 65, 67, 84, 182
cheerfulness and melancholy 107,
    110, 123, 126, 140, 141
children and infants 19, 26, 27, 94,
    98, 150, 153, 139, 194

Churchland, P. 64
common notions 67, 82, 85, 89
common properties 82, 157, 160,
    162–3
conatus (endeavour) 99, 100,
    104–5, 108, 113, 116, 118, 125,
    132–3, 146
consciousness 61, 83–4, 93–4, 97,
    108, 112, 167, 168
contingency 41, 49–51, 71, 84 *see
    also* necessity
Copernicus, Nicholaus 6
Curley, Edwin M. 59, 107, 110,
    112, 114, 148, 197

Davidson, Donald 64, 91
de Witt, Cornelius 143, 150
de Witt, Jan 4, 5, 143, 150, 196
death 69, 133, 138–9, 151, 152–4,
    158, 159, 169, 170
Deleuze, Gilles 197
Descartes, René 6, 7, 14, 36, 39, 45,
    49, 51, 53, 72, 75, 81, 88, 160
on emotions 114–16
on knowledge 65–6, 84, 86
on mind 61–2
desire 24–5, 27, 28, 31, 36, 38, 39,
    51, 60, 99, 101, 102–6, 108,
    112, 113, 114, 115, 117, 118,
    125–6, 130–1, 132, 133, 140,
    146, 191 *see also* appetite,
    conatus
devil 149–50
divine law 177, 178, 181–3
Donagan, Alan 76
duration 74, 75, 81, 150, 165, 166,
    170 *see also* time

ecology *see* ethics, environmental
Einstein, Albert 197
Ellis, Albert 156
emotion 17, 28, 31–2, 37, 99–100,
    102–3, 105, 108–11, 111–12,
    117–18, 122, 123, 124–5, 127,
    129–30, 130–1, 135, 137, 145,
    150, 156–7, 157–9, 160–5, 168,
    171–2 *see also* actions and
    passions

of animals 112
assessment of 140–3
definition of 103, 112–13
Descartes' account of 114–16
Hobbes' account of 113–14
how destroyed 128–9
introduction to 95–9
primary 99, 106–8
translation of terms for 107
emotional disease 141
Empiricism *see* Rationalism vs
    Empiricism
endeavour *see* conatus
epistemology *see* knowledge,
    theories of
essence 62, 77, 99, 102, 108, 111,
    123, 131, 132–3, 158, 162, 166
actual or given 101, 104, 105
formal 68, 70, 75–6, 81, 89,
    90–1
of God 37, 38, 39, 40, 44–5,
    47–8, 50, 55–6, 69, 72, 85, 89
eternity 17, 20, 21, 22, 23, 24, 43,
    49, 76, 91, 98, 147 *see also*
    duration, time
of the intellect 32, 69, 89, 157–8,
    159, 165–6, 167, 169–70,
    172–3, 184–5, 186
ethics 18, 20, 22, 31, 32, 54, 121–2,
    124, 146–7, 147–50, 183, 197
emotivist 130
environmental 137
introduction to 119–21
Euclid 33, 54, 57, 75, 83, 89
existence
compared with motion 105
conceived in two ways 58, 75–6,
    90, 166, 170, 172

faith 177, 179
Fermat, Pierre de 7
final cause *see* teleology
folk psychology 38, 96, 99
Fox, Margaret Fell 11
Frankena, William 120–1
free man 127, 144, 145
free will 37, 38, 42, 49, 50, 52, 71,
    85–6, 103, 147, 169

freedom *see* blessedness, free will
freedom of thought and speech
    180–1
Freud, Sigmund 155, 156, 168,
    197
Freudenthal, Jacob 197

Galileo 6, 7, 14
Gebhardt, Carl 197
Geulincx, Arnold 63, 64
God 36–7, 37–40, 72, 74, 85, 88–9,
    92, 94, 104, 115, 121, 123, 125,
    131, 134–5, 148–9, 149–50,
    159–60, 163–4, 166, 167, 169,
    170–1, 178, 179, 182–4, 185,
    188, 191, 195, 196, 197 *see also*
    substance, attribute
  causality of 47–8, 49, 73
  existence of 43–5
  freedom of 48–9
  Greek conception of, 52
  uniqueness of 45–6
  what God is 56–9
good and bad 16–18, 20–1, 24–6,
    51, 81, 98, 99, 102–3, 113, 115,
    120, 122, 123–4, 129–30, 131,
    132, 133–4, 135, 136, 137, 138,
    139, 140, 141, 142, 143–4, 147,
    149, 151–4, 169, 183, 184, 187,
    192, 195 *see also* highest
    good
  relativity of 17, 18, 39, 52, 106,
    123, 124, 131, 132
government *see state*
Grice, Paul 153–4
Gueroult, Martial 197

Hampshire, Stuart 171, 197
happiness 20, 21–2, 24, 39, 40, 120,
    122, 135, 146, 183 *see also*
    blessedness
hate 113, 135, 141, 145, 157, 189
    see also love and hate
heaven and hell 61, 69, 98
hedonism 20–1
Hegel, Gottfried W. 197
Heidegger, Martin 156
hell *see* heaven and hell

highest good 16, 17–18, 21, 24–5,
    123, 125, 127, 132, 134–5, 136,
    151–3, 178, 182
Hobbes, Thomas 24, 53, 61, 137,
    196
  on mind 63, 64
  on natural rights 186
  on passions 113–14
hope and fear 52, 113, 124, 126,
    142, 143, 172, 187
Hudde, John 7
human nature 18, 21–2, 59, 103,
    123, 132, 135, 136, 142–3, 152,
    188–9
Hume, David 48, 54, 86–9, 196
humility and repentance 124, 126,
    143
Huxley, T.H. 64
Huygens, Christian 7, 14

idea 65–6, 68, 74–5, 76–9, 86–9,
    110–11 *see also* knowledge
imagination 28, 52, 56, 67, 84–5,
    88, 116, 149, 159, 173, 178 *see
    also* opinion and imagination,
    perception
immortality 169–70, 173 *see also*
    eternity of intellect
infants *see* children and infants
intellectual love 116, 158, 159,
    166–7
intuition 32, 67, 69, 70, 71, 79, 81,
    83, 85, 89, 116, 157–8, 159,
    165, 170–1

Jacobi, Friedrich Heinrich 196
James, William 64, 155
joy and sadness 17, 20, 21, 22, 98,
    99, 101–2, 103, 106–8, 109–10,
    111, 112–13, 114, 115–16, 126,
    129, 140, 143, 144, 158, 172
Jung, Carl 156
justice & injustice 137–8, 180, 188

Kant, Immanuel 86, 87, 89, 120,
    144, 147, 170–1, 173
Kepler, Johannes 7, 14
Kierkegaard, Søren 156

Klever, Wim 10
knowledge
  of good and bad 143–4
  kinds of 15, 16, 19, 67–8, 70–1,
    79, 83, 114 *see also* opinion
    and imagination, perception,
    reason, intuition also
    imagination?
  theory of (introduction to)
    65–6
Koerbagh, Adriaan 177
Koistinen, Olli 91, 171

La Mettrie, Julian Offray de 61
laws of nature 148, 181–2
Leibniz, Gottfried Wilhelm 5, 7,
  13, 14, 45, 51, 54, 63, 64, 86,
  87
Lessing, Gotthold 196
Locke, John 54, 65, 81, 86, 87, 195
love 98, 140–1, 142, 150, 158, 194
  of God 20, 21, 27, 40, 98, 115,
    116, 150, 157, 158, 159, 160,
    163–4, 166, 178, 179, 182–3
    see also intellectual love
  and hate 99, 101–2, 104, 108,
    109–10, 111, 113, 114, 114–16,
    123, 126, 162, 164–5, 172, 189
    see also hate
Luther, Martin 4
lying 144, 151, 153

Maimonides, Moses 37, 40, 179
Malebranche, Nicholas 62, 64
Marx, Karl 197
mass terms and count nouns 57–8
mathematics 7, 34, 65, 87
Matheron, Alexandre 197
Matson, Wallace 61, 64
May, Rollo 156
Meinsma, K.O. 197
memory 71, 80, 110, 139, 164, 166,
  169
Mendelssohn, Moses 196
mental illness 155, 156 *see also*
  emotional disease
metaphysics 53–4, 58, 61, 113, 121,
  146, 154, 173, 197

introduction to 35–6
Mill, John Stuart 120
Milton, John 195
mind 61–4, 65, 66–7, 68–9, 70–1,
  72, 73, 74–5, 76, 77, 78, 80,
  81–2, 85–6, 87, 88, 89–91,
  91–2, 94, 100, 101, 102, 103–4,
  105–6, 107, 108, 110, 112, 115,
  122–3, 133, 138, 151, 157,
  157–8, 159, 160–1, 163, 165,
  166, 167, 170, 172, 173, 181,
  192, 194 *see also* eternity of
  the intellect
  theories of (introduction to)
    61–4
miracle 149, 177, 178
mode 36, 41, 42–3, 46, 49–50, 51,
  53, 55, 56–7, 58, 59, 60, 63, 68,
  70, 73, 74, 75, 76, 103, 115
  infinite 36, 41, 49, 55, 58, 59,
    72
modification *see* mode
morality & self-interest 150–4,
  169–70
Moreau, Pierre-François 196–7

Nadler, Steven 4, 5, 10
Natura Naturans & Natura
  Naturata 39, 50, 57, 59, 185
natural right 137, 179, 184–8,
  190–1, 195
naturalism 68
necessity 36, 38, 41, 42, 44–5, 47–8,
  49, 50, 71, 76, 84, 60, 132, 145,
  166, 167, 184 *see also*
  contingency
Negri, Antonio 197
Newton, Isaac 7, 14, 78
Nietzsche, Friedrich 28, 156, 197
Nozick, Robert 97

Oldenburg, Henry 7, 8, 11, 13, 32,
  178
ontological argument 43–5, 50
opinion and imagination 67, 70, 71,
  79–82, 83, 92, 114
ownership of property 138, 188,
  195

pain 62–4, 137 *see also* pleasure and pain
panpsychism 67, 70, 78
pantheism 59, 196
Pantheismusstreit 196
Pascal, Blaise 7
Pavlov, Ivan 155, 156
perception 63, 65–7, 80–2, 86–9, 92–3, 111, 115, 171
perfection and imperfection 17–18, 19, 21, 22–4, 45, 51, 107, 122, 127–8, 131–2, 135, 144, 149, 150, 159, 183–3, 184
Perls, Fritz 156
pity 124, 126, 142
Plato 6, 14, 35, 61, 122, 138, 146
pleasure 19, 20, 25, 27, 118, 141, 152, 158, 167 *see also* hedonism and pain 103, 107, 113–14, 126, 131, 137, 140 *see also* pain
promise *see* social contract
property *see* ownership
psychotherapy 32, 155–7, 158–9, 160–5, 168–9, 171–2
Ptolemy, Claudius 6
purposiveness *see* teleology

Rationalism vs Empiricism 86–9
reason 28, 67, 70, 71, 79, 82–4, 89, 99, 116, 121, 126, 130, 133–4, 135, 136–7, 138–9, 141, 142–3, 144, 145, 146, 147, 148, 149, 154, 155, 159, 160, 163, 167, 177, 179, 183, 185–7, 192, 191, 193 *see also* knowlege
precepts of 125, 127, 131–2, 157, 158
teleological concept of 185–6
religion and the state 4–5, 40, 61, 69, 98, 153, 179, 180, 188, 192, 193
Rembrandt 5, 6
revelation 188
Rieuwertsz, Jan 12, 177
right and wrong 31, 51, 52, 119, 120–2, 137–9, 147–50, 151, 158, 164, 167, 180, 181, 185, 188 *see also* natural rights

Rogers, Carl 156
Russell, Bertrand 64, 197

salvation *see* blessedness
Sartre, Jean-Paul 156, 169
science 6–8, 13–15, 19, 32, 53, 65, 95–6, 103, 119, 155–6, 179
sin 148–9, 179, 186, 188, 191–2
and merit 137–8
Skinner, B.F. 156
Smart, J.J.C. 61, 64
social contract 186–7, 191, 195
social harmony 125, 139
state (civil) 124, 127, 137–8, 139, 141, 145, 149, 177, 179, 180–1, 184, 186–7, 188, 189–92, 194–5 *see also* social contract
aristocracy 179, 193, 194
democracy 179, 193–4
Hebrew 180
monarchy 179, 180, 190, 192–3
purpose of 181, 192
state of nature 137–8, 188
Steinberg, Diane 151–2
Stoics 52, 98, 122, 146, 157, 160, 168
Strawson, Peter 64
Suárez, Francisco 6, 55, 56
substance 42–3, 53–4, 72, 86–7, 88, 170–1 *see* God, attribute
suicide 132–3
summum bonum *see* highest good

teleology 6, 36, 42, 51–3, 60, 81, 116–18, 183, 185–6, 192
The Netherlands 3–6
theology 13–15, 31, 32, 35, 40, 179
Thorndike, Edward Lee 155
time 14, 23, 36, 58, 67, 69, 72, 74, 75, 76, 81, 82, 84, 85, 90, 101, 106, 109, 110, 147, 150, 151, 154, 160, 166, 169, 170–1, 173 *see also* duration
Tolstoy, Leo 25
truth 54, 83, 84, 89, 130, 145, 153, 184
Tschirnhaus, Ehrenfried Walther von 7, 47, 49, 55

unconscious 93–4, 156 *see also*
    consciousness
universals 35, 83

van den Enden, Clara Maria 10
van den Enden, Franciscus 10, 11,
    13
van Leeuwenhoek, Anton 7, 14
Vermeer, Johannes 6
virtue 112, 121, 122, 123, 124,
    125–7, 132, 133, 136, 143–4,
    146–7, 150–2, 158–9, 166, 167,
    173 *see also* blessedness,
    salvation

Watson, John 155, 156
weakness of will 130–1
will 48, 48, 50, 51–2, 58, 59, 71,
    85–6, 101, 104, 105–6, 122,
    181, 184–5, 192, 193 *see also*
    weakness of will, free will,
    freedom
Wolf, A. 11, 38
Wolfson, Harry Austryn 197
women 194
Wundt, Wilhelm 155

Yovel, Yirmiyahu 197